American Literature Readings in the 21st Century

Series Editor: Linda Wagner-Martin

American Literature Readings in the 21st Century publishes works by contemporary critics that help shape critical opinion regarding literature of the nineteenth and twentieth century in the United States.

Published by Palgrave Macmillan:

Freak Shows in Modern American Imagination: Constructing the Damaged Body from Willa Cather to Truman Capote
By Thomas Fahy

Women and Race in Contemporary U.S. Writing: From Faulkner to Morrison
By Kelly Lynch Reames

American Political Poetry in the 21st Century
By Michael Dowdy

Science and Technology in the Age of Hawthorne, Melville, Twain, and James: Thinking and Writing Electricity
By Sam Halliday

F. Scott Fitzgerald's Racial Angles and the Business of Literary Greatness
By Michael Nowlin

Sex, Race, and Family in Contemporary American Short Stories
By Melissa Bostrom

Democracy in Contemporary U.S. Women's Poetry
By Nicky Marsh

James Merrill and W.H. Auden: Homosexuality and Poetic Influence
By Piotr K. Gwiazda

Contemporary U.S. Latino/a Literary Criticism
Edited by Lyn Di Iorio Sandín and Richard Perez

The Hero in Contemporary American Fiction: The Works of Saul Bellow and Don DeLillo
By Stephanie S. Halldorson

Race and Identity in Hemingway's Fiction
By Amy L. Strong

Edith Wharton and the Conversations of Literary Modernism
By Jennifer Haytock

The Anti-Hero in the American Novel: From Joseph Heller to Kurt Vonnegut
By David Simmons

Indians, Environment, and Identity on the Borders of American Literature: From Faulkner and Morrison to Walker and Silko
By Lindsey Claire Smith

The American Landscape in the Poetry of Frost, Bishop, and Ashbery: The House Abandoned
By Marit J. MacArthur

Narrating Class in American Fiction
By William Dow

The Culture of Soft Work: Labor, Gender, and Race in Postmodern American Narrative
By Heather J. Hicks

Cormac McCarthy: American Canticles
By Kenneth Lincoln

Elizabeth Spencer's Complicated Cartographies: Reimagining Home, the South, and Southern Literary Production
By Catherine Seltzer

New Critical Essays on Kurt Vonnegut
Edited by David Simmons

Feminist Readings of Edith Wharton: From Silence to Speech
By Dianne L. Chambers

The Emergence of the American Frontier Hero 1682–1826: Gender, Action, and Emotion
By Denise Mary MacNeil

Norman Mailer's Later Fictions: Ancient Evenings through Castle in the Forest
Edited by John Whalen-Bridge

Fetishism and its Discontents in Post-1960 American Fiction
By Christopher Kocela

Language, Gender, and Community in Late Twentieth-Century Fiction: American Voices and American Identities
By Mary Jane Hurst

Repression and Realism in Postwar American Literature
By Erin Mercer

Writing Celebrity: Stein, Fitzgerald, and the Modern(ist) Art of Self-Fashioning
By Timothy W. Galow

Bret Easton Ellis: Underwriting the Contemporary
By Georgina Colby

Amnesia and Redress in Contemporary American Fiction: Counterhistory
By Marni Gauthier

Vigilante Women in Contemporary American Fiction
By Alison Graham-Bertolini

Queer Commodities: Contemporary US Fiction, Consumer Capitalism, and Gay and Lesbian Subcultures
By Guy Davidson

Reading Vietnam Amid the War on Terror
By Ty Hawkins

American Authorship and Autobiographical Narrative: Mailer, Wildeman, Eggers
By Jonathan D'Amore

Readings of Trauma, Madness, and the Body
By Sarah Wood Anderson

Intuitions in Literature, Technology, and Politics: Parabilities
By Alan Ramón Clinton

African American Gothic: Screams from Shadowed Places
By Maisha Wester

Exploring the Limits of the Human through Science Fiction
By Gerald Alva Miller Jr.

A Companion to David Foster Wallace Studies
Edited by Marshall Boswell and Stephen J. Burn

The Middle Class in the Great Depression: Popular Women's Novels of the 1930s
By Jennifer Haytock

Charles Bukowski, King of the Underground: From Obscurity to Literary Icon
By Abel Debritto

Urban Space and Late Twentieth-Century New York Literature: Reformed Geographies
By Catalina Neculai

Revision as Resistance in Twentieth-Century American Drama
By Meredith M. Malburne-Wade

Rooting Memory, Rooting Place: Regionalism in the Twenty-First-Century American South
By Christopher Lloyd

Kate Chopin in Context: New Approaches
Edited by Heather Ostman and Kate O'Donoghue

Kate Chopin in Context

New Approaches

Edited by

Heather Ostman and Kate O'Donoghue

palgrave
macmillan

KATE CHOPIN IN CONTEXT

First published in 2015 by
PALGRAVE MACMILLAN®
in the United States—a division of St. Martin's Press LLC,
175 Fifth Avenue, New York, NY 10010.

Where this book is distributed in the UK, Europe and the rest of the world, this is by Palgrave Macmillan, a division of Macmillan Publishers Limited, registered in England, company number 785998, of Houndmills, Basingstoke, Hampshire RG21 6XS.

Palgrave Macmillan is the global academic imprint of the above companies and has companies and representatives throughout the world.

ISBN: 978–1–137–55179–5

Library of Congress Cataloging-in-Publication Data

Kate Chopin in context : new approaches / edited by Heather Ostman and Kate O'Donoghue.
pages cm.—(American literature readings in the twenty-first century)
Includes bibliographical references and index.
ISBN 978–1–137–55179–5 (hardback : alk. paper)
1. Chopin, Kate, 1850–1904—Criticism and interpretation. I. Ostman, Heather, editor. II. O'Donoghue, Kate, 1974– editor.

PS1294.C63K35 2015
813′.4—dc23 2015011425

A catalogue record of the book is available from the British Library.

Design by Newgen Knowledge Works (P) Ltd., Chennai, India.

First edition: September 2015

10 9 8 7 6 5 4 3 2 1

Contents

Acknowledgments

We would like to thank our contributors and colleagues for their good work and tireless support. In particular, we would like to thank the Kate Chopin International Society, which has given us the opportunity to know and learn from notable and rising Chopin scholars, as well as thousands of students, teachers, and readers from around the world.

Heather Ostman and Kate O'Donoghue

INTRODUCTION

Kate Chopin in Context: New Approaches

Heather Ostman and Kate O'Donoghue

After finishing *The Awakening*, Kate Chopin's groundbreaking novel, many first-time readers leave the text admitting that they feel transformed. The novel becomes a kind of rite of passage: their lives, their outlooks, or their relationships may never look quite the same after Edna takes her final swim. Every year, the Kate Chopin International Society welcomes new members who send e-mail messages such as: "I was in college when I read this novel for a lit survey and it changed my life," or "I was going through a really difficult time, and Edna was such an inspiration." Part of what makes the novel transformational for so many readers is its consistent relevance to people's lives. Emily Toth remarks in *Kate Chopin*, her landmark biography, that in 1970, while attending an antiwar march, her friend gave her "a copy of *The Awakening* and said, 'You have to read this.' I did, and was astonished that a woman in 1899 had asked the same questions that we, in the newly revived women's movement, were asking seventy years later" (9). In Europe, Helen Taylor has written that she links the novel with her time as an international student visiting the United States in 1969, during "the most exciting years in recent American history" (48). Since those earlier decades, in the generations that have followed, readers have responded similarly.

Even when many readers return to reread the novel, the narrative resonates with their experiences and the changes over the course of their lives. Chopin's returning fans and critics respond to Edna with appreciation, admiration, disdain, or contempt for Edna—as a young woman, a wife, a mother, and/or a woman of means—and frequently the second response is quite different from the first one they had to Edna and the novel overall. How they read Edna's awakening more often than not reflects the moments of their lives: what seemed like sweet rebellion the first time a young person reads *The Awakening* in college looks like irresponsibility as a parent, for instance—or vice versa: whereas a reader might have judged Edna for abandoning the life she had, a more seasoned reader might understand the challenges and the struggles of adulthood that make such sacrifices necessary. Either way, it is very rare to remain neutral to Chopin's most famous novel, whenever a reader encounters it.

Chopin's fiction enables highly personal relationships with it because the universality of the human experience in her work, the stark observation of human behavior, and the beauty of her linguistic choices. Chopin's fiction is not so different from the "voice of the sea" in *The Awakening*, which "is seductive; never ceasing, whispering, clearing, murmuring, inviting" (14). We come back to Chopin, older, more experienced, maybe a little less naïve, and we find ourselves and the people we meet along the way within her pages. Even as early as 1911, before Chopin's literary celebrity status faded, Orrick Johns wrote in the *Mirror*: "To one who has read her as a boy and come back to her again with powers of appreciation more subtly developed, she breathes the magic of a whole chapter in his life" (qtd. in Toth 261).

After Per Seyersted reintroduced Kate Chopin to the world over 40 years ago, her fiction found a solid place in the American literary canon; her stories have become a staple in anthologies, theoretical applications, and dissertations. She published *The Awakening* in 1899, but it enjoyed its greatest notoriety decades after her death in 1904, after many American critics initially panned the novel because of Edna's rebelliousness. Since then, hundreds of thousands of readers, after encountering Chopin, have transformed into true believers in her fiction and its power to articulate women's experience, and even more broadly, the human experience. Chopin's keen observation skills and clear renditions of human responses to passion, children, religion, and marriage capture her readers. Now, *The Awakening* has been translated into multiple languages, including French, Chinese, Czech, Dutch, Galician, German, Hungarian, Japanese, Korean, Polish, Portuguese, Serbian, and Spanish, and her fiction—her novels and her short stories—is taught around the world.

These days, readers often come to Chopin's work through school: secondary schools, colleges, and universities across the United States and over the globe assign *The Awakening* as part of a literature survey of American classics or women's literature. And if a student does not encounter Chopin's most famous novel, he or she will surely come across one of her heavily anthologized short stories, such as "The Story of an Hour," "Desirée's Baby," or "The Storm."

These and many of Chopin's other stories lend themselves extraordinarily well to academic discourse. Another of the unique staying features of Chopin's fiction has been its versatility. Since Seyersted's 1969 landmark volume, *The Complete Works of Kate Chopin* and *Kate Chopin: A Critical Biography*, biographers and critics, such as Emily Toth, Bernie Koloski, Barbara Ewell, Janet Beer, and others, have worked to install Chopin as one of the most widely read female authors of the nineteenth and early twentieth centuries. Her fiction seems both at home in the modern age and adaptable to quickly changing agendas and literary fads. Her novels and short stories, apart from captivating late-twentieth century literary critics, have moved well beyond this singular approach and offered scholars a stunning, wide range of theoretical approaches, including formalism, psychoanalytic criticism, Marxist criticism, reader–response criticism, structuralism, poststructuralism/deconstruction, New Historicism/cultural studies, race theory, as well as gender and queer studies. Similar to English and American writers such as Shakespeare, Milton, Pope, Melville, and Twain, whose work provides new insights to scholars, students, and readers, Chopin's body of work continues to invite new perspectives, especially as the twenty-first century classroom fosters deeper and more complex understandings of her fiction, and as today's students continue to diversify into higher education, both in the United States and abroad.

The notion of the "return" to Chopin forms the premise of *Kate Chopin in Context: New Approaches*, a collection of chapters that revisits familiar themes, establishes new frameworks, and then brings theory to practice in classroom settings, where so many of us encounter Chopin as readers and as teachers. Building on the existing scholarship that first resuscitated Chopin's fiction and then established its literary and critical significance, this collection draws on the work of seasoned and new scholars to provide diverse perspectives that span history, culture, and generations. Notably, this volume also includes the essays of several international scholars, heralding from Europe, the Middle East, and South America, which offer readers glimpses into the multinational appreciation and versatility of the author's work, but which indeed also broaden conventional approaches to Chopin. Last, the collection bridges theory to practice, bringing readers into the classroom, where much of Chopin theory has originated and developed in more recent years, with chapters that incorporate a range of pedagogical approaches for the modern student, including, necessarily, technological applications to teaching Chopin's fiction.

Therefore, the collection is divided into two sections. "Part One: New Contextual Approaches" explores Chopin's fiction through the lens of new angles and provides modern contexts on some well-known and some lesser known stories and characters. The chapters in this section, as well as the second, offer fresh readings by a range of scholars—new and seasoned, American and international. Chapter 1, in part one, "Chopin's Enlightened Men" by Bernie Koloski, sets the tone for the entire collection: Koloski, like all of the contributors, seeks to view Chopin in a new, modern light—outside the traditional and usual parameters. Since the 1960s, Chopin's fiction has been embraced and celebrated by feminist critics. Her female characters such as Edna Pontellier, Desirée, and Calixta have served feminist concerns and illuminated political ideologies. But in chapter 1, Koloski turns the focus on Chopin's male characters, particularly those largely ignored by feminist critics but who also manifest similar feminist attributes, complementing Chopin's strongest female characters.

Koloski's chapter looks beyond the disappointments the men in Chopin's best-known fiction turn out to be: the neglectful Leoncé Pontellier, the frightened Robert Lebrun, the womanizing Alcée Arobin, the controlling Brently Mallard—to say nothing of the inhuman Armand Aubigny. They are men who cannot begin to understand the needs of the women around them. Teachers and students familiar with widely taught works like *The Awakening*, "Desirée's Baby," or "The Storm" might easily conclude that Chopin specializes in creating strong, intuitive women and weak, indifferent men. But, Koloski reminds us, such a conclusion would cherry-pick the facts and focus on works that support the idea and ignore those that don't. Chopin's works include more than a few astute, compassionate men, characters in touch with their own promptings, to be sure, but also with those of the women they care about. Breaking ranks with the more familiar critique of Chopin's male characters, Koloski explores several texts, including "A Respectable Woman," "Athénaïse," and even *The Awakening*, in which Chopin offers readers perceptive, enlightened men—men who would be worthy partners for her powerful women.

Chapter 2 shifts gears and provides a reflective analysis of individualism and Chopin's specific rejection of it. Here, Rafael Walker argues that the literary work of Chopin—including "A Pair of Silk Stockings" and her 1899 novel *The Awakening*—should be viewed as a transitional moment in the history of literary realism. Scholars of classical literary realism, from Ian Watt to Nancy Armstrong and

Gillian Brown, have understood the realist novel as a vehicle for propagating liberal individualism. As Jürgen Habermas (among others) has shown, this form of selfhood depended on "separate spheres" ideology, a system of beliefs that confined women to domesticity and figured domesticity (and women) as an expansion of the liberal individual. This configuration made liberal individualism almost exclusively available to men. Walker claims that Chopin's work shows how the cultural turn to consumerism and self-indulgence at the turn of the twentieth century radically transformed bourgeois domesticity in America. As much scholarship has shown and as Chopin was keenly aware, this shift helped to redirect women's attention from the home to their own personal fulfillment. Yet Chopin did not believe that women would find fulfillment as liberal individualists, historically a male form of self-realization. Her heroine fails in her attempt to live out liberalism, rejecting liberal individualism. Walker presents Chopin as a transitional figure in the history of literary realism, one who provides a pivot between the liberal-individualist protagonists that dominate nineteenth-century literature and the scores of interminably desirous female protagonists of early twentieth-century fiction. These later heroines exhibit nonindividualist, other-directed forms of subjectivity—particularly, the protagonists of Theodore Dreiser's *Sister Carrie*, Edith Wharton's *The Custom of the Country*, Robert Herrick's *One Woman's Life*, and Booth Tarkington's *Alice Adams*—to name just a few. Although Chopin, unlike these later novelists, does not depict an alternative model for female subjectivity in her time, her work constitutes an important step in the realist novel's attempt to move beyond its reliance on the liberal individual—outdated in this era of consumption and alienated labor—to represent modern life.

In chapter 3, Amy Branam Armiento opens a discussion of "Désirée's Baby" with a compelling legal analysis in "A quick conception of all that this accusation meant for her": The Legal Climate at the Time of 'Désirée's Baby.'" Using legal cases and contemporary newspaper coverage, she analyzes the motivations of Désirée, Armand Aubigny, and Madame Valmonde in the story. Many scholars have looked at the role of Louisiana's code noir in the shaping of racial policies, but Armiento moves beyond this assumption and other generalizations such as the lack of enforcement of the code noir in the Louisiana territory and state, to interrogate just what types of consequences were likely for people in situations similar to those of Désirée and Armand. Désirée's decision to end her own life and her child's is much more complex than initial readings of shame or thwarted love, once readers understand the ramifications confronting her when she is suspected of being colored. Armiento concludes her discussion with a reflection on the intersectionality of race and gender and how this nodal point portended different social and legal consequences for men and women of color in Louisiana.

In chapter 4, Aparecido Donizete Rossi, a Brazilian scholar, examines the Gothic elements in Chopin's works. In *Patriotic Gore* (1962), Edmund Wilson makes the following statement about the property where Kate Chopin spent her years in Cloutierville: "This Place-du-Bois had a sinister history. It had belonged to a New Englander called Robert McAlpin, who had lived alone with his slaves and who had become a local legend for his cruel treatment of them" (588). Such legendary horrific treatment of human beings emerges in the character of Armand in Chopin's short story "Désirée's Baby." In his *American Gothic: An Anthology* (1999), Charles Crow identifies this short story as representative of the American Gothic tradition. In Crow's words, "Armand [Aubigny] is revealed as simply a monster" (339), and ten years later Crow states, in *American Gothic* (2009), that "Kate Chopin's 'Désirée's Baby' is perhaps the most complex and subtle of Creole Gothic tales" (92). Apart from "Désirée's Baby," Chopin never wrote any other text that could be placed within the tradition of the literature of terror and horror; however, Rossi examines how she uses Gothic elements in the creation of some scenes in *At Fault* and *The Awakening*, and shows how the Gothic works as a critical strategy to cope with rationalism, patriarchy, and phallogocentrism in her work.

Chapter 5 features the Spanish scholar Eulalia Piñero Gil's essay, "The Pleasures of Music: Kate Chopin's Artistic and Sensorial Synesthesia." Most critics stress the fact that Kate Chopin reflects her passion for music in her fiction. But she was also a synesthete, like her most well-known protagonist Edna Pontellier. In *The Awakening* music evokes transformation, awareness, and initiation; in fact, Edna's awakening is accompanied by different melodies throughout the novel. Still, critics have ignored the decisive role music has played as a sensory structure, particularly in terms of synesthetic imagery, but Gil takes an interdisciplinary look at how Chopin creates an enduring and multiple-sensory synesthesia in *The Awakening* through the extensive use of music and how this structure enables the protagonist's complete transformation.

Then in chapter 6, Heather Ostman explores essentialism and motherhood represented primarily through the narrative of "Regret," a Chopin story that has been often ignored by critics. She traces how the opposing forces of nineteenth-century essentialism and the development of the "New Woman" as they manifest in Chopin's 1894 short story. In this story, Chopin presents the female character of Mamzelle Aurélie as a figure of conventional masculinity. In her "man's hat" and "old blue army coat," Chopin tells us, she is essentially alone, except for the companionship of her dog. However, Mamzelle Aurélie learns there is more to mothering—to her surprise—than just feeding and sheltering children. Through the education of Mamzelle Aurélie, the author raises the question of women's essential nature. In contrast to other Chopin stories, such as *The Awakening* and "Athénaïse," which raise similar questions, "Regret" reconfigures conventional Victorian assumptions about woman's maternal "instinct" and suggests that it is the presence of children—not solely biology—that unlocks the maternal response. The character of Mamzelle Aurélie enables Chopin to construct a far less conventional role for women, one that draws upon the two predominant feminist schools of thought at the time: the essentialist and the antiessentialist approaches to woman's "nature." Ostman traces Chopin's development of an older female character whose newly found maternal instincts and inherent independence anticipate the "New Woman" of the next century and collapse the binary categories of feminist thought in the late nineteenth and early twentieth centuries.

"Part Two: New Pedagogical Approaches" moves the critical discussion to a pedagogical discussion. The final section in *Kate Chopin in Context: New Approaches* provides a range of scholar-teachers' experience and knowledge and the varied contexts of their classrooms for teaching Chopin's works. As such a widely taught author, Chopin offers teachers and students multiple and diverse opportunities to discover—and rediscover—her work. And as all seasoned instructors know, teaching enables one to master a subject; it broadens knowledge and critical thought. Therefore, this section provides a bridge from the theoretical and critical work in the preceding section to the practical application in the classroom, where deeper understandings continue to manifest and augment Chopin's importance within the American literary canon.

Part two opens with chapter 7, "The "I Hate Edna" Club," in which Emily Toth traces the variety of student responses to Chopin's famous protagonist, Edna Pontellier, over the course of 40 years and spanning critical responses and institutions across the nation. Beginning with Willa Cather, whose review of *The Awakening* calls Edna "one of many foolish, limited women who expect the passion of love to fill and gratify every need of life," Toth includes a variety of responses that invite analysis but that also paradoxically provides insight into the genius of Chopin. The "I Hate Edna" tracing leads to present-day students, including plagiarists, and provides the foundation for a commentary on students, American higher education, and literary responses through the late twentieth century and up to the twenty-first century.

In chapter 8, "Pioneering Kate Chopin's Feminism: Elizabeth Stoddard's *The Morgesons* as Patchwork Precursor to *The Awakening*," Diana Epelbaum traces the ancestry of Chopin's masterpiece, *The Awakening* (1899), to Elizabeth Stoddard's neglected 1862 novel, *The Morgesons*, and reopens for students the exploration of Chopin's best-known novel through the lens of feminism, as compared to Stoddard's radical work. *The Morgesons* illuminates several provocative points of intersection between the feminist readings of these two novels. A stylistically singular, deeply ambivalent articulation of rebellious American womanhood, *The Morgesons* is a patchwork text of nineteenth-century domestic, romantic, and naturalistic styles that hovers dangerously, only to at key moments retreat, on the brink of the feminist perspective espoused in *The Awakening*. *The Morgesons*'s awkward fusion of conventions and styles lends the text a certain strangeness that underscores its imperfect vision. It is not until *The Awakening* that the complex negotiation of mixed genre forms and women's writing shapes itself into a more fully realized, coherent iteration of early feminist literature. Cassandra Morgeson's inner life and her systematic self-repression is the *The Morgesons*'s intensive focus, a subject reintroduced and finally catapulted into the next century by Chopin, whose character Edna Pontellier attains the full psychological expression and physical freedom Cassandra Morgeson cannot.

In chapter 9, "'I'm So Happy; It Frightens Me': Female Genealogy in Kate Chopin's and Pauline Hopkins's Fiction," Correna Catlett Merricks examines Chopin's short stories "Désirée's Baby" and "La Belle Zoraïde" and Pauline Hopkins's novel *Contending Forces*, which tells the story of the plantation in American culture through the lens of female genealogy, a subject ignored by most Chopin critics. Hopkins's work focuses on how the images of "haunting" convey the way these stories emphasize genealogical history and how the violence of the past seeps into the present and translates into pervasive anxiety that impacts relationships between women and mother–child relationships. She argues that linking these two stories can enable students to understand how Chopin's work subverts the patriarchal order of the plantation South. The texts that Merricks compares here center on motherhood and mother–child relationships, but they destabilize the plantation's traditional hierarchy by connecting black women and white children and by reminding readers of the sexual relationships between white men and black women. The presence of women of color and mixed-race children in these stories disrupts a binary understanding of race and subverts the patriarchal order of the plantation south because it exposes what George Handley calls "the ellipses of the planter's scheme, the moments of contact with those who have been excluded" (15). On the plantation, the lives of black and white women were intricately intertwined in a complex hierarchical system; they often had sexual relations with the same men, had children at the same time, and raised them together. Merricks argues that Chopin and Hopkins boldly depict the oppressive nature of the plantation system, but they are limited by how their relationships with the plantation past impact their views of femininity; the texts primarily work to subvert the plantation hierarchy, but they also uphold it at times. However, she also argues that Chopin's and Hopkins's writings allow students to see when a linear understanding of the plantation is troubled: female characters who are orphans or foundlings, Gothic imagery, and monstrous depictions of the female body shift the audience's gaze toward women, relationships between women, and the violence women experienced in the American South.

In chapter 10, "American Refusals: A Continuum of "I Prefer Not Tos" As Articulated in the Work of Chopin, Hawthorne, Harper, Atherton, and Dreiser," Patricia J. Sehulster argues that given the ways students tend to categorize texts and authors and relegate them to separate entities without connection to one another, teachers need to demonstrate that all literature represents a continuum and an ongoing dialogue among intersecting texts. She uses the women characters of Hawthorne's *Blithedale Romance* (1852), Harper's "The Two Offers," Atherton's *Hermia Suydam* (1889) and *Patience Sparhawk* (1903), Dreiser's *Sister Carrie* (1900), as compared to those in Chopin's "Désirée's Baby" (1893) and "A Pair of Silk Stockings" (1896), as examples of that continuum and conversation through the lens of the growth and ambiguities inherent in the "New Woman" of the nineteenth century. Encompassing differences of gender, race, and perspective of a 50-year historical context, Sehulster writes, these authors nonetheless demonstrate a continuum and stylistic progression of American literature connected by time and nation. Sehulster's study derives from her experience in a diverse community college setting, but it extends well to most classrooms, even in other types of institutions. The teacher who uses this lens of discovery can lead students on a journey that codifies a method of inquiry that seeks connection instead of separation and a shift that displaces the rules of canon in favor of the rules of a symphony of literary voices in ongoing and related movements.

In a move around the globe, chapter 11, "What Did She Die of? 'The Story of an Hour' in the Middle East Classroom," by Mohanalakshmi Rajakumar and Geetha Rajeswar, brings a Qatari perspective to the well-known short story. They assert that teaching "The Story of an Hour" during the first part of a two-course series for first-year writing students in the Middle East has revealed compelling parallels between the sensibilities of Chopin's era and attitudes toward women and marriage in contemporary Arab society. Qatar, an emirate the size of Connecticut, perches on the Arabian peninsula above the kingdom of Saudi Arabia. With one of the wealthiest native populations in the world, Qatari citizens have access to all the commodities of modern life found in the Western Hemisphere. But their consumption of electronics and popular culture does not mean they ascribe to modern, Western social values. Examining students' reading logs, essays, and comments in class discussion, Rajakumar and Rajeswar show how female Arab students in Qatar read this text, a story ostensibly about a woman who dies from surprise at the sight of her husband, and demonstrate the parallels between modern Qatar and Chopin's day, as well as demonstrate viable ways to approach teaching the text, given this context.

Finally, in chapter 12, "Teaching Chopin Using Multimedia," Kate O'Donoghue encourages instructors to assign their students multimedia projects. O'Donoghue argues that multimedia approaches enliven the discussion of literature for today's students and deepen their knowledge of Chopin's contributions to American cultural and historical life. O'Donoghue contributes to recent work in the digital humanities that seeks to collapse the gap between pedagogy and research, and maintains that students can work along with instructors to create online, collaborative, and open-source scholarship. Here, O'Donoghue outlines an ongoing project that maps places in Kate Chopin's 1892 short story, "Miss McEnders," in order to highlight regional changes resulting from the social and economic inequality that developed in St. Louis after the Civil War.

Together, the chapters in this volume present fresh, new, and renewed looks at Chopin's work. The contributors have read and reread the author's stories, applying the broad range of their experience and knowledge to reaffirm the relevance of the once controversial author to our own times. Through the multiple efforts of several contributors to this collection, as well as many others, Chopin has remained popular with modern readers; however, this was not always the case—as her absence from the canon and the literary market for most of the twentieth century warns us. *Kate Chopin in Context: New Approaches* uses the work of existing scholarship that revived Chopin's literature and cemented her significance as an American author as a jumping off point for new scholarly perspectives—from outside and inside the classroom—and reminds us how relevant her work is to past generations and future generations, here in the United States and around the world.

Works Cited

Chopin, Kate. *The Awakening*. Ed. Margo Culley. 2nd ed. New York: 1994. Print.

Handley, George. *Postslavery Literatures in the Americas: Family Portraits in Black and White*. Charlottesville: UP of Virginia, 2000. Print.

Taylor, Helen. "Bringing Kate Chopin to Britain: A Transatlantic Perspective." *Awakenings: The Story of the Kate Chopin Revival*. Ed. Bernard Koloski. Baton Rouge: Louisiana State UP, 2009. 47–60. Print.

Toth, Emily. *Kate Chopin*. Austin: U of Texas P, 1990. Print.

PART I

New Contextual Approaches

CHAPTER 1

Chopin's Enlightened Men

Bernard Koloski

What a disappointment, what a disgrace, the men in Kate Chopin's best-known fiction turn out to be: the neglectful Léonce Pontellier, the frightened Robert Lebrun, or the womanizing Alcée Arobin in *The Awakening*,[1] the controlling Brently Mallard in "The Story of an Hour," or the repulsive Armand Aubigny in "Désirée's Baby." These men cannot begin to understand the needs of the women around them. Only Alcée Laballière in "The Storm," driven by the same desires as Calixta, is attuned to his lover—for the moment at least.

Readers familiar solely with widely taught Chopin works like these might well conclude that Kate Chopin specializes in creating strong, intuitive women and weak, indifferent men. It is certainly true that many of Kate Chopin's sensitive, intelligent characters are women, and it is true that readers and critics today tend to focus their attention on these women. The Norwegian critic Per Seyersted set the tone for discussing Kate Chopin in 1969 by publishing almost all her fiction and by positioning her in his critical biography as an essential figure in the realm of women's literature. Critics and scholars since Seyersted draw heavily upon his work and upon the 1999 Chopin biography by Emily Toth, which is also woman-centric.[2]

But Kate Chopin's works include more than a few astute, compassionate men, characters in touch with their own promptings, to be sure, but also with those of the women they care about. They are modern men, men ahead of their times, products of the same cultural forces sweeping across Europe and America in the 1880s and 1890s that gave rise to Chopin's modern women. They embody the emerging dynamic—the diminishing religious influence, the openness about sex, the questioning of gender roles, the intellectual audacity—that was playing out in advanced Western circles at the close of the nineteenth century. The intellectual group that Kate Chopin belonged to in St. Louis when she was writing her stories was one of those advanced circles, and Chopin supplemented what she was discussing with American journalists, publishers, philosophers, and others by monitoring Parisian media and French Third Republic fiction (she was a native speaker of French as well as English).[3]

From Wallace Offdean in her first short story to Mr. Laborde in one of her last, from the extraordinary Gouvernail in "Athénaïse" to the fully developed David Hosmer in *At Fault*—and through characters in other stories—Chopin offers us perceptive, enlightened men, men who are worthy friends, lovers, partners, or fathers for her powerful women.[4]

Offdean in "A No-Account Creole"

Wallace Offdean, the young businessman through whose consciousness we enter Kate Chopin's imaginative world, is "a sure-footed fellow," we learn on the opening pages of "A No-Account Creole," Chopin's first short story (drafted in 1888, revised in 1891, and published in 1894), determined to "get his feet well planted on solid ground, and to keep his head cool and clear." Above all, Chopin tells us, Offdean "would keep clear of the maelstroms of sordid work and senseless pleasure in which the average American business man may be said alternately to exist, and which reduce him, naturally, to a rather ragged condition of soul" (166).[5]

Offdean hopes to purchase a neglected Louisiana Red River plantation that he admires and to marry the woman he loves. The obstacles he deals with to fulfill his hopes define his character. Although he is deeply drawn to Euphrasie, the daughter of the plantation's caretaker, he at first controls himself. He understands that "overwhelming passion was taking possession of him" but he knows, too, that he is still financially insecure and is not in a position to enter marriage (180).

Only when he realizes that he can use his new inheritance to purchase the plantation does he conclude that he can propose to Euphrasie. He imagines a "delicious" life on the Red River plantation with Euphrasie as his wife and an existence that "imposing bodily activity, admits the intellectual repose in which thought unfolds" (184).

Yet, although he has spent many days with Euphrasie examining the plantation and has met her again at Mardi Gras in New Orleans, and although he rightly believes that she returns the passion that he feels for her, he is not aware that she is engaged to Placide, whom she had grown up with and likes well enough and whose proposal she had accepted because "she saw no reason why she should not be his wife when he asked her to" (171).

Placide is, Chopin tells us, an impetuous, hot-blooded, "no-account" Creole, and he is infuriated when he learns that Offdean loves Euphrasie and that she returns his love. Driven by "brute passion," he sets out with his gun to kill his rival (187). But Offdean, who is unarmed, shows great courage in talking calmly to Placide, appealing to his sense of honor.[6] "The way to love a woman," he tells the Creole, "is to think first of her happiness. If you love Euphrasie, you must go to her clean. I love her myself enough to want you to do that" (188).

Offdean prevails, Placide backs off and leaves the plantation, and Euphrasie can have the husband she yearns for. It's true that Offdean wants Euphrasie "for his very own" (184), just as Placide does, both exhibiting what Chopin in the short story "Her Letters" calls the "the man-instinct of possession" (781). Peggy Skaggs writes that in her fiction Chopin reveals "an awareness that women find their sense of identity largely through their relationships with other people, especially their husbands. And she observes that too often these relationships are made painful and unrewarding by male possessiveness" (277).

Kate Chopin offers us few ideal characters, female or male. Yet because of his level-headedness, his courage, and what Barbara Ewell calls the "rational moderation" of his goals, Wallace Offdean emerges as an engaging young man, a good partner for Euphrasie, along with—as Ewell also points out—a representative of "the new order in the South" since he will draw upon his business experience and his resources to restore prosperity to the Red River plantation (56).

And Linda Wagner-Martin notes that "while we rightly valorize Kate Chopin for being a champion of realistic characterization of women, for creating women who recognize—and often act on—physical passion, her earliest fiction reminds us that she began her career drawing loving and yet realistic portraits of a bevy of young men whose youthful charm remains vivid" (205). Wallace Offdean is one of those men.

Mr. Laborde in "Charlie"

"A No-Account Creole," Kate Chopin's first story, offers us young Offdean setting out in life. "Charlie," one of her last (written in 1900 but first published only in 1969)—and her longest—gives us

Mr. Laborde, an older man, a widower raising seven daughters whose ages run from 5 to 19.

We come to understand Offdean from inside and outside—from his own thoughts and from the impressions he makes on others. But we know Mr. Laborde almost entirely from outside, from the consciousness of a tomboy, 17-year old Charlie (Charlotte), his second child, who loves him dearly.

When we meet her, Charlie is eager to behave like the son Mr. Laborde hoped for but did not have. She gallops her horse at breakneck speed, carries a pistol, and is constantly late for her lessons and therefore in trouble with the governess who is charged with the girls' education. Charlie "really felt that nothing made much difference so long as her father was happy," Chopin writes. "Her actions were reprehensible in her own eyes only so far as they interfered with his peace of mind" (991).

Mr. Laborde nevertheless treasures having time alone with her. When he visits her in the seminary in the city where he had sent her after she accidentally hit and wounded a visitor to the plantation during her target practice, "he was like a school boy on a holiday" (1010).[7] He is impressed with the soft, womanly hands she has worked so hard to cultivate, and tells her so, but he gently reminds her of other important things. "You know you mustn't think too much about the hands and all that," he says. "Take care of the head, too, and the temper" (1012).

Yet at the close of the story, after Mr. Laborde has lost his right arm—and nearly his life—in an accident at his sugar mill, it is the now more womanly Charlie who firmly refuses to follow the other older girls as they head off to marriage, to boarding school, or to Paris with an aunt. "I know as much about the plantation as you do, dad; you know I do," she insists. "From now on I'm going to be—to be your right hand—your poor right hand" (1018). And she tells her suitor that she will in time accept his offer of marriage, but only after the younger children are raised. In the meantime, she will care for her father and manage the plantation.

She will act the role of the son she seemingly yearned to be. Per Seyersted notes that at the end of the story, Charlie "again assumes that self-assertive posture which men like to see as their prerogative" (*Biography* 183). Barbara Ewell adds that "like a Shakespearean comic heroine, Charlie enlarges herself by trying on the roles of each sex" (179). And Bonnie James Shaker argues that Charlie "returns to the androgyny of her youth, although her masculine freedoms are checked by her feminine familial responsibilities" (105).

Charlie matures in the story in good part because she is so confident in her father's love for her. Mr. Laborde will not part from his daughters and will not turn over their upbringing to someone else. He supports each of his girls in their endeavors and gives them the freedom to be different from one another and from him. He looks after them and does what is good for them. He does the same for his employees. He loses his arm because of "an accident at the sugar mill; a bit of perilous repairing in which he chose to assume the risk rather than expose others to danger" (1013). He is an endearing man—and an admirable father.

Yet Kate Chopin portrays Mr. Laborde, too, as less than ideal in character. He enjoys what is pleasant about fatherhood, but he resents needing to discipline Charlie: "Every one assumed an air of irresponsibility in regard to Charlie which was annoying to Mr. Laborde as it implied that the whole burden of responsibility lay upon his own shoulders, and he was conscious of not bearing it gracefully" (997–98). In her treatment of Mr. Laborde, Kate Chopin offers us what Lewis Leary calls her "tenderness, compassion, and sympathy" as well as her "underlying honest questioning which usually avoids irony as deftly as her compassion avoids sentimentality" (vi).

Gouvernail in "Athénaïse"

"Athénaïse" (written in 1895, published in 1896) is not so well known as the celebrated "Story of an Hour," "Désirée's Baby," or "The Storm," but it is a superb work, one of Kate Chopin's very best—an "American classic," as Susan Lohafer argues, a Library of America "Story of the Week," and a featured story on Voice of America broadcasts to people studying English around the world.

It is about a young girl who marries an older man, a plantation owner, a widower. But Athénaïse is not ready for marriage, she misses her family, especially her brother Montéclin, and she cannot deal with her husband's sexual passion. Gouvernail is the man whom she meets when Montéclin arranges for her to run away from the plantation and to live secretly in a boarding house in the French Quarter of New Orleans.

Gouvernail is remarkable among Kate Chopin's male characters, appearing not only in "Athénaïse" but playing a major role in "A Respectable Woman" and attending Edna Pontellier's party late in *The Awakening*. He is a New Orleans journalist, a man of "quick intelligence" (375), and is "older than thirty and younger than forty" (372), Chopin suggests. His dwelling is full of books of philosophy and poetry, and "it was his almost invariable custom," Chopin says, "to spend Sunday evenings out in the American quarter, among a congenial set of men and women,—*des esprits forts*, all of them, whose lives were irreproachable, yet whose opinions would startle even the traditional 'sapeur,' for whom 'nothing is sacred'" (373).

Gouvernail travels in a social circle that resembles the high-powered St. Louis intellectual company Kate Chopin kept during the 1890s when she was writing her fiction—a company that included journalists like Gouvernail—and it is not surprising that he comes close to seeing life in the way that she herself does. Joyce Dyer notes that "Gouvernail highlights themes, establishes moods, and indicates, in subtle ways, the direction of Chopin's art and philosophy" (54). He is the most articulate of Chopin's men, and the most insightful.

In "A Respectable Woman," he quotes lines from Walt Whitman's *Leaves of Grass* that show he is aware of the sexual arousal of the married woman he is sitting next to. In *The Awakening*, among the guests at the dinner party Edna throws to mark her leaving her husband's house, he quotes an Algernon Charles Swinburne sonnet, suggesting an ominous atmosphere of death in the room.[8] In "Athénaïse," after an hour of talk with the story's title character, he understands her very well. "It was not so much what she had said as what her half saying had revealed to his quick intelligence," Chopin tells us. "He had gathered that she was self-willed, impulsive, innocent, ignorant, unsatisfied, dissatisfied" (375).

Yet troubled as she is, Athénaïse is also charming, open, honest, and very beautiful—Gouvernail finds her face "radiant" (376). He is drawn to her. He explores New Orleans with her, and, as the days pass, becomes her confidant, falls in love with her. When he finds her crying one night, "a wave of pity and tenderness swept through him. He took her hands and pressed them against him. He wondered what would happen if he were to put his arms around her" (379). He is unprepared when Athénaïse instead puts her arms around him and weeps bitterly on his shoulder. Chopin describes his impulse to pull her to himself and kiss her—and then explains in one of the more extraordinary passages in her fiction why he does not:

> He understood a thousand times better than she herself understood it that he was acting as substitute for Montéclin. Bitter as the conviction was, he accepted it. He was patient; he could wait. He hoped some day to hold her with a lover's arms. That she was married made no particle of difference to Gouvernail. He could not conceive or dream of it making a difference. When the time came that she wanted him,—as

> he hoped and believed it would come,—he felt he would have a right to her. So long as she did not want him, he had no right to her,—no more than her husband had. (379–80)

As impressive as his "advanced" line of thought (373) is Gouvernail's response when Athénaïse discovers she is pregnant and rushes home to the plantation, forgetting about—embarrassed about— the intimacy she has been building with him. He takes her to her train and is "kind, attentive, and amiable, as usual, but respected to the utmost the new dignity and reserve that her manner had developed.... He was a man of intelligence, and took defeat gracefully; that was all. But as he made his way back to the carriage, he was thinking, 'By heaven, it hurts, it hurts!'" (383–84).

Chopin does not show us where Gouvernail's life leads him. But his eagerness to take up with a married woman seems likely to cause him and others eventual pain. And his "courtliness" toward Athénaïse, Barbara Ewell notes, "is only a style of hard-won restraint; his passions are as turbulent as [her husband's] and would doubtless be expressed in a similar way if Athénaïse would respond" (110).

Hosmer in *At Fault*

David Hosmer in Chopin's early novel *At Fault* (written in 1889 and 1890, published in 1890) is an older, more experienced businessman than Wallace Offdean in "A No-Account Creole." He has been married, but he divorced his wife when she turned to alcohol after their child died. He is successful in his business ventures and works extremely hard to earn money, but he is generous with his resources. He doubled the court's alimony payment to his former wife, and he seeks to build a financially secure future for his sister, because he is her sole support since their parents died.

He loves the widowed Thérèse Lafirme, who—in spite of her neighbors' doubts—is herself managing the four-thousand acre plantation she inherited when her husband died and upon whose land Hosmer operates a sawmill. Thérèse returns his love, but she is a Roman Catholic, and although (like Kate Chopin herself) she is Catholic more in tradition than in conviction, she refuses his declaration of affection. "You married a woman of weak character," she tells Hosmer. "You furnished her with every means to increase that weakness, and shut her out absolutely from your life and yourself from hers. You left her then as practically without moral support as you have certainly done now, in deserting her. It was the act of a coward"

(37). Hosmer, Thérèse insists, should remarry his former wife, seek to rehabilitate her, and make the best life he can with her.

Like Wallace Offdean who, in times of trouble, turns for advice to a "stoic philosopher" (178), David Hosmer consults an alter ego, as he calls his friend Homeyer. "And what had Homeyer said" about Thérèse's suggestion? "He had startled and angered Hosmer with his denunciation of Thérèse's sophistical guidance. Rather—he proposed—let Hosmer and Thérèse marry, and if Fanny were to be redeemed—. . . let the redemption come by different ways than those of sacrifice: let it be an outcome from the capability of their united happiness" (46).

As Chopin phrases it, "Hosmer did not listen to his friend Homeyer. Love was his god now, and Thérèse was Love's prophet" (46), so he follows Thérèse's advice, and the rest of the novel details a succession of turbulent events, although driven only in part by Hosmer's actions, that leads to Fanny's death—and the death of other characters, including Gregoire, the brother of Placide of "A No-Account Creole." A year after Fanny's death, Hosmer marries Thérèse Lafirme, and the novel ends on a note of hope.

Modern readers may respond with incredulity to Thérèse's insistence that Hosmer return to the woman he divorced, but the ethics of divorce was very much a matter of public discussion in the late nineteenth century (William Dean Howells had published a novel, *A Modern Instance*, about the subject in 1882), and fierce arguments in the secular and religious press were common. Chopin would surely have been aware of those arguments, and, as Donna Campbell observes, she explores them by following the pattern of nineteenth-century social problem novels (40–41). Per Seyersted argues that *At Fault* is "the first American novel to treat divorce amorally" (*Biography* 93).

Clearly Hosmer does not see the matter in moral terms. "Do you know, Mrs. Lafirme," he tells Thérèse, "it's one of those things to drive a man mad, the sweet complaisance with which women accept situations, or inflict situations that it takes the utmost of a man's strength to endure" (90). He insists that "there would be more dignity in putting an end to my life" (92). And Thérèse in time confesses that "I have seen myself at fault in following what seemed the only right. I feel as if there were no way to turn for the truth. Old supports appear to be giving way beneath me. They were so secure before" (154).

No doubt, Hosmer—whom we come to know better than Offdean, Mr. Laborde, or Gouvernail because Chopin develops his character over the length of a novel—brings about some of his own problems. Years earlier, he had rushed into marriage with Fanny shortly after meeting her. "I am a poor hand to analyze character: my own or another's," he admits. "I have never schooled myself to inquiry into my own motives for action. I have been always thoroughly the business man. . . . Socially, I have mingled little with my fellow-beings, especially with women" (34).

Jane Hotchkiss speaks of "the extent to which David Hosmer, the romantic hero, is 'at fault' in the events culminating in the death of his weak but certainly not evil wife, Fanny. One can easily read Hosmer as the earnest love martyr, the hapless victim of two women: one whose life is steeped in error, another who in spite of her many virtues and attractions is guilty of a fatal error in judgment" (35). But "in the course of the story," Hotchkiss adds, "Hosmer repeatedly refuses responsibility for the misguided scheme to redeem Fanny, in which he is nevertheless the primary actor" (36).

And Barbara Ewell notes that "Hosmer's dulled emotional life represents a defection from his moral responsibility to participate fully in the human community." It's true, she notes, that he doubled his wife's alimony, but his "material generosity is his means of satisfying social obligations and of salving his conscience." For Kate Chopin, she argues, his "shortcomings" are those of "American male individualism generally. Dramatizing increasingly specialized functions of male and female, Hosmer acknowledges with complacency his inability to comprehend human emotions and relationships. Neither the inner life nor society holds much interest for him. These are the province of women" (38–39).

Ewell's argument rings true for David Hosmer, but not for other Chopin characters, not for Wallace Offdean—who sets out to avoid precisely the businessman's "rather ragged condition of soul" that Hosmer finds himself saddled with—nor for Mr. Laborde or Gouvernail. And foolish as Hosmer may have been to marry Fanny initially and then to follow Thérèse's advice, he has grown by the end of *At Fault*. When Thérèse tells him that she feels "as if there were no way to turn for the truth," he replies, "the truth in its entirety isn't given to man to know—such knowledge, no doubt, would be beyond human endurance. But we make a step towards it, when we learn that there is rottenness and evil in the world, masquerading as right and morality—when we learn to know the living spirit from the dead letter" (154).

Enlightened Men

The critic George Arms notes that in her fiction Kate Chopin "presents a series of events in which the truth is present, but with a philosophical pragmatism she is unwilling to extract a final truth. Rather, she sees truth as constantly re-forming itself and as so much a part of the context of what happens that it can never be final or for that matter abstractly stated" (222).

There may be no final truth to be extracted from the appearance of Wallace Offdean, Mr. Laborde, Gouvernail, and David Hosmer in Kate Chopin's works. But other short stories help place such characters in context. Chopin wrote stories about a considerate man meeting and then falling in love with a poor woman ("Love on the Bon-Dieu"), with an impetuous woman ("A Night in Acadie"), or with a proud, independent woman ("The Wood Choppers"). She wrote stories about a man with a great sense of loyalty to the family of his former white master ("Nég Créol"), to a former black cook ("Ozème's Holiday"), or to his former neighbor who is devastated by his wife's abandoning him while he is fighting in the Civil War ("After the Winter"). She wrote a story about a heartbroken man yearning for the woman he loves long after she has lost her youth and beauty ("A Visit to Avoyelles"). She wrote one about an innocent, troubled, torn adolescent ("A Vocation and a Voice").[9]

When she offers us a man who is objectionable, she sometimes redeems him. Cazeau, for example, the husband Athénaïse escapes from before turning for comfort to Gouvernail, suffers at least as much as his young wife from the apparent failure of their marriage. He is horrified in realizing that he may be treating Athénaïse as his father once treated an escaped slave, and he sends her a letter "in which he disclaimed any further intention of forcing his commands upon her. He did not desire her presence ever again in his home unless she came of her free will, uninfluenced by family or friends; unless she could be the companion he had hoped for in marrying her, and in some measure return affection and respect for the love which he continued and would always continue to feel for her" (367). Chopin's men can at times adapt.

They live in an era of vast cultural transformations in the United States and Europe, and they embody characteristics of both the old order and the new. Their male possessiveness is on full display, but so is their questioning of traditional morality and the roles that men and women assume. When Thérèse in the closing chapter of *At Fault* suggests to Hosmer, her new husband, that he could now help her run her successful plantation, he simply laughs. "No, no, Madame Thérèse," he says, "I'll not rob you of your occupation. I'll put no bungling hand into your concerns" (156).

We may not want to think of Offdean, Mr. Laborde, Gouvernail, Hosmer, and other Chopin male characters as paragons of virtue or strength, but they are honest and affectionate, sometimes courageous, occasionally uncommonly insightful. They seek to make the most of what they have to work with. They seek the best possible lives for themselves and for the women they care about.

In *Lélia* (Kate Chopin called her only daughter Lélia, apparently in appreciation of this 1833 French novel), George Sand writes that "l'homme que je pourrais aimer n'est pas né, et il ne naîtra peut-être que plusieurs siècles après ma mort" (124)—["the man whom I would be able to love has not been born, and he will, perhaps, be born only several centuries after my death"].

If Kate Chopin shared such a conviction, some of her best stories and her early novel do not show it.

Notes

1. Robert C. Evans offers a vigorous defense of Robert Lebrun (146–61). And Catherine Mainland points to male characters in *The Awakening*—Edna's two sons, Victor, Arobin, and Dr. Mandelet—who "represent the four stages of childhood, adolescence, young manhood, and maturity. The influence these characters have on Edna follows a chronological progression through the natural stages of development of man, as might be encountered in a traditional, masculine narrative" (75). Dr. Mandelet might be thought of as one of Chopin's enlightened men, because he is known for his wisdom. But he does not have a close relationship with Edna Pontellier. He understands that she is troubled, but as a Creole and an old friend of her husband, he does not have a way to intervene—and he does not want to be involved with other people's inner lives and secrets. He is insightful but ineffective. When he reaches out to Edna the day before she dies, it is too late.
2. Extensive, up-to-date, easily searchable bibliographies of books and articles about Chopin's works, as well as lists of translations of those works into other languages and scholarship written in those languages, can be found on *KateChopin.org*, the website of the Kate Chopin International Society.
3. Per Seyersted's and Emily Toth's Chopin biographies describe the changing culture of Kate Chopin's America. My study of the short fiction focuses on the importance of Chopin's bilingual and bicultural imagination.
4. Pearl Brown rightly argues that "Chopin scholarship has understandably concentrated on the awakening of her women, but the awakening of her men also deserves attention. In Chopin's vision

of a progressive society, both men and women must strive for autonomy" (81).

5. Page references in the text refer to Sandra Gilbert's Library of America edition of Chopin's fiction. There is a list of composition and publication dates for Kate Chopin's works in that volume as well as on the closing pages of Per Seyersted's *Complete Works of Kate Chopin*.
6. Emily Toth argues that "men's character conflicts, especially over notions of honor as in Chopin's story, were what grabbed [Richard Watson] Gilder," the editor of the *Century* magazine, where the story appeared in 1894 (132).
7. Anne M. Blythe objects to Per Seyersted's suggestion that there may be a "fixation" between Charlie and her father (207).
8. Texts of the Whitman lines and the Swinburne sonnet are included in several printed editions of Chopin's works, as well as on *KateChopin.org*, in the Questions and Answers section of pages devoted to the novel and the short story.
9. Chopin also wrote stories about a man obsessively attached to a woman ("Azélie" and "At Chênière Caminada").

Works Cited

Arms, George. "Kate Chopin's *The Awakening* in the Perspective of Her Literary Career." *Essays on American Literature in Honor of Jay B. Hubbell*. Ed. Clarence Gohdes. Durham, NC: Duke UP, 1967. 215–28. Print.

Blythe, Anne M. "Kate Chopin's 'Charlie.'" *Kate Chopin Reconsidered: Beyond the Bayou*. Ed. Lynda S. Boren and Sara deSaussure Davis. Baton Rouge: Louisiana State UP, 1992. 207–15. Print.

Brown, Pearl L. "Awakened Men in Kate Chopin's Creole Stories." *American Transcendental Quarterly* 13 (1999): 69–82. Print.

Campbell, Donna. "*At Fault*: A Reappraisal of Kate Chopin's Other Novel." *The Cambridge Companion to Kate Chopin*. Ed. Janet Beer. Cambridge, England: Cambridge UP, 2008. 27–43. Print.

Dyer, Joyce. "Gouvernail, Kate Chopin's Sensitive Bachelor." *Southern Literary Journal* 14 (1981): 46–55. Print.

Evans, Robert C. "In Defense of Robert Lebrun in Kate Chopin's *The Awakening*." *Critical Insights: The Awakening*. Ed. Robert C. Evans. Ipswich, MA: Grey House, 2014. 146–61. Print.

Ewell, Barbara C. *Kate Chopin*. New York: Ungar, 1986. Print.

Gilbert, Sandra M. ed. *Kate Chopin: Complete Novels and Stories*. New York: Library of America, 2002. Print.

Hotchkiss, Jane. "Confusing the Issue: Who's 'At Fault'?" *Louisiana Literature* 11.1 (1994): 31–43. Print.

Koloski, Bernard. *Kate Chopin: A Study of the Short Fiction*. New York: Twayne, 1996. Print.

———, ed. KateChopin.org. Kate Chopin International Society, 1 July 2014. Web. 1 July 2014.

Leary, Lewis, ed. Introduction. *The Awakening and Other Stories by Kate Chopin*. New York: Holt, Rinehart and Winston, 1970. iii–xx. Print.

Lohafer, Susan. *Coming to Terms with the Short Story*. Baton Rouge: Louisiana State UP, 1985. Print.

Mainland, Catherine. "Chopin's Bildungsroman: Male Role Models in *The Awakening*." *Mississippi Quarterly* 64 (2011): 75–85. Print.

Sand, George. *Lélia*. Paris: Calmann Lévy, 1894. Print.

Seyersted, Per, ed. *The Complete Works of Kate Chopin*. Baton Rouge: Louisiana State UP, 1969. Print.

———. *Kate Chopin: A Critical Biography*. Baton Rouge: Louisiana State UP, 1969. Print.

Shaker, Bonnie James. *Coloring Locals: Racial Formation in Kate Chopin's Youth's Companion Stories*. Iowa City: U of Iowa P, 2003. Print.

Skaggs, Peggy. "'The Man-Instinct of Possession': A Persistent Theme in Kate Chopin's Stories." *Louisiana Studies* 14 (1975): 277–85. Print.

Toth, Emily. *Unveiling Kate Chopin*. Jackson, MS: UP of Mississippi, 1999. Print.

Wagner-Martin, Linda. "Kate Chopin's Fascination with Young Men." *Critical Essays on Kate Chopin*. Ed. Alice Hall Petry. New York: G. K. Hall, 1996. 197–206. Print.

CHAPTER 2

Kate Chopin and the Dilemma of Individualism

Rafael Walker

In an exquisitely compact piece titled "Emancipation: A Life Fable," Kate Chopin narrates the journey of a beast that has spent his entire life hitherto locked in a cage. Thanks to the "care and protection of an invisible protecting hand," this creature has never wanted for anything: "When he thirsted, water was brought, and when he felt the need of rest, there was provided a bed of straw upon which to lie."[1] This snug existence has satisfied the creature so much that he had come to believe that there couldn't possibly be more to the world than what experience has already shown him—that the narrow ray of sun that penetrates his dwelling "existed but to lighten his home." But everything changes when, one day, the door accidentally swings open (presumably as a result of the owner's carelessness). According to the narrator, the creature is initially quite put out to find the door ajar and would have closed it if not for the fact that "for such a task his limbs were purposeless." Unable to shut himself off from the world outside, he finally pokes his head through the door. However, the immensity of the open sky and wide world prove overwhelming for this being that had never before seen beyond the four walls of his cage.

At least, it does at first. Try as he might, the creature cannot rest with the door open, "for the spell of the Unknown was over him," leading him to venture farther and farther out, for increasingly longer spans of time. Eventually, though, the discovery that there was so much more to see and desire than food, water, and a warm place to sleep overcomes him, and he bolts full-speed out of the cage—"seeing, smelling, touching of all things." Although there are times when he can find nothing to eat, he never returns to his former haven. "So does he live, seeking, finding, joying and suffering." There the short fable ends—in Chopin's characteristically suggestive fashion—with no explanation of why this lowly creature would prefer a life of scarcity to the easy existence he had enjoyed within the iron bars. All we know is that the creature is somehow fundamentally changed through his acquaintance with desire, for "the cage remains forever empty!"

This odd little fable, only a single page long, touches briefly but provocatively on a subject that Chopin would spend much of her short career exploring: the transformative potential of desire. Caged and sated, the creature of the fable remains immune to the pangs of desire until his horizons expand, revealing lacks in his life that he formerly had no way of knowing existed. The real-life referent of this fable becomes more explicit in Chopin's short story "A Pair of Silk Stockings." When its protagonist, Mrs. Sommers, finds herself "the unexpected possessor of fifteen dollars," her actions take a considerable turn away from her characteristically maternal ways. Initially presented as a paragon of maternal self-effacement—earlier that very day, having forgotten to eat because absorbed by domestic chores—Mrs. Sommers at first resolves to spend almost every cent of the fortuitous $15 on her children: a sturdy pair of shoes for Janie, yards of percale for new shirts for the entire Sommers brood, a beautifully patterned gown for Mag, caps for the boys, sailor hats for the girls. The one personal extravagance Mrs. Sommers permits herself—two pairs of stockings (and these only after she has calculated the costs of her children's new things)—she considers not for her own enjoyment but for her housekeeping efficiency: "what darning [their purchase] would save for a while!" (*KC* 816).

But the many appeals of the department store bewitch Mrs. Sommers out of her customary asceticism, and her concern quickly shifts away from the children's needs, to her own suppressed longings. Thanks to Chopin's richly sensuous language, we are able to proceed step by step through the total seduction of Mrs. Sommers by the marketplace. By the end of her encounter with the silk stockings, Mrs. Sommers is said to have gone on "feeling the soft, sheeny luxurious things—with both hands now, holding them up to see them glisten, and to feel them glide serpent-like through her fingers" (817). When she eventually grows hungry from her busy day of shopping, the mysterious hedonistic "impulse that was guiding her" impels her to take a toothsome lunch of a half dozen bluepoints, a "plump chop," crème frappée, a glass of Rhine, and, as a digestif, a cup of black coffee. "Another time," we are told, "she would have stilled the cravings for food until reaching her own home, where she would have brewed herself a cup of tea and taken a snack of anything that was available" (819). But not on this day. Clearly, the impulse buyer we observe here has come a long way from the self-denying mother who would often get so caught up in ministering to her family's needs that she would forget to eat altogether.

As Mrs. Sommers runs through $15, snatching up every manner of costly apparel and feasting like a queen, her children have all but disappeared from her thoughts, and, indeed, we hear no more of them beyond the story's first page. Yet, despite Mrs. Sommers's unwonted self-indulgence, the short story terminates on a cable car, in a scene of unmixed longing: "A man with keen eyes, who sat opposite to her, seemed to like the study of her small, pale face. It puzzled him to decipher what he saw there. In truth, he saw nothing—unless he were wizard enough to detect a poignant wish, a powerful longing that the cable car would never stop anywhere, but go on and on with her forever" (820). These cryptic last sentences leave us in a quandary. For one, who is this nonplussed male spectator—nonplussed because not "wizard enough" to detect Mrs. Sommers's desire to prolong her day? Moreover, how do we explain the puzzling fact that, although she has splurged much more than ever before, rather than being surfeited or at least satisfied, she wants more? Paradoxically, Mrs. Sommers's appetite swells as she consumes.

The two questions with which this closing passage leaves us—about the significance of the staring stranger and the paradoxical nature of Mrs. Sommers's desire—are linked. As Nancy Bentley suggests, Mrs. Sommers's "opacity signifies a new kind of interpretive problem" (145).[2] The fact that Mrs. Sommers, in her altered state, remains so inscrutable to the pensive gentleman is indeed full of metaphorical significance. Chopin's contemporaries believed that the onset of consumer culture created a chasm between the sexes. One reviewer of Edith Wharton's novel *Custom of the Country* from the *Nation* (clearly more interested in expounding his theory of civilization than reviewing her novel) reminds his reader of the "inherent difference in faculty between men and women, and an equally apparent difference in adaptability." "The aspirations for the softer, finer things of life," he continues, "are stronger in the female of the species. The advent of leisure gives more immediate freedom to feelings long repressed." Women were better able to adapt to the nation's rise from scarcity to abundance, he suggests, and, as a result, "we are undoubtedly in the position of having placed woman on a pedestal and left her there lonely and rather dizzy." While their male counterparts maintain the pioneering spirit of their ancestors (only now in the sphere of commerce), women alone have adapted to a new order of self-indulgence, queens among a throng of male drudges.

This reviewer's description of the American woman left alone and "dizzy" on a pedestal aptly characterizes the daydreaming Mrs. Sommers—described at one point as "not thinking at all." In this short story, Chopin, like the reviewer, signals the celerity with which consumer culture was changing prevailing stereotypes of middle-class women, who were thought to be immersed in the endless pleasures of self-gratification. This metamorphosis was imagined to occur at a rate so rapid that it rendered women incomprehensible—almost unrecognizable—to their less adaptive male counterparts. After only a single day of shopping, Mrs. Sommers has been transformed from the self-abnegating mother of Victorian lore into the self-centered, prodigal woman who mystifies men. The "interpretive problem" to which Bentley refers turns out to stem from the power of consumer culture to engender a form of desire that radically alters the imagined relations between the sexes, transforming middle-class women from the selfless stewards of the private sphere into opaque seekers after self-gratification.

This cultural shift is central to Chopin's most famous work, *The Awakening*, which attempts to elaborate what is only hinted in "Emancipation" and "A Pair of Silk Stockings." In this novel, Chopin speculates more daringly than ever before on the consequences for middle-class women of society's authorization of female desire. Although *The Awakening* does not draw the explicit connection between the consumer-oriented market and female desire that we find in "A Pair of Silk Stockings"—set primarily in a shopping center—the novel nonetheless attributes the erosion of the nineteenth-century ideal of womanhood and domesticity to the unleashing of female desire. As is true of Mrs. Sommers, the emergence of desire renders Edna Pontellier unrecognizable to the other characters of the novel, the male characters especially. The novel begins with Edna's husband, Léonce, complaining that she is "burnt beyond recognition" after indulging in a swim that pleases her much more than it does him. The narrator suggests that it is her violation of convention that upsets her husband and renders her "beyond recognition": "What folly! to bathe at such an hour in such heat," he raves (*KC* 522). As was true of Mrs. Sommers, in Edna's case, "beyond recognition" becomes synonymous with "beyond convention." Later, when Léonce upbraids Edna for neglecting her household duties, the narrator notes that "He could see plainly that she was not herself." But, just when we think that Léonce understands his wife, we are assured of his misrecognition: "That is, he could not see that she was becoming herself and daily casting aside that fictitious self which we assume like a garment with which to appear before the world" (*KC* 586–7). Her self-indulgence appears to have made her a stranger to the very person who should know her best.

The predominance of the word *self* in this passage and throughout the novel offers an important clue to what the awakening of desire within Edna has done to her. Where desire leads Edna shares much with Mrs. Sommers's "poignant wish . . . that the cable car would never stop anywhere, but go on and on with her forever"—a wish that, if fulfilled, would separate her from her children and obligation forever. Initially intending to title the novel "A Solitary Soul," Chopin changed it only at her editor's urging. But, in retitling the novel, Chopin may have detracted from the fact that her heroine's greatest wish is simply to be left alone. Edna and the narrator express this sentiment frequently enough to make it clear: "[The absence of her children] seemed to free her of a responsibility which she had blindly assumed and for which Fate had not fitted her" (541); "Every step which she took toward relieving herself from obligations added to her strength and expansion as an individual" (629); "But I don't want anything but my own way" (650), she insists, and, even more succinctly, "I want to be let alone" (649).

Despite the simplicity of this wish—to be left alone—critics have often understood Edna's longings as fantastical. In agreement with Willa Cather's scathing review of *The Awakening*, for instance, Susan Rosowski conflates Edna Pontellier's problem with Emma Bovary's, proposing that her dilemma lies in the fact that "woman must choose between her inner life of romance and the outer world of reality" (54). In a more charitable interpretation of the novel, Sandra Gilbert argues that "*The Awakening* is a female fiction that both draws upon and revises *fin de siècle* hedonism to propose a feminist and matriarchal myth of Aphrodite/Venus as an alternative to the masculinist and patriarchal myth of Jesus" (91).[3] According to Gilbert, the novel "shows, from a female point of view, just what would 'really' happen to a mortal, turn-of-the-century woman who tried to claim for herself the erotic freedom and power owned by the classical queen of love" (92).

My more sublunary contention, *pace* Gilbert, is that *The Awakening* shows just what would really happen to a turn-of-the-century mother who tried to claim for herself the privileges of liberal individualism. An ideology that framed the way people conceived of the self in the nineteenth century, liberal individualism stresses the autonomy, self-enclosure, and privacy of the individual. For many widely noted reasons, this form of self-realization was, practically, only available to white men.[4] This is what makes Edna's urge so transgressive, for her desire to be left alone amounts to a liberal wish for self-possession.[5] This fact is doubtless at the root of Andrew Delbanco's suggestion that *The Awakening* be read as a "novel of passing"—not "about a light-skinned black passing for white" but about "a woman passing for a man" (104). While I do not believe that Edna's story truly counts as one of passing (a process requiring much more dissembling than could be expected from this uncompromising heroine), I concur with Delbanco's conviction that Chopin's frequent masculinization of Edna is hardly accidental. When Chopin notes that Edna had "strong, shapely hands" (in contrast to the other ladies' "dainty and discriminating fingers") (522), that she is "rather handsome than beautiful" (524), that she "drank the liquor from the glass as a man would have done" (612)—when Chopin describes her heroine in these masculine ways, she is metaphorically demonstrating that the liberal privileges of self-possession of which Edna is increasingly trying to avail herself are essentially male privileges. Put differently, to be a liberal individual is, in Chopin's mind, to be a white man.

Even before her transformative swim at Grand Isle—commonly understood as the turning point in the novel—the narrator carefully distinguishes Edna from the "mother-women" around her in order to establish her incongruence with idealized nineteenth-century femininity. Mother-women "idolized their children, worshiped their husbands, and esteemed it a holy privilege to efface themselves as individuals and grow wings as ministering angels" (*KC* 529). But Edna is simply "fond of her husband," possessing "no trace of passion or excessive and fictitious warmth " and "fond of her children in an uneven, impulsive way" (541). The consummate mother-woman, Edna's friend Adèle Ratignolle, serves to throw Edna's unconventionality into relief. Adèle is feminine to the point of cliché: "There are no words to describe her save the old ones that have served so often to picture the by-gone heroine of romance and the fair lady of our dreams" (529). Significantly, she is customarily cloaked in "a fluffiness of ruffles," which "suited her rich, luxuriant beauty as a greater severity of line could not have done" (*KC* 536–7). In contrast, Edna is sharply delimited: the "lines of her body were long, clean and symmetrical"; she displays a striking "severity of poise and movement"; her hat "clung close to her head" (536). These casually mentioned details hint at these women's differently constituted ego boundaries, the integrity and autonomy of Edna's self versus Adèle's psychological fluidity and organic oneness with her community. This contrast is brought into view once more when Edna withdraws from the sewing circle one afternoon at Grand Isle, where we find Adèle thriving among her fellow mother-women. Here, Edna abandons this scene of female sociability—a visual representation of the intense bonding that suffuses the idealized "woman's sphere"—in favor of a more solitary, stereotypically more masculine exercise. While these women tranquilly knit away, symbolizing the intertwinement of their lives, Edna extracts herself from the communal web of love and ritual to paint an impressionistic portrait of Adèle.[6]

After her first swim at Grand Isle, Edna's differences from the women around her grow even more explicit. What was merely hinted at before finds clear expression in Edna's bold declarations. For instance, whereas the other women take pride in self-effacement, after the swim, Edna insists on the sanctity of her self. "I would give up the unessential; I would give my money, I would give my life for my children," Edna explains to Adèle, "but I wouldn't give myself" (575). Adèle replies, "I don't know what you would call the essential, or what you mean by the unessential... but a woman who would give her life for her children could do no more than that—your Bible tells you so. I'm sure I couldn't do more than that." As the bemused response of this spokeswoman for mother-womanhood suggests, Edna's reference to a metaphysical self that is irreducible to her life seems nonsensical coming from the mouth of a married woman. What more, Adèle asks, does a woman have to give up than her life? In her insistence upon an inalienable self—"I wouldn't give myself"—Edna rehearses one of liberalism's dearest tenets, that individuals have property in their persons.[7] Yet, as a woman of the nineteenth century, Edna is presumed to be the property of her husband, hence the novel's opening passage, in which Léonce eyes his sunburned wife "as one looks at a valuable piece of personal property which has suffered some damage" (522).

But what is it about the swim that so profoundly dissatisfies Edna with being owned? Though readers have perceived the centrality of Edna's sublime attempt to swim "where no woman had swum before," this pivotal moment remains ill understood in existing scholarship on the novel. Attention is usually reserved for the novel's other important swim, in which Edna ends her life (on which, more later). This scene, however, is likely the novel's most concentrated expression of the feeling animating Edna—of what the narrator obliquely dubs "more wisdom than the Holy Ghost is usually pleased to vouchsafe to any woman" (535). The swim dramatizes the birth of Edna's ego, of consciousness of "her relations as an individual to the world within and about her" (535).

The felicity of swimming as a figure for Edna's awakening into desire for full autonomy lies in the way that submersion in water envelopes the entire body in a uniform sensation, thereby generating a feeling of the body's wholeness. Moreover, the act of swimming places the swimmer's survival completely into her own hands. These are precisely the aspects of Edna's swim on which the novel dwells. "She would not join the groups in their sports and bouts," we are told, "but intoxicated with her newly conquered power, she swam out alone" (552). This brief swim allows Edna to luxuriate in the semi-conscious feeling of oneness and self-sufficiency that will ultimately prove illusory outside of swimming.

Given the deep solipsism of this episode, it is puzzling that so much effort has been spent on attempting to designate a person outside of Edna as the inspiration for her awakening. For instance, Kenneth Eble, one of the novel's earliest admirers within the academy, concludes, "Quite frankly, the book is about sex," nominating the novel's men (central among whom the craven Robert Lebrun) as the initiators of Edna's awakening (9). Kathleen Lant dissented from such readers as Eble, arguing for Adèle's influence on Edna. Elaine Showalter likewise asserted the importance of women in Edna's development, adding Mademoiselle Reisz to the mix (45–6). Yet Chopin seems intent on portraying Edna's awakening as an event entirely internal to her—as an enthusiastic response to the sea's invitation to "the soul to wander for a spell in abysses of solitude; to lose itself in mazes of inward contemplation" (*KC* 535). The novel appears to anticipate readers' temptation to attribute Edna's awakening to sources outside herself when, during her swim, it pokes fun at the onlookers who each "congratulated himself that his special teachings had accomplished this desired end" (552).

Immediately after her brief but life-altering dalliance with pure autonomy, Edna's sense of self broadens to the point of eclipsing her view of the personhood of others. "The people about me," she notes on her way up from the shore, "are like some uncanny half-human beings" (553). At this moment, she is speaking in the register of fantasy, playfully swapping improvised fairytales with Robert, but the altered view of herself that she expresses here is meant in earnest. Awakened to the great magnitude of her self, she has come to regard the property she possesses in it as too precious to yield to another. This sentiment first manifests itself as a refusal to bend to the will of others, most importantly her husband's. When Léonce returns from the shore, he finds Edna lying awake in the hammock right in front of their Grand Isle house. Notwithstanding his many injunctions to abandon the hammock and join him for bed, Edna resolutely declines, countering his commands with a stiff-necked "Léonce, go to bed" (556). "Another time," the narrator notes, "she would have gone in at his request" (555). This we know to be true, for, only a few nights earlier, she had instinctively obeyed him when, on his late-night return from the men's club, he churlishly demanded that she rise from her sleep to check on one of the children (though she had been "quite sure Raoul had no fever"). However, as she reflects on moments such as this one while in the hammock, her past responses seem entirely foreign to her: "she could not realize why or how she could have yielded, feeling as she then did" (556).

For an awakened Edna, all externally imposed conventions come to seem deep infringements on her desire for self-determination, and the remainder of the novel—all the way to the very last page—traces her attempt to discard them. After a heated disagreement with her husband over her neglect of "les convenances," for instance, Edna retreats to her bedroom to throw a tantrum. Desiring simply to "destroy something," she smashes a vase against the hearth and hurls her wedding ring to the floor, stomping it with the heel of her boot. We are meant to view this frenzied display as Edna's revolt against the institution most threatening to her personal freedom, wedlock. But the outcome of her rebellious paroxysm bodes poorly for her emancipatory enterprise: "her small boot heel did not make an indenture, not a mark upon the little glittering circlet" (581).

In Edna's ensuing quest for liberation, proprietary issues come to occupy a place of increasing importance in the novel. We have already noted her desire for self-possession—her resolve "never again to belong to another than herself" (613). However, as Delbanco notes, Edna comes to develop a more expansive "taste for ownership" (98). When, for instance, Mlle. Reisz asks why she has opted to move out of the Pontellier home and into a dwelling modest enough to merit the name "the Pigeon house," Edna explains, "The house, the money that provides for it, are not mine" (613). Mlle. Reisz replies, "They are your husband's," puzzled by Edna's complaint. But Edna clarifies that it is a room wholly her own that she seeks, by detailing the independent means that have enabled her to procure the space: "I have a little money of my own from my mother's estate, which my father sends me by driblets. I won a large sum this winter on the races, and I am beginning to sell my sketches.... I know I shall like it, like the feeling of freedom and independence" (613).

Had Chopin stopped here, we may well have ended up with the tale of female liberation that much feminist criticism has found in *The Awakening*. But Chopin makes clear that the kind of liberty that Edna seeks—pure autonomy, complete freedom from relation—is impossible. As a few critics have pointed out, Edna's quest for independence is predicated upon dependence. Right before she gushes to Mlle. Reisz about the "feeling of freedom and independence" she anticipates in removing to the Pigeon house, for instance, she notes that "Old Celestine," one of the black servants employed in the Pontellier home, "says she will come stay with me and do my work" (613). Elaine Showalter was one of the first critics to point out the illusory nature of Edna's independence:

> Floating along in her "mazes of inward contemplation," Edna barely notices the silent quadroon nurse who takes care of her children, the little black girl who works the treadles of Madame Lebrun's sewing machine, the laundress who keeps her in frilly white, or the maid who picks up her broken glass. She never makes connections between her lot and theirs. (51)

For Showalter, this is not just Edna's problem but Chopin's as well. Just as Edna "never moves from her own questioning to the larger social statement that is feminism" (51), Chopin, in her "literary solitude" and refusal to situate her work within a "woman's tradition," failed in her novel "to work out something different and new" (48).

Similarly, Michele Birnbaum demonstrates the many ways in which Edna's erotic emancipation depends on appropriation and exploitation. According to Birnbaum, "Edna locates in racial and ethnic Others a territory necessary for a liberating alterity: in their difference, she finds herself" (303). Although Birnbaum does not as explicitly conflate Edna and Chopin, the suggestion that they might share the same blind spot appears in her essay nonetheless, if for no other reason than that Birnbaum depicts Chopin as the unself-conscious creator of an objectionable heroine. I echo Jennifer Fleissner in posing to such critics as Showalter and Birnbaum the following question: if there is no suggestion that Edna sympathizes with the many women around her, "what should we say of the author who has brought that dissatisfaction to our attention in the first place?" (244).

In Fleissner's study, the question does not stay long enough for an answer, but it is indispensable to any understanding of the novel. The details in the narration undermining Edna's claim to unbridled autonomy are too numerous and too conspicuous to seem unintentional.

It seems more reasonable to assume that both we and the author perceive the gap between Edna's individualistic aspirations and her reality. As we shall see, the significance of the narrator's attempt to belie Edna's autonomy is significant. First, however, it is important to note the way in which Edna's quest for freedom hinders her relationships, thereby alienating her to a point that ultimately proves unbearable. Besides Edna's unacknowledged reliance upon the labor of her domestic servants, Chopin portrays all of Edna's relationships as exploitive, as crucial instruments whose importance Edna must ignore in order to maintain the illusion of her autonomy. In Edna's relationship with Mlle. Reisz, we find the most salient proof that her exploitive tendencies infect more than just her relations with her black servants. Edna's disdain for this ostracized spinster is hardly concealed (548). When, for instance, Mlle. Reisz tells Edna, "I really don't believe you like me," Edna strains at civility, replying, "I don't know whether I like you or not" (592). Yet Edna continues her relationship with Mlle. Reisz because it is through her alone that she can nourish her passion for Robert, who writes his most confidential letters to this eccentric woman. Though Edna may remain unaware of her need to exploit Mlle. Reisz, Reisz herself is certainly not. When Edna marches into her home imperiously issuing demands—"Show me the letter and play for me the Impromptu"—Reisz complies but not without revealing that she is aware of being used. With a "wriggling laugh," just before she fetches the letter and sets herself to playing the requested composition, she describes herself as "a foolish old woman whom you have captivated" (594).

In her pursuit of freedom, Edna seeks independence and solitude, admitting relations only insofar as they enhance her ability, as she puts it, to "have my own way" (650). As the novel suggests, Edna is not the only woman seeking to have her own way and trying to exceed the limitations of the traditional "woman's sphere." When Léonce first consults Dr. Mandelet about his wife's erratic behavior, the doctor instantly asks, "Has she been associating of late with a circle of pseudo-intellectual women—super-spiritual beings?" (596). Of course, Dr. Mandelet is referring to the many feminist circles of the turn of the century. Interestingly, had those circles been to blame for Edna's puzzling actions, Léonce, as he himself suggests, might have been slightly more at ease: "That's the trouble . . . she hasn't been associating with any one" (596).

The nature of Edna's quest for freedom, centering on freedom from relation—on the achievement of unencumbered autonomy—unfits her not only for friendship (as we see in her exploitive tendencies toward those around her) but also for the kind of collaboration that feminism would require and that we see transforming US culture in general, in its turn to more associational forms (e.g., corporate capitalism).[8] As historian James Livingston explains, many contemporary intellectuals believed that the "'socialization' of modern industry via corporate devices" and "the implication of the family in a new universe of 'social organizations'" were driving American society away from individualistic forms of self-definition and toward more associational forms (11). Examining the attempts of pragmatist philosophers and feminists of the era to understand self-formation in more radically associational terms, Livingston sees in Chopin's nonliterary contemporaries the capacity to "suffer the dissolution of...the form of subjectivity specific to the 'era of the ego,' circa 1600–1900" (10). As Livingston's study suggests, for many at the time, individualism had lost its relevance as a model for middle-class life.

However, in the epoch that thinkers extending from Chopin's time to our own have characterized as the age of association, the oddly literalized Emersonian self-reliance that Edna seeks turns out to be not only chimerical but lethal as well. Toward the end of the novel, during her suicidal swim, Edna appears to catch a glimpse of the role her self-sequestration has played in her demise, musing, "Perhaps Doctor Mandelet would have understood if she had seen him—but it was too late..." (655). Even in the sea—the birthplace of her desire for pure autonomy and the only place where she had felt anything remotely like it—even here, thoughts of relationality and interdependence haunt her, including the relation that has loomed largest throughout the novel. In addition to faint speculations on the difference the doctor might have made, images of family—of her father and sister Margaret—flash before her, culminating in the final "hum of bees, and the musky odor of pinks" that bookend the novel and her life (655). These are symbols of generation and motherhood, and they bring Edna's mind back to the one relation that she could elude only through sacrificing her life—which, we should recall, she groups with the "unessential," in contradistinction to the inviolable metaphysical self that she earlier tries to describe to Madame Ratignolle. "Remember the children!"—the penetrating admonition that Madame Ratignolle had voiced to her while in the throes of labor—thrusts before Edna that one unshakable relation, her relation to her children and concomitant responsibility to them. "She had said over and over to herself: 'To-day it is Arobin; to-morrow it will be some one else. It makes no difference to me, it doesn't matter about Léonce Pontellier—but Raoul and Étienne!'" (653). Through Adèle's indelible reprimand, Edna realizes that preserving what she had come to regard as the unessential, the property she has in herself, would, in fact, require her death.

Some critics have provocatively argued that we ought not assume that Edna commits suicide, believing such an interpretation too defeatist for a novel so revolutionary.[9] However, these readers have had great difficulty accounting for the hard distinction between the essential and unessential self—the metaphysical (her intellectual and spiritual autonomy) and the physical (her life)—on which Edna insists. When we observe how much of Edna's preparation for the swim involves shedding—of "the unpleasant, pricking garments"—we are prompted to recall that distinction; the discarded bathing suit symbolizes the "unessential" (her life) that she must now sacrifice to preserve the essential. Given the limitations on women's lives in the nineteenth century, suicide was practically the only way for Edna to live out liberal individualism, with its commitment to freedom (as opposed to the "soul's slavery" that living has come to represent for her) (654). Therein lies Chopin's quarrel with her era. Though Chopin is indeed disapproving of her heroine's individualistic ways—hence the sometimes unflattering portrayal of Edna—she nonetheless deplores the fact that individualism remained nonviable for women like Edna solely because of their gender, race, and class.

Patricia Yaegar helps us to see just how constricted Edna's possibilities are. Bringing poststructuralist theory to bear on the novel, Yaegar has suggested, "*The Awakening*'s most radical awareness is that Edna inhabits a world of limited linguistic possibilities, of limited possibilities for interpreting and re-organizing her feelings, and therefore of limited possibilities for action" (200). Put differently, Edna cannot work out a solution for her dilemma because she lacks the language necessary for even conceiving of what she wants. Hence her vague and convoluted complaints: "But I don't want anything but my own way. That is wanting a good deal, of course, when you have to trample upon the lives, the hearts, the prejudices of others—but no matter—still, I shouldn't want to trample upon the little lives" (650).

Suggesting that the absence of a speech community is central to Edna's conflict, Yaeger's interpretation of the novel seems right insofar as it highlights Edna's "need for a more passionate and intersubjective speech." However, instead of nominating the language of romance as the idiom that most clouds the heroine's judgment, as Yaeger does, I would suggest the language of liberal individualism. For one, understanding Edna's story in this way would prevent the overestimation of Robert Lebrun's importance in the novel that results from such interpretations as Yaeger's and many others'. Love, after all, is but one of multiple avenues through which Edna seeks solitary fulfillment (we mustn't forget her passion for art and economic independence). And, perhaps more importantly, it would help us to grasp why relation in general—a concern that, in some way or another, links most critical treatments of *The Awakening*—becomes such a crucial problem in the novel.

It is clear that, in writing *The Awakening*, Chopin was seeking a way of imagining women's lives that differed from the prevailing options, embodied by the two enigmatic figures amid whom Edna so often finds herself—the young lovers and the doleful widow in black. Larzer Ziff has suggested that these two figures represent "the horizons of experience" (20). He appears to imply the antipodal experiences of bliss and mourning, but I believe that Chopin has in mind the narrow range of experience afforded women in fiction. Though the young lady doting on her suitor and the widow in mourning exist on opposite ends of the continuum of heterosexual love, their lives nonetheless remain tethered to that continuum—one ceaselessly basking in love, the other ceaselessly grieving its loss. However, in Chopin's mind, the turn of the twentieth century, so to speak, opened the door of the stupefying love-cage that had falsely restricted women's desire, much as entrapment initially restricts the freed beast with which this essay begins.

We see Chopin's exhaustion with the limitations that literary convention had placed on the writing of women's lives in her short story "Miss Witherwell's Mistake." There, Mildred Witherwell is sent to live with her aunt after her father learns of her dalliance with a young man of modest wealth. Her aunt, though a spinster, espouses the most conventional ideas about women and marriage, and even earns a living from writing stories and short tracts upholding all things traditional, including the widespread stereotypes about women (in addition to love stories, treatises titled "Security Against Moths," "A Word to Mothers," and so forth). It just so happens that the lover Mildred left in St. Louis found employment as an editor at the very periodical that publishes her aunt's paeans to the status quo. The two eventually meet and covertly resume where they left off in St. Louis. Apparently attempting to figure out her dilemma through writing a story of her own, Mildred consults her aunt when the story's protagonist reaches, as she herself has, the point where her desires and convention diverge. "Bear in mind that being brought—almost forced together—through outside influences, they grow to love each other to desperation," Mildred explains (*KC* 689). Without the slightest hesitation, her aunt replies, "Your hero must now perform some act to ingratiate himself to the obdurate parent." When Mildred objects that she "can't force the situation"—being as she is "extremely realistic"—an "aghast" Miss Witherwell retorts, "The poison of the realistic school has certainly tainted and withered your fancy in the bud, my dear, if you hesitate a moment. Marry them, most certainly, or let them die" (690).

Of course, this scene enables Chopin to enact another of her signature plot twists—the aunt inadvertently encourages her niece to violate her father's wishes and marry the impecunious editor—but I think there is yet more to grasp here. In her orthodox response to her niece's attempt to imagine new directions for her life, the aunt closes off potentially fruitful veins of thought—ones that might lead her niece to discover new modes of artistic expression as well as new, possibly more fulfilling ways to live. Miss Witherwell's titular mistake consists not simply in the fact that she sent her niece to the publishing office unaccompanied or that she accidentally encouraged her to defy her father's wishes. Her mistake is that she enabled the conventions of love to falsify a work of art and to detour a life from what might have been a more salutary course.

Edna, too, might have thrived had she been able to find a viable third path beyond the dichotomy of love and death endorsed by that parrot of tradition, the elder Miss Witherwell. Such a path, Chopin makes clear, would not lead to the embrace of unencumbered individualism—a way of life hardly viable for men in this era (even Edna's husband makes his living from joint-stock ventures in New York) and much less so for a mother. It would seem that Edna's task lay not in the impossible act of ridding herself of relations. It lay in finding some way to reconfigure relatedness—inevitable always but, at this moment in history, undeniable—into a more endurable state of being.

Chopin does not say how she might do so. But what Chopin does make clear is that, though women's desires were beginning to exceed the narrow scope usually afforded them in nineteenth-century fiction, their lives would not conform to the shape of liberal individualism. Indeed, they would not follow the path long imagined for men. Although she does not present a version of what form female subjectivity might more viably take in this age of awakened desire, her work constitutes an important step in reimagining women in fiction at a moment when gender relations were rapidly changing in the real world.

Notes

1. Kate Chopin, "Emancipation: A Life Fable," in *Kate Chopin: Complete Novels and Stories*, ed. Sandra Gilbert (New York: Library

of America, 2002), 656. All references to Kate Chopin's literary work derive from this collection; subsequent references are cited parenthetically with the abbreviation *KC*.

2. Bentley argues that Chopin's fiction overturns the more analytical, almost scientific literary realism practiced by earlier male novelists (such as William Dean Howells) in favor of a more fantastical realism attuned to "desire and bodily pleasure" (145). Accordingly, Bentley construes the gentleman's inability to understand Mrs. Sommers as Chopin's way of exposing the inadequacy of a purely analytical literary realism.
3. We find a similar fixation on the novel's mythic dimension in Cristina Giorcelli's study of *The Awakening*. "In a very unobtrusive and apparently unconscious manner," she claims, "Chopin appears to have seized upon mythic figures to help unravel both the complexity and the mystery of human existence" (127).
4. For a more extended treatment of liberal individualism, see Steven Lukes's *Individualism* (1973). For examinations of liberal individualism in fiction specifically, see Gillian Brown's *Domestic Individualism* (1991), Nancy Armstrong's *How Novels Think* (2005), and Elaine Hadley's *Living Liberalism* (2010).
5. It is worth repeating Wai Chee Dimock's observation that, just nine years before the publication of *The Awakening*, Louis D. Brandeis and Samuel D. Warren had published "The Right to Privacy," "an essay arguing for 'the right of the individual to be let alone'" (192). Dimock's legalistic interpretation—which situates the novel within the prevailing rights-based paradigm of the nineteenth century—bears certain resemblances to my own understanding of the novel. But our differences are significant. In Dimock's discussion, Edna's gender would appear unimportant, but I see it as paramount. Moreover, Dimock joins a host of other critics of the novel who erroneously align Chopin's views with Edna's. In suggesting that "*The Awakening*...would seem to embody the language of rights up to the last," Dimock neglects the dismissal of liberal individualism that Chopin enacts through killing off her heroine (221).
6. Artistry for Edna means something completely different from what it means to Adèle. The latter "was keeping up her music on account of the children" and "because she and her husband both considered it a means of brightening the home and making it attractive" (*KC* 547). However, individualist that she is, Edna expresses more self-serving reasons for practicing art: "I believe I ought to work again. I feel as if I wanted to be doing something" (584). Moreover, in her isolation from the group—her refusal to sacrifice her individuality for fusion with the female community—Edna clings to what political philosopher Norman Barry refers to as "that 'separateness' and 'identity' of individual persons that is at the heart of the libertarian ethic" (20).

7. According to one of the fathers of classical liberalism, John Locke, "Though the Earth, and all inferior Creatures be common to all Men, yet every Man has a *Property* in his own *Person*. This no Body has any Right to but himself" (287).
8. In the words of one of the contemporary economists whom James Livingston quotes, the period witnessed the "regress of self-sufficiency and the progress of association."
9. For different variations of this position on the novel, see Sandra Gilbert's "The Second Coming of Aphrodite" and Anca Parvalescu's "To Die Laughing and to Laugh at Dying."

Works Cited

Barry, Norman. *On Classical Liberalism and Libertarianism*. New York: St. Martin's, 1987. Print.

Bentley, Nancy. *Frantic Panoramas: American Literature and Mass Culture, 1870–1920*. Philadelphia: University of Pennsylvania Press, 2009. Print.

Biggs, Mary. "'Si tu Savais': The Gay/Transgendered Sensibility of Kate Chopin's *The Awakening*." *Women's Studies* 33 (2004): 145–81. Print.

Birnbaum, Michele A. "'Alien Hands': Kate Chopin and the Colonization of Race." *American Literature* 66.2 (1994): 301–23. Print.

Chopin, Kate. *Kate Chopin: Complete Novels and Stories*. Ed. Sandra M. Gilbert. New York: Library of America, 2002. Print.

Delbanco, Andrew. "The Half-Life of Edna Pontellier." Ed. Wendy Martin. *New Essays on The Awakening*. New York: Cambridge, 1988. 89–107. Print.

Dimock, Wai Chee. *Residues of Justice: Literature, Law, Philosophy*. Berkeley: University of California Press, 1997. Print.

Eble, Kenneth. "A Forgotten Novel." *Kate Chopin*. Ed. Harold Bloom. Philadelphia: Chelsea House Publishers, 1987: 7–16. Print.

Gilbert, Sandra M. "The Second Coming of Aphrodite." *Kate Chopin*. Ed. Harold Bloom. Philadelphia: Chelsea House Publishers, 1987: 89–113. Print.

Giorcelli, Cristina. "Edna's Wisdom: A Transitional and Numinous Merging." *New Essays on* The Awakening. Ed. Wendy Martin. New York: Cambridge UP, 1988: 109–48. Print.

Lant, Kathleen Margaret. "The Siren of Grand Isle: Adèle's Role in *The Awakening*." *Kate Chopin*. Ed. Harold Bloom. Philadelphia: Chelsea House Publishers, 1987: 115–24. Print.

Locke, John. *Two Treatises of Government*. Ed. Peter Laslett. New York: Cambridge UP, 2005. Print.

Lukes, Steven. *Individualism*. Oxford: Basil Blackwell, 1973. Print.

Parvalescu, Anca. "To Die Laughing and to Laugh at Dying: Revisiting *The Awakening*." *New Literary History* 36.3 (2005): 477–95. Print.

Rev. of *The Custom of the Country*, by Edith Wharton. *The Nation* 15 May 1913: 494. Print.

Rosowski, Susan J. "The Novel of Awakening." *The Voyage in: Fictions of Female Development.* Ed. Elizabeth Abel, Marianne Hirsch, and Elizabeth Langland. Hanover, NH: University Press of New England, 1983: 49–68. Print.

Showalter, Elaine. "Tradition and the Female Talent: *The Awakening* as a Solitary Book." *New Essays on The Awakening.* Ed. Wendy Martin. New York: Cambridge UP, 1988: 33–57. Print.

Yaeger, Patricia S. "'A Language Which Nobody Understood': Emancipatory Strategies in *The Awakening.*" *NOVEL: A Forum on Fiction* 20.3 (1987): 197–219. Print.

Ziff, Larzer. "An Abyss of Inequality." *Kate Chopin.* Ed. Harold Bloom. Philadelphia: Chelsea House Publishers, 1987: 17–24. Print.

CHAPTER 3

"A quick conception of all that this accusation meant for her": The Legal Climate at the Time of "Désirée's Baby"

Amy Branam Armiento

Although Kate Chopin lived in Louisiana until she was five years old, her adult experience in Louisiana coincided with the "carpet-bagger" days of state government. One contemporary described this period as one in which "all the honesty and intelligence of the country were driven out of sight into nooks, corners, and rat-holes, and the Southern States were delivered to the merciless legislation of the ignorant negroes, acting blindly under the guidance of white leaders, the majority of whom will be eternally gibbeted in history under the appellations of carpet-baggers and scalawags" (Gayarre 480). This atypical period in Louisiana history was the direct consequence of northern pressures to extend equality to African Americans in the wake of the Civil War. The North had recently terminated its occupation of the South when the Louisiana Code of 1870 was adapted to incorporate laws and amendments passed since its last revision in 1825, and the new code also excised all references to slaves and slavery. From 1870 to 1894, Republicans—not Democrats—clung to their majority in the Louisiana legislature and many African American men served as well (Yiannopoulus 10–11). However, by 1894, the political tides had changed. The southern Democrats regained power, and Jim Crow loomed large, influencing a resurgence of segregation laws (Wallenstein 104).

From 1870 to 1884, Chopin experienced a Louisiana that had strict social codes governing race; however, these codes were undermined by the northern ideas of equality that pressed upon a culture that had outlawed intermarriage (also referred to as hybridization, miscegenation, amalgamation, and mongrelism in the parlance of the time) since the state had joined the union in 1812. By 1884, she had returned to St. Louis, Missouri, and begun her writing career. In 1893, as racial tension increased in Louisiana and initiatives were sought to reinstitute the separation of the races with the introduction of Jim Crow laws, Chopin penned one of her most intriguing and enduring tales, "Désirée's Baby" (Toth, *Kate Chopin* 204). Chopin's *Bayou Folk* appeared on *The Literary World's* "The Best Books List of 1894," which appeared January 12, 1895. In 1977, Thomas Bonner distinguishes "Désirée's Baby" from the rest of collection when he refers to it as "[Chopin's] best story" in *Bayou Folk* (8).

Set during the antebellum period, the story is hard to fix in a specific point of time or even within a decade. It is clearly set when fair-skinned African Americans were commonplace, which had occurred by the turn of the nineteenth century. Detecting an exact time for the narrative is somewhat beside the point, for, as Heather Kirk Thomas points out, "The New South, not a romanticized antebellum version, was [Chopin's] primary focus, and it is equally clear that she was never keen on attracting a Southern audience" (Thomas 107–8). Thomas further argues that "Désirée's Baby" is one of many stories in which Chopin uses an unreliable narrator to convey to northern readers that the southern "insider" who serves as the narrator is a perspective fraught with tricks and encodings to which northern "outsiders" who serve as the primary audience are not privy but anxious to decipher. The use of this southern point of view results in the unexpected endings that are readily apparent upon a second read (Thomas 97).

In addition to a preoccupation with placing the story within its proper historical context, numerous literary scholars have been interested in analyzing the formal aspects of the story, including character study, theme, and irony. For instance, Roslyn Foy explores Armand's characterization, focusing on how Chopin sketches his "dark side of personality" (222). Ellen Peel analyzes how Désirée functions as a floating signifier on which the other characters project their desires (223). In contrast to a focus on character development, Emily Toth asserts that Chopin invokes literary conventions "to attract readers—and then to lead them beyond convention to new insights" ("Kate Chopin and Literary Convention" 202). Elizabeth McMahan argues that Chopin wrote "Désirée's Baby" to illustrate how the theme of marrying for love is just as problematic as marrying for any other motive because that type of love depends too much, or worse solely, on the approbation of the husband (32–5). Other scholars, such as Catherine Lundie and Marcia Gaudet, have focused on the treatment of women of color in Chopin's texts by researching Chopin's interactions with and knowledge of mulatto and black women during her lifetime. Chopin's reworking of the tragic mulatta storyline is the focus of Dagmar Pegues's argument. Dan Shen uses Wayne Booth's theory of the implied author to deduce Chopin's attitude toward race relations. Similarly, Robert Arner revisits the story and posits that Chopin strives to demonstrate that "there is no absolute distinction between white and black, but rather an imaginary line drawn by white men and crossed at their own choosing" (140). He continues to prove his thesis by dissecting how Chopin alludes to light/dark and heaven/hell.

Very few scholars have argued for Louisiana law as a significant contributor to the story's plot, particularly its denouement. Guadet and others refer to Louisiana marriage laws cursorily. Margaret D. Bauer's essay, "Armand Aubigny, Still Passing after All These Years: The Narrative Voice and Historical Context of 'Désirée's Baby,'" however, delves more deeply into the relationships between law and text by connecting the laws to the character motivations in the story, but she neglects to address the period in Louisiana pre-statehood history when intermarriage was legal. Under Spanish rule, priests performed interracial marriages because they viewed this act as preferable to the sin of fornication (Aubert 461).This essay elaborates on Bauer's argument, by contending, in line with Thomas's assertion regarding Chopin's interest in the present, that the antebellum laws against comingling help to illuminate an important facet of character motivations in the story and that the reentrenchment of these antimiscegenation laws in the period when Chopin writes the story provide a compelling exegesis. By bringing together newspaper accounts, court cases, and sociohistorical scholarship, this essay speculates on the laws that existed and could have been used to persecute the transgressive relationships of Monsieur Aubigny, La Blanche, Désirée, and Armand.

Monsieur and Madame Aubigny

The sordid and tragic plot of Kate Chopin's "Désirée's Baby" originates with the marriage of Armand Aubigny's parents. Toth observes, "It was the old indulgent master, Armand's father, who broke the color taboo, marrying a woman considered black" ("Kate Chopin and Literary Convention" 207). Ostensibly, Armand's father returns to France, being descended from an illustrious family whose name refers to Brittany, for a visit and, while there, unexpectedly falls passionately in love. Slavery in France was an antiquated notion by the nineteenth century. In the early fourteenth century, France passed a progressive decree that granted amnesty to any slave that set foot on its shores (Palmer 101). For a brief period in the late eighteenth century, France had banned interracial marriage due to anxiety surrounding the increasing black population. However, the decree was short lived, and the country began to recognize marriages between blacks and whites in the early nineteenth century. Any ambiguity in the law was resolved in April 24, 1833, when France declared that all free men would receive equal protection under its laws (Frederickson 106,110).

While in France, Aubigny apparently marries a black woman who is probably fairly complected, for Armand, although eight at the time of her death, does not identify her with the black race. In Gaudet's research on Chopin's allusions to the Cane River Creoles, she presents a convincing case that Madame Aubigny may have been one of the free women of color (f.w.c.'s) who lived on the prosperous L'Isle des Mulâtres. This colony was founded by a freed slave whose former master had provided her with her own plantation in this area. Such wealthy landowners helped to carve out a new social class, which was much higher in the social hierarchy than the slave but not quite as equal as the white plantation owners. The convention of adding "f.m.c." or "f.w.c." in all documentation to denote free men and women of color was just one way in which their nascent rights as freedmen and women were protected while simultaneously ensuring that no "flaw" would allow their "children [to] claim equality with his betters" (de Gournay 511). Gaudet asserts, "Chopin may have intended that [Armand's] mother was a Creole of Color from Isle Brevelle [present day L'Isle des Mulâtres'] who left the area to 'pass for white' and thus be able to marry a white man" (Gaudet 49–50).

Yet, Armand's mother does not pass for white. Rather, Monsieur Aubigny is quite aware of his wife's race, which is evident when the letter is discovered. One can presume that Monsieur Aubigny and his future wife were in the habit of corresponding. One can even infer that the letter fragment was part of a scheme to unite the couple in a safe place that would sanction their marriage. Armand's parents probably met in Louisiana. Assuming that Aubigny's plantation was in or near Natchitoches, which is where many of Chopin's stories are located, he would have been within 15 miles of L'Isle des Mulâtres. His proximity to this wealthy area, known for its attractive inhabitants, would have facilitated an acquaintance with Armand's mother.

If the two of them had had a dalliance that resulted in a pregnancy, the two would be unable to legitimate their union and their child through marriage. Therefore, the future Madame Aubigny immigrated to France, and Monsieur Aubigny accompanied her shortly after. In France, they could marry and raise their child legitimately. Although Madame Aubigny probably passed for white in France, it was unnecessary for her to do so. Since she was known to be an f.w.c. in Louisiana, she and her husband could not return to his plantation or to her isle.

The end of the letter is telling, for Madame writes, "his mother, who adores him, belongs to the race that is cursed with the brand of slavery" (Chopin 245). One wonders what has prompted this exclamation, especially if one were tempted to read her as a native-born French woman. It is possible that Monsieur Aubigny may not have decided to join his future wife until after the birth of his child, and she is informing him of this boon. Once he has learned that Armand can pass for white, he relocates to France to build a life where he and his wife can be free to pursue their relationship and a family. After the birth of Armand, who can pass, the Aubignys do not have any more children. Therefore, Aubigny is free to travel between France and his Louisiana plantation and account for his wife's absence and his frequent excursions to France by using the simple and plausible excuse that Aubigny's wife "loved her own land too well ever to leave it" (Chopin 241). The couple had orchestrated the whole situation so that no one in Louisiana was the wiser regarding their illicit marriage.

In a real-life situation that parallels the Aubignys' plan to marry despite southern antebellum laws, Jean Dupre, a white man, and Elizabeth Boulard, noted in the newspapers as an "f.w.c.", eloped to France in 1835. They remained together in France for ten years without having any children, and then, when the marriage floundered, Elizabeth returned to Louisiana in 1845 ("The Courts" 4). Their illegal marriage became public when Dupre filed suit against Boulard's heirs in *J. M. Dupre v. the Executor of Boulard, f.w.c., et al.* The union would not have been newsworthy, but for the fact that Dupre wanted to claim her property. Although Boulard had anticipated this move by Dupre, he ignored the suit that was filed by her in 1845, which granted separation of their property, and he alleged that a will that she drew up in 1835 in France was still valid. The case persisted in the courts, and Dupre eventually appealed to the Louisiana Supreme Court. Judge Henry Martyn Spofford heard the case and wrote a brief opinion. Essentially, the court refused to acknowledge the marriage enacted in France as well as the purported earlier will because to acknowledge one act as legal and binding would be to deem the other the same. Spofford insisted that the plaintiff's relationship with an f.w.c. as an "unnatural alliance."

While many southern states repealed their antimiscegenation laws during Reconstruction, Missouri held fast to its statue against intermarriage, which had been passed in 1835. In the "Missouri Supreme Court Abstract" published March 28, 1885, in *The Albany Law Journal*, the State of Missouri, as did many other states, ruled that its antimiscegenation law did not violate the Fourteenth Amendment ("Missouri Supreme Court" 254). In an attempt to circumvent these prohibitions, similar to the action taken by Monsieur Aubigny, couples eloped to jurisdictions that did not have antimiscegenation laws. A highly publicized case of this subterfuge appeared in 1879.

Edmund Kinney, a black man, and Mary Susan Hall, a white woman, had been living together for many years in Virginia and had heard that they were going to be arrested for fornication. In an effort to elude this crime, the two traveled to Washington, D.C., where intermarriage was legal, and married. However, when they returned to their home in Virginia, the authorities arrested them, citing the fact that Virginia did not recognize their marriage; therefore, it was null and void. Essentially, in this case, the State of Virginia refused to acknowledge D.C.'s law since it contradicted its own ("Imprisonment" 6). The couple was sentenced to five years in the state penitentiary for their defiance ("Testing" 324). Case after case came before state courts, and case after case was upheld on appeal when anti-miscegenation laws were at stake in the years following the Civil War. Although late to join with the other southern states, Louisiana also reenacted these antebellum laws by 1894, so the debate surrounding these legal changes was contemporaneous with the composition of Chopin's story.

La Blanche and Désirée

Once Désirée's child is born and his African American heritage manifests itself in his physical person, Armand's view of his wife shifts diametrically from idolatry to contempt. When confronted by Désirée about his icy treatment, he expresses his distaste toward her by likening Désirée to his concubine, scoffing that her skin is "[a]s white as La Blanche's" (Chopin 243). In this statement, Armand expresses that Désirée is no better than a concubine, and he no longer esteems her in a manner that befits a husband for a wife.

Toth writes, "Armand appears to have a sexual relationship with La Blanche, one of his slaves, but he violates no social rules: he simply takes his right to her because he is master" ("Kate Chopin and Literary Convention" 207). The evidence for this liaison is alluded to in one line of the story. While Désirée is recovering from her childbirth, it is apparent that Armand has either maintained or resumed his affair with the light-skinned slave. In a conversation with her adopted mother regarding how strong her son is becoming, Désirée says, "Armand heard him the other day as far away as La Blanche's cabin" (241). If the reader misses this first reference, a second opportunity is presented when, later in the story Désirée becomes conscious of her son's color only when she sees him next to "one of La Blanche's little quadroon boys" (242).

Without the second reference in the story, the way in which Armand has situated La Blanche—in her own cabin—and his visits to her so "far away" from the main house mirrors the practice of setting up slave mistresses. Comely slaves were especially at risk for being singled out by white men (Malone 219). Ann Patton Malone observes, "It was a brutal rite of passage for planter-class youth to sneak down to the quarters and compel slave girls to have sex" (229). One can imagine a young Armand participating in this same ritual by seeking out La Blanche. However, as Malone also notes, "these men were supposed to cease these activities once they married" (220). Once married, the husband usually sent the former concubine away, by selling her (and any offspring) or relocating her (and any offspring) to a place where they could live as if free (Malone 220–21). Armand, on the other hand, chooses a less popular route. He keeps her and her multiple children, likely all fathered by him, on his plantation. In a sense, Armand has realized the very arrangement that Dr. Flint had hoped to effect in Harriet Jacobs's slave narrative, *Incidents in the Life of a Slave Girl* (84). The comparison between Dr. Flint and Armand also reveals that either La Blanche was much more willing to accommodate her master's desires than Linda Brent or that Armand resorted to rape, whereas Dr. Flint wanted Linda to renounce her own morals and succumb to his will.

Once Armand's son is born and Désirée's color becomes suspect, under Louisiana law the marriage is null and void. The result is that Désirée's position in the household becomes untenable: she is no better than La Blanche. Armand's assumption that Désirée is the one who possesses the African ancestry is supported by antebellum research on mulattos. In 1843, a medical essay by J. C. Nott appeared in the *Boston Medical and Surgical Journal*, and asserted that the "Anglo-Saxon and Negro races are [. . .] distinct species and that the offspring of the two is a hybrid" (2). He further argues, "A general law laid down by naturalists is, that the hybrid derives its size and internal structure principally from the mother" (3). Assuming "internal structure" refers to genetics, the notion that the child's black skin reflects the mother's black heritage becomes linked to scientific fact. Later in this essay, the author also posits that the father's head shape is manifested in the child, which explains why Armand's sons share physical traits, particularly from the waist up, as is apparent when Chopin describes both of Armand's children as "half naked" at the moment Désirée discovers their shared racial heritage (242; Nott 4).

For these reasons, readers can assume that Désirée believes that she is African, albeit a free African. Due to her free status, readers may wonder why she opts for suicide. Elizabeth McMahan suspects that Désirée's decision is based on her lack of a separate identity. Since she defines herself in relation to Armand, his rejection terminates her raison d'être (34). Catherine Lundie, however, contends that Chopin's text obfuscates Désirée's fate: "Although the reader can know neither Désirée's fate nor the reasons for her actions, the text strongly implies that she has taken her baby and walked out into the bayou, committing suicide and infanticide because she thinks she is a black woman" (131). This implication of *felo de se*, as Toth notes in "Kate Chopin and Divine Love and Suicide," seems to be the interpretation that many contemporary readers assume in Chopin's other ambiguous ending of *The Awakening*. In uncovering contemporary criticisms of the novel, Toth discovered an article that reported four suicides caused by "sympathetic motives" (119). Whether Chopin overtly stated how these two female protagonists died or not, the assumptions by most readers was to rule these deaths as suicides.

By interrogating the life awaiting Désirée as a free black woman with an infant, the conclusion that she committed suicide becomes all the more persuasive. Despite Madame Valmondé's entreaty for Désirée to return to her, in this case, Désirée's options were bleak at best. As an African woman with a child, she may have been able to depend on the Valmondés temporarily, but after their passing, Louisiana law could be quite whimsical when it came to last wills and testaments involving adopted parties as well as persons of color. Désirée's orphan status at the time the Valmondés discovered her may have either helped or hurt her in court after the passing of her adoptive parents. In Louisiana, adoption took the form of "a transfer of authority from the birth to adoptive parent" (Bardaglio 166). If a relative materialized after the deaths of Monsieur and Madame Valmondé, Désirée would be hard-pressed to produce the "formal evidence" of such a transaction, for she was either lost or abandoned rather than deliberately given into someone else's custody (Bardaglio 166, 170). During the antebellum period, the courts considered blood ties to be much stronger than adoptive ties, thereby Désirée's chances of being left destitute, financially and materially, following the death of the Valmondés were likely.

Furthermore, if Désirée were to return to the Valmondés' home, theoretically Armand would be able to petition for a marriage annulment on the basis of mistake respecting the person as formulated in the Louisiana Civil Code (1825), Article 92. In practice, George Snellings finds that marriages were not dissolved under this aspect of the article in practice because courts interpreted this criterion as mistaken identity (566). Snellings could only locate one case that had seemed to fit this statute, a case in which a person married a slave but was under the impression that that person was free, but this case occurred before the Napoleon Code had been instituted (566, n. 16). To take the matter to the courts, however, would result in negative attention that most likely neither husband or wife would want to draw. Besides, the marriage was already void under the Louisiana Civil Code (1825), Article 95, which forbade intermarriage of "free white persons with free people of color."

In consideration of these laws, if Désirée and Armand had reconciled and continued to live as husband and wife, they would have been engaging in concubinage. Furthermore, Armand would now have two concubines. In 1851, the court ruled in the case of *Vail v. Bird* that a slave could consent to concubinage, and in Désirée's case, her free status indicts her as one who freely chose this illegitimate arrangement. Assuming that Armand never remarries and only has children by La Blanche and Désirée, which would be advisable considering any wife would be able to divorce him under Article 137 for keeping "his concubine in their common dwelling" or under the 1837 statute that also extended this right to divorce for reasons of a concubine if she were kept "openly or publicly in any other," La Blanche and Désirée fair differently under the inheritance laws due to their slave and free statuses, respectively.

If Armand writes a will that leaves any possessions to La Blanche and Désirée and/or he manumits La Blanche and her children, the deceased's final wishes are likely to be thwarted by Louisiana law. In a best case scenario, Armand has no ascending or descending forced heirs. Then, no matter what Armand designates for La Blanche and Désirée in his will, the concubine is only entitled to one-tenth of the estate in movables (e.g., slaves, livestock, furniture, produce) under Article 1468. In the *Vail v. Bird* case, the judge strictly adhered to this rule, which meant that all slaves had to be apprised as part of the estate. In case after case, slave concubines who were granted manumission through their masters' wills were unable to attain their freedom because their individual value exceeded the one-tenth rule. If La Blanche had to remain a slave due to her value, then Désirée could possibly inherit La Blanche or one of her sons, or their values if they were sold, if Armand had also named her in his will. If Armand had attempted to free La Blanche and/or her children in his will and they were valued at less than one-tenth of the estate, this gesture would still be meaningless if he dies after 1857. In the Act of 1857, Louisiana no longer allowed any slaves to be freed by masters. In 1858, in the case of *Price v. Ray*, the court ruled that the slaves who were manumitted in a will could not be freed because it was now against the state law.

All of these "what-if" scenarios spinning from this story had received a renewed relevance in the years preceding the publication of "Désirée's Baby." After the reign of northern federals in the southern states ended, white men in particular fought hard to pass legislation that banned the mixture of the races. State courts, in the North as well as the South, had overturned antebellum antimiscegenation laws. In the confusion that followed during the transition from allowing mixed marriages to banning them, some couples paid a hefty price. For instance, in *Hoover v. State [Alabama]* (1877), a black man and white woman were charged with fornication even though they had believed that they were married because, as Robert Hoover testified, they were told that it was within their Fourteenth Amendment rights to do so. The state of Alabama disagreed. In 1883, in *State [Missouri] v. Jackson* it explained that the citizens' rights were not violated by preventing intermarriage because it was akin to a state enforcing incest laws. In the case of Hoover, the couple became victims of the deterrence against such unions as defined by Section 4184:

> [I]f any man and woman live together in adultery or fornication, each of them must, on the first conviction of the offence, be fined not less than one hundred dollars, and may also be imprisoned in the county jail or sentenced to hard labor for the county for not more than six months. On the second conviction for the offence, with the same person, the offender must be fined not less than three hundred dollars, and may be imprisoned in the county jail, or sentenced to hard labor for the county for not more than twelve months; and for a third or any subsequent conviction with the same person, must be imprisoned in the penitentiary, or sentenced to hard labor for the county for two years.

Newspaper stories appeared, showing the obstinacy of some couples who pushed against society's norms. In 1880, a story out of New

Paris, Ohio, was reported in *The National Police Gazette,* a notorious tabloid of the day. It featured a black man and white woman who cohabitated ("Miscegenation" 6). When her stepfather threatened to involve the law, the two eloped to Indiana so that they could not be prosecuted for fornication. The article ended by noting that there was really nothing the community could do about this socially transgressive couple because it was within the law for them to marry.

Despite the lack of legal measures, social consequences in the North and South served as a deterrent. As early as the late 1850s, southern opinion on intermarriage in the North brought the two geopolitical factions into conflict. In a dialogue of newspaper snippets published in the *Cleveland Leader*, the writer presented the statistic that, in 1858, only nine intermarriages of black men to white women and no white men to black women took place in Boston. However, the writer was exasperated by the accusation in the *National Democrat* that there is no woman so low as one that would marry a black man. He is alarmed at the *National Democrat's* hypocrisy, which criticizes the rare phenomenon of intermarriage in the North yet ignores the rampant, illegitimate (as in extramarital) relations between blacks and whites in the South as evidenced by the indubitable numbers of mulatto offspring ("Amalgamation" 1).

Still, the writer of the *National Democrat* is correct in purporting that white women who were involved with black men were considered to be absolutely degraded in the North and the South. Therefore, if Désirée had been exonerated in the sense of proving herself to be white, her affinity for a black man may have proven just as disastrous to her reputation as the discovery that she was of mixed race. In the story, Désirée has a glimmer of defiance when she says, "Look at my hand; whiter than yours, Armand" (243). If in this moment, she suspects that he may be the person of color; however, she does not press it, for either way, the marriage will not be sustained. Moreover, as a white woman, she was in no position to fight for her attachment to Armand. Her attempt to do so would be mocked and characterized as a clear sign of her debauchery. For instance, in 1854, *The Daily Picayune* referred to this type of relationship as a "new Othello and Desdemona" ("Practical Amalgamation").

This same predicament affecting women's reputations existed in the years preceding Chopin's composition. Catherine Lundie argues that this story focuses on "[Chopin's] contemporaries' preoccupations with miscegenation" rather than a look back at a historical situation (132). The white women linked to black men in news stories from the 1860s to the 1880s are depicted as evil, conniving, and perverse. In

1862, a writer for the *Liberty Tribune* (Missouri) takes a jab at the abolitionists, informing readers that a runaway slave had taken many household items, including a man's wife, and the write-up concludes, "and if Mrs. Whitney can live with her sable lover it will be another feather in the cap of the Abs" ("Bethany Union" 1). The humor gives way to terror in the wake of the emancipation. In 1866 in Detroit, a lengthy, lurid account appeared alongside graphic illustrations. A white woman and black man had planned to marry and open a grocery in Canada after the wife approached him to kill her husband ("Lake Snore" 1). The stories continued to appear into the 1870s. In North Carolina, an article titled "Lust at Its Lowest" detailed how a black man and white woman conspired to kill her white husband. The man claimed his innocence in the homicide but confessed to sexual relations with the woman. He was hanged, and she received life in prison ("Lust at Its Lowest" 6).

Miscegenation became a topic of heated discussion in the aftermath of the Civil War. Once the South regained control over its legislatures, it enacted laws overturning northern-influenced laws to allow marriages between races. Furthermore, while the laws were in place to protect intermarriage, social commentary lambasted white women's reputations in particular. In the midst of this public controversy, Chopin may have thought about how her social climate in St. Louis had come to resemble the one she had undoubtedly heard rumors about while residing in New Orleans.

Désirée's Babies

What the mixed marriage of Jean Dupre and Elizabeth Boulard eschews is the consequences faced by mulatto children in antebellum Louisiana. Similarly, Kate Chopin's short story "Désirée's Baby," included in her 1894 collection titled *The Bayou Folk*, remains silent on this point. However, Chopin's silence opens a space for exploration. Rather than devise a dénouement for this story that engages social and legal ramifications for Désirée, Armand, and their child, Chopin hints at the terrible consequences that awaited them by sacrificing Désirée and her child to the bayou.

Not only were marriages forbidden but also sexual relations. Historically, these statutes were less concerned with the sex act itself than with the social complexities of how to categorize offspring. Because the United States' institution of slavery had evolved into a racial slavery system (i.e., black corresponded to slave and white to free) by the nineteenth century, bizarre paradoxes began to appear in its culture and laws. For instance, Barbara J. Fields identifies "the well-known anomaly of American racial convention that considers a white woman capable of giving birth to a black child but denies that a black woman can give birth to a white child" (qtd. in Hodes 9). Moreover, once the United States shifted classification of a child's race from a patrilineal to a matrilineal inheritance in colonial court cases, double standards based on gender became commonplace (Bardaglio 53). According to Bardaglio, the white male hegemony deterred white women from pursuing relationships with black men because their mixed children would be born free. The deterrents relied on social mechanisms that insisted that white women who preferred dalliances with black men were depraved and lascivious (Bardaglio 61). Martha Hodes observes that not only black women but "white women were also supposedly endowed with dangerously strong sexual desires" and that "poor white women [were] especially prone to sexual depravity and dishonor" (65). In divorce documents, Hodes discovered descriptive phrases of white women who committed adultery with and/or left their husbands for black men, including "a notorious whore" and "guilty of acts of the greatest lewdness, immorality, and vice" (79).

Despite the social pressures exerted to prevent white women from engaging in sexual relations with black men, it still occurred to the extent that the courts invented devious interpretations of the current laws to address legitimacy and inheritance (Hodes 50). The laws of Louisiana and other states sought to ensure that any issue from these relationships, consensual or nonconsensual, would prohibit access to the rights granted to free whites. The cases of Désirée's baby and La Blanche's babies offer an illustration of the possibilities.

The children born of a slave woman followed the condition of the mother. Thus, as is seen in the story, La Blanche's boys are slaves. In a fashion similar to their mother, if Armand had any provisions for them in his will and he died while they remained slaves, they could inherit nothing, for slaves, as property, could not own property. If he had a clause that freed these slaves upon his death, other heirs could dispute the will on the grounds that Armand had denied them some of the value of the estate and sue in court for his slave offspring's reenslavement. Courts may or may not have ruled in favor, for some judges decided that the lack of manumission before the master's death meant that the master did not really intend for the slave to be freed ("Turner"). If Armand had died in 1857 or after, the desire to free these children would not be deemed valid. Also, Armand would be wise to obfuscate that these children were his own because the courts looked unfavorably on any flaunting of immoral behavior ("Robert"). For instance, in

Barrow v. Bird (1870), slaves could not be emancipated and could not receive property if born in concubinage. In sum, La Blanche's children had very little to hope for from their father ("Barrow").

Similarly, the children born of a free black woman were denied rights to patrimony. Operating under the notion that she and her child are black, Désirée would have been thwarted by the Louisiana Civil Code. Legitimate children are defined by the code as "those born of a marriage lawfully contracted." This is not the case for Armand and Désirée; therefore, their son is considered illegitimate. Article 217, revised in 1831, clearly states that no "white parent [may] legitimate a colored child." However, Désirée's son, most likely through his baptism, would have been acknowledged by Armand, which means that, although illegitimate, he is Armand's natural child. Once this relationship is established, Armand is required under Article 260 to provide for his colored child's "board and lodging, and to enable [him] to learn to read and write, and a trade." In some cases, masters were aware of the limits imposed by the law, and they attempted to circumvent these barriers through creative means. Antoine Lacour tried to leave more money than permitted to his heirs by stating that he owed them money for "an unpaid accumulated debt" (Thompson 36). As long as Armand does not remarry, Armand's son by Désirée will be his heir after his death, even if Armand does not name him as such, for, in accordance with the Civil Code, Armand appears to have no "descendants nor ascendants, nor collateral relations, nor surviving wife." If Armand remarries, Désirée's child will inherit only if there is no issue and if Armand's widow is deceased.

In the interim, Désirée's child's quality of life is debatable. Malone writes, "In all cases, the offspring occupied a very shaky and confusing position" (222). They suffered under insulting appellations, including half-breed, mongrel, hybrid, amalgam, and, obviously, mulatto, a reference to the hybrid between a horse and an ass, the mule. The child served as the signifier for the illicit relationship, a sign that most white women wanted to hide from others because it meant isolation. Two notable newspaper stories in 1867 spoke to the desperate lengths women would go to in order to erase the existence of their mulatto children. In Pendleton County, Kentucky, a white woman crushed the head of her mulatto child as soon as it had been born in order to hide her illicit relationship with a black man. The child's remains were discovered in the barn. Her Negro lover had fled, and she was to be charged with murder ("Correspondence" 3). In a less horrific expediency, in Missouri, a white family checked in at a hotel, and to the consternation of the employees, the mother and child remain secreted in the room. The authorities were contacted, and the community learned that an adoption of her mulatto child had been effected (Domestic Criminal" 4). In line with these contemporary incidents, Pegues's postcolonial reading of Chopin's story explains, "Désirée's internalized system of oppression to black identity allows her to commit infanticide of her mulatto baby." The Louisiana laws both uphold and direct society's views on miscegenation, and Désirée's actions prove that she is a product of her environment. Toth argues that this object is dominant in Chopin's work: "'Désirée's Baby' is about environment, the effect of slavery on men's character" ("Kate Chopin and Literary Convention" 205). Not only men's character but also women's is at play here, for Désirée is adversely impacted by the patriarchal culture in which she dwells, and she feels compelled to end her baby's life.

Armand and Désirée

This tragic love story between Armand and Désirée continues to capture the imaginations of readers today. In an age that wants to believe that love can conquer all, the disintegration of their relationship caused by the impervious nature of the color line is heart-wrenching. Still, the story is not simply one of a man now believing that his white wife is black. The situation is much more complex. The realities of race in antebellum, Reconstruction, and post-Reconstruction America stretched men and women to their emotional limits at times. Social, financial, and legal barriers imposed upon transgressors were realities that even love could not conquer. Charles Chesnutt articulates a fear that many white Americans felt at the time of the story's composition, particularly as the number of light-skinned blacks increased. In "The Future American: A Complete Race-Amalgamation," he writes, "If it is only by becoming white that colored people and their children are to enjoy the rights and dignities of citizenship, they will have every incentive to 'lighten the breed,' to use a current phrase, that they may claim the white man's privileges as soon as possible" (134). In "The Future American: A Stream of Dark Blood," he even remarked on the phenomenon that Armand had experienced when he discussed the obsession one family had over hiding its African ancestry. Chesnutt writes, "One child of this generation emigrated to what was then the Far West, married a white woman and reared a large family, whose descendants, now in the fourth or fifth remove from the Negro, are in all probability wholly unaware of their origin" (127). This light-skinned ancestor had moved to a place where he could pass, and he succeeded, thus far, in diluting the line and ensuring the obfuscation of his ancestry by never returning to his hometown.

For Désirée and Armand, even though their true origins were unknown to themselves, their families were not successful in keeping their heritages absolutely secret (for as is often pointed out, one is never sure if Désirée is white). When the narrator tells the readers that Désirée had "[a] quick conception of all that this accusation meant for her" (Chopin 243), one needs to think beyond love and consider what this line means in relation to Désirée, a woman and a single mother living in the nineteenth-century South, in order to understand fully why she chooses death.

Works Cited

"Amalgamation." *Liberator* 29.17 (1859): 1. American Periodical Series. Web. 17 Sept. 2013.

Arner, Robert D. "Pride and Prejudice: Kate Chopin's 'Désirée's Baby.'" *Critical Essays on Kate Chopin*. Ed. Alice Hall Petry. New York: G.K. Hall, 1996. 139–46. Print.

Aubert, Guillame. "'The Blood of France': Race and Purity of Blood in the French Atlantic World." *The William and Mary Quarterly* 61.3 (2004): 439–78. Print.

Bardaglio, Peter. *Reconstructing the Household: Families, Sex, and the Law in the Nineteenth-Century South*. Chapel Hill: The University of North Carolina Press, 1995. Print.

Barrow v. Bird. 22 La. Ann. 407. Supreme Court of Louisiana, New Orleans. 1870.

Bauer, Margaret D. "Armand Aubigny, Still Passing after All These Years: The Narrative Voice and Historical Context of 'Désirée's Baby.'" *Critical Essays on Kate Chopin*. Ed. Alice Hall Petry. New York: G.K. Hall, 1996. 161–83. Print.

"The Best Books List of 1894." *The Literary World* 12 Jan. 1895.

"Bethany Union." *Liberty Tribune* 5 Dec. 1862: 1.

Bonner, Thomas. "Bayou Folk Revisited." *The New Laurel Review* 7.2. (1977): 8. Print.

Chesnutt, Charles W. "The Future American: A Complete Race-Amalgamation Likely to Occur." *Essays & Speeches*. Eds. Joseph McElrath, Robert Leitz, and Jesse Crisler. Stanford: Stanford UP, 1999. 131–5. Print.

———. "The Future American: A Stream of Dark Blood." *Essays & Speeches*. Eds. Joseph McElrath, Robert Leitz, and Jesse Crisler. Stanford: Stanford UP, 1999. 126–31. Print.

Chopin, Kate. "Désirée's Baby." *The Complete Works of Kate Chopin*. Vol. I. Ed. Per Seyersted. Baton Rouge: Louisiana State UP, 1969. 240–5. Print.

Civil Code of the State of Louisiana: With the Statutory Amendments, from 1825 to 1853, Inclusive. New Orleans: Bloomfield and Steel, 1861. Duke University Libraries Confederate Imprints. Web. 15 Mar. 2014.

Code Napoleon; or, the French Civic Code. London: William Benning, 1827. Internet Archives. Web. 15 Mar. 2014.
Correspondence of National Police Gazette. "Cincinnati." *The National Police Gazette* 5 Oct. 1867: 3. American Periodical Series. Web. 23 Dec. 2013.
"The Courts." *The Times-Picayune* 1 March 1852: 4.
de Gournay, P. F. "The F.M.C.'s of Louisiana." *Lippincott's Monthly Magazine* Apr. 1894: 511–18. American Periodical Series. Web. 17 Sept. 2013.
"Domestic Criminal News." *The National Police Gazette* 2 Feb. 1867: 4. American Periodical Series. Web. 23 Dec. 2013.
Foy, Roslyn Reso. "Chopin's Désirée's Baby." *Explicator* 49.4 (1991): 222–3. Print.
Fredrickson, George M. "Mulattoes and *Métis.* Attitudes toward Miscegenation in the United States and France since the Seventeenth Century." *International Social Science Journal* 57.83 (2005): 103–12. PsycINFO. Web. 4 Feb. 2014.
Gaudet, Marcia. "Kate Chopin and the Lore of Cane River's Creoles of Color." *Xavier Review* 6.1 (1986): 45–52. Print.
Gayarre, Charles. "Art. V.—The Southern Question." *North American Review* Nov./Dec. 1877: 472–97. Print.
Hodes, Martha. *White Women, Black Men: Illicit Sex in the 19th-Century South.* New Haven: Yale UP, 1997. Print.
Hoover v. the State. 59 Ala. 57. Supreme Court of Alabama. 1887. *LexisNexis Academic.* Web. 18 Sept. 2013.
"Imprisonment for Miscegenation." *The National Police Gazette* 19 April 1879: 6. American Periodical Series. Web. 23 Dec. 2013.
Jacobs, Harriet A. *Incidents in the Life of a Slave Girl. Written by Herself: Electronic Edition.* Ed. Lydia Maria Francis Child. Boston: Published for the Author, 1861. Documenting the American South. Web. 15 Mar. 2014.
J. M. Dupre v. the Executor of Boulard, f.w.c., et al. 10 La. Ann. 411. Supreme Court of Louisiana, New Orleans. 1855.
Lake Snore. "Negro Paramour of a White Wife." *The National Police Gazette* 17 Nov. 1866: 1. American Periodical Series. Web. 23 Dec. 2013.
Lundie, Catherine. "Doubly Dispossessed: Kate Chopin's Women of Color." *Louisiana Literature* 11.1 (1994): 126–42. Print.
"Lust at Its Lowest." *The National Police Gazette* 30 Aug. 1879: 6. American Periodical Series. Web. 23 Dec. 2013.
Malone, Ann Patton. *Sweet Chariot.* Chapel Hill: U of North Carolina P, 1992. Print.
McMahan, Elizabeth. "'Nature's Decoy': Kate Chopin's Presentation of Women and Marriage in Her Short Fiction." *Turn-of-the-Century Woman* 2.2 (1985): 32–35. Print.
"Miscegenation." *The National Police Gazette* 3 Jul. 1880: 6.
"Missouri Supreme Court Abstract." *The Albany Law Journal* 28 Mar. 1885: 254. American Periodical Series. Web. 23 Dec. 2013.

Nott, J. C. "The Mulatto a Hybrid—Probable Extermination of the Two Races if the Whites and Blacks Are Allowed to Intermarry." *The Boston Medical and Surgical Journal* 29.2 (1843): 1–5. American Periodical Series. Web. 23 Dec. 2013.

Palmer, Vernon Valentine. "The Strange Science of Codifying Slavery—Moreau Lislet and the Louisiana Digest of 1808." *Tulane European and Civil Law Forum* 24 (2009): 38–113. Hein Online. Web. 17 Sept. 2013.

Peel, Ellen. "Semiotic Subversion in "Désirée's Baby.'" *American Literature* 62.2 (1990): 223–37. Print.

Pegues, Dagmar. "Fear and Desire: Regional Aesthetics and Colonial Desire in Kate Chopin's Portrayals of the Tragic Mulatta Stereotype." *Southern Literary Journal* 43.1 (2010): 1–22. Print.

"Practical Amalgamation." *The Daily Picayune* 25 Jul. 1854. Newspapers. com Web. 1 Oct. 2013.

Robert Monatt v. E.T. Parker. 30 La. Ann. 585. Supreme Court of Louisiana, New Orleans. 1878.

Shen, Dan. "Implied Author, Overall Consideration and Subversion in "Désirée's Baby.'" *Poetics Today* 31.2 (2010): 285–311. Print.

Snellings, George. "Louisiana Law on the Nullity of Marriage." *Louisiana Law Review* 20.3 (1960): 563–83. Print.

"Testing the Virginia Miscegenation Laws." *Christian Advocate* 22 May 1879: 324. American Periodical Series. Web. 23 Dec. 2013.

Thomas, Heather Kirk. "The White League and Racial Status: Historicizing Kate Chopin's Reconstruction Stories." *Louisiana Literature* 14.2 (1997): 97–115. Print.

Thompson, Harry. *A Miscarriage of Justice: Miscegenation Laws in Louisiana in the Eighteenth and Nineteenth Century.* Thesis. Southern University, 2001.

Toth, Emily. *Kate Chopin.* New York: William Morrow, 1990. Print.

———. "Kate Chopin and Literary Convention; Désirée's Baby." *Southern Studies* 20.2 (1981): 202. Print.

Turner v. Smith. 12 La. Ann. 417. Supreme Court of Louisiana, New Orleans. 1857.

Vail v. Bird. No. 2129, 6 La. Ann. 223. 1851.

Wallenstein, Peter. *Tell the Court I Love My Wife: Race, Marriage, and Law—An American History.* New York: Palgrave McMillan, 2004. Print.

Yiannopoulus, A. N. "Two Critical Years in the Life of the Louisiana Civil Code: 1870 and 1913." *Louisiana Law Review* 53.1 (1992): 5–33. Print.

CHAPTER 4

The Gothic in Kate Chopin

Aparecido Donizete Rossi

Since 1932, only a few critics have attempted to address the presence of the Gothic in Kate Chopin's fiction, beginning with Daniel Rankin, who wrote that *The Awakening* was a "curious morbid pathos of mental dissection" (140) and "morbid in theme" (175). The recurrence of the word "morbid" in Rankin's appraisals is curious, for it can also be found in a review contemporary to the publication of the novel: "unhealthily introspective and morbid" (12), proclaimed *The Los Angeles Sunday Times* on June 25, 1899. It may be difficult for modern readers to find gloomy or gruesome excerpts in Chopin's masterpiece, though it was understood as "diseased" or "unhealthy" by the patterns of the fin de siècle Western society.

Thirty years after Rankin's statement, in a different historical and critical background, Edmund Wilson revealed a surprising history of the property where Chopin spent her years in Cloutierville:

> This Place-du-Bois Plantation had a sinister history. It had belonged to a New Englander called Robert McAlpin, who had lived alone with his slaves and who had become a local legend for his cruel treatment of them.... The tradition of brutality had been carried on by Kate Chopin's father-in-law, whose money was mostly in French railroads and who spent a good deal of his time in France, so that it touched Kate herself uncomfortably. (588)

This place, with its "sinister history," may have darkly inspired Chopin, who transformed some of its real features into literature. In this perspective, Place-du-Bois is the name of Thérèse Lafirme's property in *At Fault*, where an important location was violently and meaningfully destroyed by fire, and Wilson's references to Chopin's father-in-law (his brutality with the slaves and his long times spent in France) resemble the Aubigny family in "Désirée's Baby," particularly Armand Aubigny's extreme cruelty and brutality with the slaves and old Monsieur Aubigny's preference of residing in France.

Almost 40 years separate Wilson's words from the next Gothic insight into Chopin's work, and this more contemporary insight addresses "Désirée's Baby." In a 1999 anthology, Charles Crow selected this short story as a representative text of the American Gothic. Later, in his 2009 study on the subject and on the story, Crow wrote that "Kate Chopin's 'Désirée's Baby' is perhaps the most complex and subtle of Creole Gothic tales" (92). Crow seems to have been the first literary critic to use the word "Gothic" as an adjective for a text written by Chopin, which is remarkable because such a statement places her in the same Gothic tradition where Ann Radcliffe, Jane Austen, Mary Shelley, the Brontë sisters, Charlotte Perkins Gilman, and Edith Wharton, as well as Charles Brockden Brown, Nathaniel Hawthorne, Edgar Allan Poe, and Ambrose Bierce can be found.

Stemming from Crow's groundbreaking study on "Désirée's Baby" and using the lens of the Gothic tradition and criticism, this chapter will approach the Gothic through a closer reading of selected scenes from *At Fault* and *The Awakening* to emphasize how Chopin uses specific elements from this literary tradition to address issues of women's experience in society.

Kate Chopin and the Gothic

The Gothic as a literary mode rose in 1764 with the publication of Horace Walpole's *The Castle of Otranto.* A development and transformation resulting from the rise of the novel in the eighteenth century, the Gothic constitutes an artistic reaction to the logic and rationality that were dominant in art and literature during the Enlightenment period. Either in novels, short stories, theatre, or poetry, the Gothic aesthetic represents the dark side of existence. The gloomy and the eerie are its imagery; the terrifying and the horrific are its diction; the awesome and the awkward are its tones; shadows and nightmares are its rhythms. It is the realm of madness and uncanniness, where the evil supernatural and terrifying mystery dwell in dreadful freedom: "Gothic writing remains fascinated by objects and practices that are constructed as negative, irrational, immoral and fantastic" (Botting 2), in a direct contrast with the positive, rational, moral, and realistic literature of the beginning of the eighteenth and the end of the nineteenth centuries. General characteristics of this genre are easily recognizable, for

> In Gothic fiction certain stock features provide the principal embodiment and evocation of cultural anxieties. Tortuous, fragmented narratives relating mysterious incidents, horrible images and life-threatening pursuits predominate in the eighteenth century. Spectres, monsters, demons, corpses, skeletons, evil aristocrats, monks and nuns, fainting heroines and bandits populate Gothic landscapes as suggestive figures of imagined and realistic threats. This list grew, in the nineteenth century, with the addition of scientists, fathers, husbands, madmen, criminals and the monstrous double signifying duplicity and evil nature. Gothic landscapes are desolate, alienating and full of menace. In the eighteenth century they were wild and mountainous locations. Later the modern city combined the natural and architectural components of Gothic grandeur and wildness, its dark, labyrinthine streets suggesting the violence and menace of Gothic castle and forest. (Botting 2)

Contrary to the emphasis of most criticism on the Gothic prior to the 1980s, the genre is not only a matter of theme, but also a matter of form. Botting reveals not only a list of thematic recurrences that are now clichés, but also a structure characterized by terminology such as "tortuous," "fragmented narratives," "specters," "the double," and "labyrinthine." As Gothic writing attempts to evoke a sense of fear, it has developed a narrative architecture of fear through its history, identified by a fragmented narrative where the spectrality and duplicity of suspense sustain tension. Together with a labyrinthine construction of space and time, the narrative tension creates an atmosphere where the emotion of fear can develop throughout the text.

The recurrent Gothic themes, with their codependent relationships to the architecture of fear, constitute the impressive foundations over which Gothic writing, fiction, and art were erected. In this codependence also dwells the critical reaction that marked the rise of the Gothic into the present—its destabilizing and deconstructive powers against the constitution of the "real," the rational, and logic in a sociopolitical, economic, and artistic status quo overwhelmed by the predominance of totalitarianisms. Beyond a matter of theme and form, the Gothic is also (and perhaps mainly) a matter of criticism.

As such, it is notable that one of the main lines of the Gothic history and tradition was established by women writers. After the publication of *The Castle of Otranto*, the works of Ann Radcliffe developed another perspective for the Gothic, the female Gothic, characterized by fainting heroines, haunted castles, exotic places, and the explained supernatural as a grand finale. Though cliché now in the twenty-first century, Radcliffe's female Gothic was responsible for giving the mode its classic shape, and her work delved deeply into the imagination of her contemporaries and generations afterward to the extent that Jane Austen felt the need to compose a kind of reviewing dialogue with Radcliffe's masterpiece in *Northanger Abbey*. And on the other side of the Atlantic, Edgar Allan Poe, one of Radcliffe's most dedicated apprentices, could not resist directly mentioning her in "Life in Death": "The chateau . . . was one of those fantastic piles of commingled gloom and grandeur which have so long frowned among the Apennines, not less in fact than in the fancy of Mrs. Radcliffe" (735).

Radcliffe's influence gave birth to a long and continually evolving tradition of female Gothic writers. Inspired by impressive novels like *The Mysteries of Udolpho* and *The Italian*, many women tried to imitate her style and themes, not always paralleling her mastery. However, writers like Jane Austen, Mary Shelley, the Brontë sisters, and Emily Dickinson transformed the genre. In *Northanger Abbey*, Austen created a metanarrative that functions as both a critique of the Gothic clichés established by Radcliffe and a Gothic novel; Mary Shelley confronted the sacred patriarchal institutions of science, religion, and myth in her *Frankenstein*; Emily Brontë turned an anodyne love story into a nightmarish plot studded with pain, curses, and creatures of darkness in *Wuthering Heights*; Charlotte Brontë unleashed the "madwoman in the attic" into the bildungsroman of *Jane Eyre*; and Emily Dickinson, with her cutleries and entombments, turned the Gothic into poetry in a way never anticipated by the Romantics.

Instead of merely reproducing the Radcliffean patterns, these women writers went a step further and turned the Gothic into a critical weapon against the patriarchal orders and burdens imposed on women, and, in doing so, they became feminist icons of the twentieth and twenty-first centuries:

> A challenge to, or interrogation of, forms of fiction dominated by patriarchal assumptions, Gothic novels have been reassessed as part of a wider feminist critical movement that recovers suppressed or marginalised writing by women and addresses issues of female experience, sexual oppression and difference. (Botting 19)

Female experience, sexual oppression, and difference were (and maybe still are) the first issues addressed by the feminist critical movement, to which another word must be added as a summary for longtime struggles: resistance. "Resistance" implies reaction and vice versa, no matter if physically or textually, which is why the relationship between feminism and the Gothic is as close as it is. Sandra Gilbert and Susan Gubar argue that a defining characteristic of women's texts is precisely a monstrously dangerous, contaminating, and Gothically Dickinsonian "infection in the sentence" (45), which shares parallels to a defining characteristic of all Gothic writing: "the danger of contamination," the principle of "originary infection" that reveals "that in the end our myths of origin are flawed, that there are areas through which the unknown and the unsolicited may none the less stray" (Punter 2).

Resistance seems to create a phantasmatic connection, a frightening repetition of spectrality, between feminism and the Gothic with Chopin's life and works. In the introduction to the second edition of *The Madwoman in the Attic*, Gilbert and Gubar explain that Chopin's *The Awakening* is one of the "key texts"" (xxviii) of the feminist critical movement. Such a statement implies that Chopin's works are key texts to Gilbert and Gubar's thinking on the female writers' literary imagination and to the theoreticians' analytic corpus that is the bulk of the female Gothic tradition. Something similar to this implication may be apprehended from some recent words written by Emily Toth, Chopin's contemporary biographer: "Kate Chopin taught me how to *resist*" (16). In this regard, Chopin has indeed been an inspiration to feminist resistance. However, her relationship to the Gothic through the phantasmatic element of this connection emerges less obviously.

Given her education, Chopin could hardly have been unaware of the works of Radcliffe, Austen, Shelley, and the Brontës, as she was not unaware of the female movements of her times. There are clear references to these movements in Chopin's texts, though she was never political. Additionally, the romantic poetry from both sides of the Atlantic was very popular and influential in her times, and she notes both Austen's *Pride and Prejudice* and Charlotte Brontë's *Shirley* at the end of her first diary (Seyersted and Toth 88).[1] However, Chopin's inclusion of the female Gothic tradition into her fiction may have happened in a more unexpected way: as life experiences turned into literature afterward.

Life experiences turning into literature may not be understood here in terms of what Elaine Showalter defines as "authority of experience," "a new language, a new way of reading that can integrate our [female] intelligence and our experience, our reason and our suffering, our scepticism and our vision" (39). In Chopin's fiction, life experiences turned into literature are much closer to "an open, infinite process that is both meaning-generating and meaning-subverting" (Johnson 40), or "the text as a signifying process" (Moi 76), or more appropriately "a unique and differentiated textual 'operation,'...whose unfinished movement assigns itself no absolute beginning, and which, although it is entirely consumed by the reading of other texts, in a certain fashion refers only to its own writing" (Derrida 3). "Textuality" threads through each of these definitions, or writing (écriture), which may be used as its correlate.

Textuality/writing is not contradictory to Showalter's authority of experience; it rather incorporates this concept, but with a single difference: Showalter's concept implies a certain naïve subjectivity, while the authority of experience as incorporated by textuality/writing implies conscious and subversive resistance and reaction. As Gilbert and Gubar state, the woman writer "can manipulate; she can scheme; she can plot—stories as well as strategies" (26). In terms of textuality/writing, the authority of experience is one of these strategies, similar to the literary technique of turning life experiences into literature.

In light of these propositions, some of Chopin's life experiences illuminate the author's phantasmatic connection with the Gothic. One of these life experiences could be framed in Freudian terms: mourning and melancholia. When Chopin started writing for publication under Dr. Kolbenheyer's encouragement, many of her loved ones had already passed away: her father, half-brother, great grandmother, grandmother, husband, and mother. Her husband Oscar's death brought her hard times for almost two years; when she returned to St. Louis in 1884, where she would live until the end of her days, she had six dependent children. When Kolbenheyer encouraged Chopin to write, he was not only "struck with the literary quality of her descriptions" (49), as Seyersted states, but also concerned about her financial situation. Nonetheless, it seems that Chopin started writing out of deep sorrow, and where there is sorrow the Gothic hovers like a vulture, for sorrow is the threshold of despair. Whether she used sorrow as a motivation to write or as a life experience turned into literature will remain forever a mystery, but "The Story of an Hour" may offer a hint of an uncanny symbiosis between both possibilities. Nonetheless, melancholia is a well-known characteristic of her writings, and mourning was certainly familiar to her in life.

Another life experience that illuminates Chopin's connection with the Gothic is her historical moment. She was 15 years old when the Civil War ended, so she had had contact with slavery, a classic theme of the American Gothic. The well-known episode of a young Chopin tearing down the Union flag from her house porch emerges here as something unexpectedly meaningful: 13-year old Chopin (O'Flaherty at that time) was a Confederate sympathizer. Despite this early sympathy, it seems that she began to develop an adverse response to slavery as she spent more time in Louisiana as an adult.

After their honeymoon, Kate and her husband Oscar decided to live in New Orleans. In 1879, they moved to Cloutierville, in the Natchitoches parish. By this time, she already knew about how terribly her father-in-law had treated his slaves. However, while the adolescent Miss O'Flaherty was a Confederate sympathizer, the young adult Mrs. Chopin was uncomfortably touched by father-in-law's antebellum practice (Wilson 588). Her time in Louisiana cultivated in Chopin an unprecedented understanding of what slavery really meant, and this changed her mind. As a result, Chopin wrote "Désirée's Baby." In this short story, slavery was painted in the entire multitude of its Machiavellian aspects, with all its shadowy, sadistic, and horrible colors. The Gothic emerges from Chopin's life experience with slavery turned into literature in this short story: it hovers like a cursed specter over the text, as if she had used textuality/writing as a ritual of exorcism. Slavery remains alive in "Désirée's Baby," though it is sealed by textuality/writing at the same time it is textuality/writing itself, so its readers will have to face the "very spirit of Satan" (Chopin 242).

Slavery was not the only influence on Chopin as writer of Gothic fiction. Her great-grandmother, Madame Charleville, was a storyteller who had grown up in New Orleans, and "[t]he joy of this remarkable and vivacious old lady was to fire the mind of the child [Chopin] with enthralling stories" (Rankin 13). These "enthralling" stories were surely related to France (Madame Charleville belonged to a first generation of French descendants) and to slavery, but not exclusively. Spanish, English, and French people, as well as the Acadians and the slaves themselves, brought to Louisiana their culture and their languages, so in the 1850s and 1860s the language of Louisiana folklore, religion, myth, and legend had already incorporated frightening elements such as changeling and foundling legends, witchcraft, the classic European Gothic pantheon (werewolves, vampires, ghosts, and specters), Voodoo, Hoodoo, Papa Legba, and the appalling names of Madame LaLaurie and Marie Laveau.[2] This language was certainly not unfamiliar to Madame Charleville and was possibly passed to Chopin when she was still a child.

Other literary influences also appear in a list at the end of the author's first diary (Seyersted and Toth, 87–88), including texts such as Edmund Burke's *A Philosophical Enquiry into the Origin of Our Ideas of the Sublime and Beautiful*, the first book to deal with the feeling of fear in its relation to the sublime, making it one of the first theoretical treatises on the Gothic; William Howitt's *Homes and Haunts of the British Poets*; *The Inferno* from Dante's *The Divine Comedy*[3] and some works by Coleridge, Lamb, and Tasso. The influence of these texts, as well as Chopin's relationship to Louisiana as a land of the Gothic, seems to be fundamental to understanding Chopin's technique of creating atmosphere in her own stories.

In her works, atmosphere is carefully connected with local color, and sometimes both are understood as the same, due to the fact that they are parts of the intricate textual structure. The struggle between love and traditional ethics creates an unstable environment in *At Fault*; solitude and existential drama occur in *The Awakening*; and fear and horror frame "Désirée's Baby." The ironical struggles against the social and artistic status quo in many of her short stories are some examples of Chopin's mastery in the artistic creation of atmosphere, a mastery inherited from Gothic experts.

Further, Guy de Maupassant influenced Chopin's style and aesthetics. About him, she wrote: "Here was a man who had escaped from tradition and authority, who had entered into himself and looked out upon life through his own being and with his own eyes; and who, in a direct and simple way, told us what he saw" (701). Maupassant modeled a detour for Chopin, one in which feminism and the Gothic are ways out from tradition, authority, and the status quo (Cixous 63). They are means of resistance, seen particularly in some of Maupassant's short stories in the Gothic tradition ("The Wolf", "A Ghost," "The Grave," "A Mother of Monsters," and "The Horla," a horror story masterpiece that inspired Lovecraft in the composition of "The Call of Cthulhu"). Maupassant figures as the central link between Chopin and the Gothic; through his influence we see Chopin's phantasmatic connection with the Gothic tradition.

The Gothic in *At Fault* and *The Awakening*

At Fault has been read in many different ways: as a novel of the Reconstruction Era after the Civil War or as a novel devoted to specific themes like divorce, racism, alcoholism, and violence, among others. However, no reading has ever emphasized its Gothic aspects, and Sandra Gilbert seems to be, until the present, the only literary critic to provide a clue that would possibly support this approach to the work:

> Like a number of other nineteenth-century female fictions, Chopin's *At Fault* depends for its drama on crucial elements of the *Jane Eyre*

> plot: specifically, on a husband helplessly shackled to a mentally "incompetent" wife (in this case an alcoholic rather than a madwoman), a "pure" woman who insists on the holiness of wedlock, a fire that destroys much of the husband's property, and a providential death that happily resolves the unhappy triangle. (14–5)

If Chopin read *Shirley*, the presupposition that she may have read *Jane Eyre* as well is not illogical. Charlotte Brontë's masterpiece was one of the most influential and popular novels of the nineteenth century, and its impressive symbiosis between theme and structure remains prominent until the present to the extent it served as a direct motivation and example for one of the most important theoretical projects of the twentieth century: Gilbert and Gubar's *The Madwoman in the Attic*. The design of *Jane Eyre* could not be a finer model for Chopin's début: a husband helplessly shackled to a mentally deceased wife (David Hosmer, Chopin's version of Edward Rochester); a mentally "incompetent" wife who is an alcoholic, a renewed version of the madwoman archetype (Fanny Larimore, Chopin's rereading of Bertha Mason); a "pure" woman who insists upon the holiness of wedlock (Thérèse Lafirme, Chopin's American Jane Eyre); a fire that destroys much of the husband's property (the burn of Hosmer's sawmill in Place-du-Bois, Chopin's review of the burn of Thornfield Hall); a providential death that happily resolves the unhappy triangle (Fanny, who, differently from Bertha Mason, died by water, not by fire). Something that must not be forgotten about *Jane Eyre*, however, is the fact that it is a novel within the female Gothic tradition, and the phantasmatic stains of the terror and horror literature it left on *At Fault* are unmistakable.

Place-du-Bois, the main setting of Chopin's first novel, can be read as a correspondent to Thornfield Hall, one of the main settings in *Jane Eyre*, though both locations are very different in their compositional atmosphere: while Thornfield Hall is a classic Gothic manor, a somber place surrounded by mist where sorrow dwells, Place-du-Bois is a classic plantation from the South of the United States, a place near the clear waters of a river, where things grow and the sun shines most of the year. Though it seems a place unfit for Gothic patterns, Place-du-Bois bears a very interesting Gothic feature: it is *isolated*. When *At Fault* begins, the reader is cast immediately into the microcosm resulting from this isolation, a microcosm fabricated with intrigues and threats of all kinds. One of these threats concerns the people who live in the place: a widow and a couple who will form the core of the tension within the plot (and where there is tension there is the specter of suspense lurking in the shadows to remind us of the architecture of fear). Also present are black people recently released from slavery who still bear its scars and people of mixed races who feel displaced, left behind in a transitional world. Both groups of people heighten the tension in the novel.

As one of the characters of mixed ethnicity, the half Native American, half African American Joçint is a free spirit who seems almost an entity of the wilds. He is David Hosmer's employee, but he hates his sawmill job of cutting and impairing the trees of his beloved forest. Under the pressure of his father to keep doing his unbearable work, Joçint burns Hosmer's sawmill down in fury and revenge. The scene, in the sixth chapter, is perhaps the highlight of the presence of the Gothic in *At Fault*: "The night," explains Chopin's narrator, "was so dark, so hushed, that if ever the dead had wished to step from their graves and take a stroll above ground, they could not have found a more fitting hour" (819). At this eerie moment, Hosmer goes out for a little walk while thinking about Thérèse's feelings towards him:

> When his measured tread upon the veranda finally ceased to mark the passing hours, a quiet that was almost pulseless fell upon the plantation. Place-du-Bois slept. Perhaps the only night in the year that some or other of the negroes did not lurk in fence corners, or male exchange of nocturnal visits.
>
> But out in the hills there was no such unearthly stillness reigning. Those restless wood-dwellers, that never sleep, were sending startling gruesome calls to each other. Bats were flapping and whirling and darting hither and thither; the gliding serpent making quick rustle amid the dry, crisp leaves, and over all sounded the murmur of the great pine trees, telling their mystic secrets to the night.
>
> A human creature [Joçint] was there too, feeling a close fellowship with these spirits of night and darkness; with no more fear in his heart than the unheeded serpent crossing his path. Every inch of the ground he knew. He wanted no daylight to guide him. Had his eyes been blinded he would no doubt have bent his body close to earth and scented his way along like the human hound that he was. Over his shoulder hung the polished rifle that sent dull and sudden gleamings into the dark. A large tin pail swung from his hand. He was very careful of this pail—or its contents, for he feared to lose a drop. And when he accidentally struck an intervening tree and spilled some upon the ground, he muttered a curse against his own awkwardness. (Chopin 819)

The ambience of this scene, full of symbols of the darkness, echoes a Voodoo-like ritual of black magic: the insinuation of a good hour for the dead to rise from their graves like zombies while an "unearthly stillness" reigns, the forest creatures of the dark, with their creeping sounds, coming forward from the shadows to share their foul secrets with the night. Within such a dreadful environment Joçint glides like a serpent and has the senses of a hunting dog.

Notably, Chopin's narrator links Joçint and those "spirits of night and darkness," the serpent (he was "with no more fear in his heart than the unheeded serpent crossing his path") and the hound ("Had his eyes been blinded he would no doubt have bent his body close to earth and scented his way along like the human hound that he was"). These links characterize Joçint as a true minion of the darkness ("He wanted no daylight to guide him"), closely related to the bestiary of the night (restless wood-dwellers, bats, serpents, the crackling pine trees, hounds), someone who was summoned to commit ruthless crimes.

Joçint, over whom "the darkness hung about...like the magic mantle of story" (Chopin 820), moved toward his target place "cautious[ly], creeping along with the tread of a stealthy beast" (820) and, by spilling the content of the pail around the place and setting fire to it, burned the sawmill down. To crown this important phantasmatic manifestation of the Gothic, Chopin concludes the famous scene of her first novel with the romantic heroine, Thérèse Lafirme, waking up from a nightmare, another classic Gothic feature:

> Thérèse was passing a restless night. She had lain long awake, dwelling on the insistent thoughts that the day's happenings had given rise to. The sleep which finally came to her was troubled by dreams—demoniac—grotesque. Hosmer was in a danger from which she was striving with physical effort to rescue him, and when she dragged him painfully from the peril that menaced him, she turned to see that it was Fanny whom she had saved—laughing at her derisively, and Hosmer had been left to perish. The dream was agonizing; like an appalling nightmare. She awoke in a fever of distress, and raised herself in bed to shake off the unnatural impression which such a dream can leave. The curtains were drawn aside from the window that faced her bed, and looking out she saw a long tongue of flame, reaching far up into the sky—away over the tree tops and the whole Southern horizon a glow. (Chopin 821)

Thérèse's nightmare (demoniac and grotesque, agonizing and appalling, the cause of fever and distress) evokes the Gothic Romance atmosphere and themes of Keats's "The Eve of St. Agnes": the heroine is afraid of losing her lover, so evil ideas disturb her imagination. On the other hand, this nightmare is an upside down flash-forward of Fanny's death at the end of the novel, which will lead Hosmer to distressfully try to save his official wife from a river flood by putting his own life in danger and Thérèse to have to look after him. Due to this nightmare, Thérèse will awaken and see the hellish flames of the sawmill on fire, flames that are not the first in Chopin's works, for they echo a more moderate, though no less hellish, fire scene, the one at the end of "Désirée's Baby" in which the Satanic Armand Aubigny burns all Désirée's remaining belongings together with a bundle of revealing letters.

The spectral or phantasmatic modes of presence of the Gothic in *At Fault* evoke Derrida's questions about the "being-there" of the specter, which also call into question the significance of "presence" in the text: "what is the being-there of a specter? what is the mode of presence of a specter?" (38). As a momentary conclusion for these considerations on the "being-there" of the Gothic in *At Fault*, it should be noted that the scene of the burning of the sawmill may also be taken metaphorically as a life experience turned into literature, since it seems to be what Kate Chopin herself, after a change of mind, would have liked to do with the homonymous Place-du-Bois, a place haunted by a "tradition of brutality [that] had been carried on by Kate Chopin's father-in-law" (Wilson 588). In this sense, the famous scene from *At Fault*, turned above into Gothic in the unveiling of its phantasmagoria, may be read as a sign of (un)conscious resistance against patriarchal impositions in the same way the madwoman in the attic functions in *Jane Eyre*.

Compared to *At Fault*, the "being-there" of the Gothic in *The Awakening* seems to be of a subtler and even more phantasmatic type due to its powerfully lyrical façade. Concealed within Whitmanian, Coleridgean and Swinburnean imagery, the Gothic pervades the novel's textuality/writing, creating the effects of isolation (by the sea, metaphor of the unconscious), mysticism, and mythology (Chopin's narrator compares Edna to Venus) in order to unveil the awakening of a woman's identity and independence—a shift away from the reductive patriarchal metaphors such as the Angel in the House.

Within this frame and differently from *At Fault*, *The Awakening* finds no model in the tradition of female Gothic novels or even in a narrative tradition. It is alone in its own kind, singular in its canonicity, a solitary book like the solitary soul who dwells in its pages, since in the composition of her masterpiece Chopin is no more a newcomer, but a mature artist aware of the far-reaching possibilities of poetry in its Heideggerian sense. *The Awakening* may in fact be better compared to poetry in prose than to narrative, as it employs subtexts that turn its textuality/writing into a palimpsest, which "invites us to engage in a relational reading, the flavor of which, however perverse, may well be condensed in an adjective . . . : a *palimpsestuous* reading. To put it differently, just for the fun of switching perversities, one who really loves texts must wish from time to time to love (at least) two together" (Genette 399).

The Gothic is one of these subtexts in *The Awakening*, a weft (maybe *the* weft) in the weaving of the novel's palimpsest that demands, for its sake, a palimpsestuous reading. A first phantasmatic presence of its subtextuality in the novel may be palimpsestuously detached from the following excerpt:

> Yes. On the twenty-eight of August, at the hour of midnight, and if the moon is shining—the moon must be shining—a spirit that has haunted these shores for ages rises up from the Gulf. With its own penetrating vision the spirit seeks some one mortal worthy to hold him company, worthy of being exalted for a few hours into realms of the semi-celestials. His search has always hitherto been fruitless, and he has sunk back, disheartened, into the sea. But to-night he found Mrs. Pontellier. Perhaps he will never wholly release her from the spell. . . . (Chopin 909–10)

Uttered by Robert Lebrun, the story of the Ghost of Grand Isle reveals itself as a classic Gothic feature in the novel. It seems to maintain an axial relation with another excerpt from the text: as Edna was fond of music, she used to listen to Adéle Ratignolle to play or practice during the morning. One of the pieces Adéle plays is called "Solitude" by Edna, and "When she heard it there came before her imagination the figure of a man standing beside a desolate rock on the seashore. He was naked. His attitude was one of hopeless resignation as he looked toward a distant bird winging its flight away from him" (Chopin 906). The naked man is related to the Ghost of Grand Isle, or rather *is* the ghost itself, since both scenes, the Ghost of Grand Isle and the Naked Man, are inspired by Walt Whitman's "Out of the Cradle Endlessly Rocking," which presents erotic visions of freedom of the body, mind, and soul.

To use Freudian terms, eroticism reveals here an unconscious work with suppressed sexual drives: the Ghost of Grand Isle holds a "penetrating vision," reminiscent of the psychoanalytic association between the vision and the phallus, and the man standing near the rock is naked, which turns him into an object of desire. These excerpts from *The Awakening* demonstrate the links between the Gothic and sexuality that also emerge in the work of Radcliffe,

Austen, Shelley, the Brontës and other women writers. As the dark side of Romanticism, the "Gothic becomes a fiction of unconscious desire, a release of repressed energies and antisocial fantasies," write Botting, so the female Gothic is "a mode of addressing fears about sexuality and childbirth. . . . A challenge to, or interrogation of, forms of fiction dominated by patriarchal assumptions" (19).

A second phantasmatic presence of the Gothic that may be palimpsestuously addressed in *The Awakening* is found at the end of its twelfth and thirteenth chapters. In their Tristan and Iseult quest for being together, Edna and Robert visit another island, Grande Terre, and attend a service in "the quaint little Gothic church of Our Lady of Lourdes, gleaming all brown and yellow with paint in the sun's glare" (Chopin 916). During the rites, Edna feels unexplainably ill, and Robert brings her to Madame Antoine's house, a local resident, where she recovers. After listening to some storytelling from the old lady, the couple leaves Grande Terre by nightfall:

> The night came on, with the moon to lighten it. Edna could hear the whispering voices of dead men and the click of muffled gold. When she and Robert stepped into Tonie's boat, with the red lateen sail, misty spirit forms were prowling in the shadows and among the reeds, and upon the water were phantom ships, speeding to cover. (Chopin 920)

A first reading of this conclusion to Chapter Thirteen would emphasize the previous storytelling moment as the thriller of such imaginative visions. Such a rational reading is not contradictory to the presence of Gothic features in the text, for the Gothic signifies "an over-abundance of imaginative frenzy, untamed by reason and unrestrained by conventional . . . demands for simplicity, realism or probability" (Botting 3).

Contradiction, however, seems to be at the core of these excerpts of *The Awakening*, as it is at the core of the Gothic. First, it is quite uncanny, in the excerpt from the end of Chapter Twelve, that a Catholic service takes place in a Gothic church, since Gothic not only comes from paganism but is pagan itself. Second, in the same excerpt, a Gothic church appears uncommonly bright in its features: "gleaming all brown and yellow with paint in the sun's glare." Usually, Gothic churches are somber because their architecture is designed to cast shadows. Third, the bulk of Chapter Thirteen is a very important part of *The Awakening* as it is the moment that highlights Edna's rite of passage from Christian humanity (Mrs. Pontellier) into pagan divinity (Venus/Aphrodite): "Having bathed, slept, feasted, communed, and received quasireligious instructions in an alternate theology, she seems definitively to have entered a fictive world, a realm of gold where extraordinary myths are real and ordinary reality is merely mythical" (Gilbert 54). The remarkable contradiction in this point is that Edna's passage from humanity to pagan divinity happens in a Christian Last Supper-like rite.

The Gothic phantasmagoria that concludes Chapter Thirteen is then a metaphor for Edna's entrance into a fictive world, the realm of mythology, which will free her body, mind, and soul from the patriarchal restraints binding her existence as a woman. This phantasmagoria is a transformation of the romantic principle of apprehending reality through imagination. It also echoes Coleridge's "The Rime of the Ancient Mariner" in its use of the classic Gothic image of the phantom ship: like Charon's ferry, it is in between life and death, real and unreal, reality and imagination, nature and culture, margin and center, independence and submission, sleep and awake. Consequently, Edna's struggles for freedom are, like all struggles of female characters or women writers from the nineteenth and the beginning of the twentieth centuries, Gothic per se in their reaction and resistance principles; *infections in the sentence*, to paraphrase Gilbert and Gubar.

Under these considerations and as an open conclusion to the issues raised in this chapter, the phantasmatic presence of the Gothic in the palimpsestuous fabric of *The Awakening* is a literal infection in the sentence found in Chapter Thirty. Edna, already transubstantiated into Venus and apparently released from patriarchal restraint, is giving a small party to commemorate her birthday. Among the guests is "a gentleman by the name of Gouvernail, connected with one of the daily papers, of whom nothing special could be said, except that he was observant and seemed quiet and inoffensive" (Chopin 970). One of the few recurrent characters in Chopin's fiction, Gouvernail murmurs to the readers, the only listeners of his whispered words, two verses of a poem in appraisal to the Dionysian scene of Edna's birthday party moving in front of him: "'There was a graven image of Desire / Painted with red blood on a ground of gold'" (Chopin 973). These very well-known verses are from Swinburne's "A Cameo," and they deserve to be quoted in their full textual frame.

> There was a graven image of Desire
> Painted with red blood on a ground of gold
> Passing between the young men and the old,
> And by him Pain, whose body shone like fire,
> And Pleasure with gaunt hands that grasped their hire.
> Of his left wrist, with fingers clenched and cold,

The insatiable Satiety kept hold,
Walking with feet unshod that pashed the mire.
The senses and the sorrows and the sins,
And the strange loves that suck the breasts of Hate
Till lips and teeth bite in their sharp indenture,
Followed like beasts with flap of wings and fins.
Death stood aloof behind a gaping grate,
Upon whose lock was written Peradventure.

Beyond a literal infection in the sentence in its two verses cited in *The Awakening* palimpsest, the novel literally becomes phantasmatic, a frightening and uncontrollable spectral repetition, through its textuality/writing.

In the way Chopin quotes the poem, and in light of the Gothic influences on Chopin, "A Cameo" points to the being-there of the Gothic in *The Awakening* and in the author's life and works as a whole: it is quoted by a recurring though supporting character in a novel that was turned into a film in contemporary times and inspired another novel that is also about to become a film.[4] Such theatricality creates an echo, an uncanny repetition, of themes developed throughout the textuality/writing of *The Awakening*, themes that can be identified by the words in Swinburne's poem: desire, pain, pleasure, satiety, hate—all engravings in a metaphoric piece of jewelry, like a Shakespearean universe in a nutshell, painted with blood by lurking death, who has marked this jewelry with the worst and unescapable condition of existence: Peradventure. Isn't it death then, the Gothic memento mori, who hides behind every single life experience Gothically turned into literature by Kate Chopin in her works?

Notes

1. *Pride and Prejudice* and *Shirley* are not Gothic novels, but they are written by women who are considered representatives of the genre. In the same list that notes these two novels, *Shirley* is attributed to "A. Bell"; "Acton Bell" was Anne Brontë's penname.
2. Voodoo and Hoodoo are religious practices of African roots very common in Louisiana. Papa Legba is a godly entity in Voodoo. Madame Marie Dauphine LaLaurie (c. 1775–c. 1842) was a New Orleans socialite and serial killer who became famous for her involvement in the torture and murdering of slaves. Marie Laveau (1794–1881) was a renowned Louisiana Creole practitioner of Voodoo better known as the Voodoo Queen of New Orleans.
3. Referred to as Dante's *The Vision*, an old allusion to the most famous part of Dante's poem in English.

4. Mary Lambert's *Grand Isle* and Bob Graham's *The End of August* are the films *The Awakening* was turned into; Robert Stone's *Children of Light* is the novel which *The Awakening* is about to be turned into a film.

Works Cited

Botting, Fred. *Gothic*. London and New York: Routledge, 1996. Print.

Cixous, Hélène. "Sorties: Out and Out: Attacks/Ways Out/Forays." *The Newly Born Woman*. Trans. Betsy Wing. Minneapolis and London: U of Minnesota P, 1986. 63–129. Print.

Chopin, Kate. "The Awakening." *The Complete Works of Kate Chopin*. Ed. Per Seyersted. Baton Rouge: Louisiana State UP, 2006. 881–1000. Print.

———. "Common Place Book, 1867–1870." *A Kate Chopin Miscellany*. Ed. Per Seyersted and Emily Toth. Natchitoches and Oslo: Northwestern State UP and Universitetsforlaget, 1979. 47–88. Print.

———. "Confidences." *The Complete Works of Kate Chopin*. Ed. Per Seyersted. Baton Rouge: Louisiana State UP, 2006. 700–2. Print.

———. "Désirée's Baby." *The Complete Works of Kate Chopin*. Ed. Per Seyersted. Baton Rouge: Louisiana State UP, 2006. 240–5. Print.

———. "At Fault." *The Complete Works of Kate Chopin*. Ed. Per Seyersted. Baton Rouge: Louisiana State UP, 2006. 741–877. Print.

———. "The Western Association of Writers." *The Complete Works of Kate Chopin*. Ed. Per Seyersted. Baton Rouge: Louisiana State UP, 2006. 691–2. Print.

Crow, Charles L. *American Gothic*. Cardiff: U of Wales P, 2009. Print.

Derrida, Jacques. *Positions*. Trans. Alan Bass. Chicago and London: U of Chicago P, 1981.

———. *Specters of Marx: The State of the Debt, the Work of Mourning, and the New International*. Trans. Peggy Kamuf. New York and London: Routledge, 1994. Print.

Franklin, Rosemary F. "Poe and *The Awakening*." *Mississippi Quarterly* 47.1 (1993/1994): 47–57. Print.

"Fresh Literature." *Los Angeles Sunday Times*. Los Angeles Sunday Times, 25 Jun. 1899. 12.

Genette, Gérard. *Palimpsests: Literature in the Second Degree*. Trans. Channa Newman and Claude Doubinsky. Lincoln and London: U of Nebraska P, 1997. Print.

Gilbert, Sandra M. "Introduction: The Second Coming of Aphrodite." *The Awakening and Selected Stories*. Ed. Sandra M. Gilbert. Harmondsworth: Penguin Books, 1984. 7–33. Print.

———, and Susan Gubar. *The Madwoman in the Attic: The Woman Writer and the Nineteenth-Century Literary Imagination*. New Haven: Yale UP, 2000. Print.

———. "The Second Coming of Aphrodite: Kate Chopin's Fantasy of Desire." *The Kenyon Review* 5.3 (1983): 42–66. Print.

Johnson, Barbara. "Writing." *Critical Terms for Literary Study*. Ed. Frank Lentricchia and Thomas McLaughlin. Chicago and London: U of Chicago P, 1995. 39–49. Print.

Lovecraft, H. P. *The Annotated Supernatural Horror in Literature*. Ed. S. T. Joshi. New York: Hippocampus, 2000. Print.

Moi, Toril. *Sexual/Textual Politics: Feminist Literary Theory*. London and New York: Methuen, 1985. Print.

Poe, Edgar Allan. "Life in Death [The Oval Portrait]." *The Unabridged Edgar Allan Poe*. Philadelphia: Running Press, 1983. 734–8. Print.

———. "The Philosophy of Composition." *The Unabridged Edgar Allan Poe*. Philadelphia: Running Press, 1983. 1079–89. Print.

Punter, David. "Gothic Origins: The Haunting of the Text." *Gothic Pathologies: The Text, the Body and the Law*. Basingstoke and London: Macmillan, 1998. 1–18. Print.

Rankin, Daniel S. *Kate Chopin and Her Creole Stories*. Philadelphia: U of Pennsylvania P, 1932. Print.

Seyersted, Per. *Kate Chopin: A Critical Biography*. Baton Rouge: Louisiana State UP, 1980. Print.

Showalter, Elaine. "Towards a Feminist Poetics." *Women Writing and Writing about Women*. Ed. Mary Jacobus. London and New York: Croom Helm; Oxford University Women's Committee; Barnes & Noble Books, 1979. 22–41. Print.

Swinburne, Algernon Charles. "A Cameo." *Poetry Foundation*. Web. 02 Feb. 2014.

Toth, Emily. "My Part in Reviving Kate Chopin."*Awakenings: The Story of the Kate Chopin Revival*. Ed. Bernard Koloski. Baton Rouge: Louisiana State UP, 2009. 15–31. Print.

Wilson, Edmund. *Patriotic Gore: Studies in the Literature of the American Civil War*. New York: Oxford UP, 1962. Print.

CHAPTER 5

The Pleasures of Music: Kate Chopin's Artistic and Sensorial Synesthesia

Eulalia Piñero Gil

> She did not sing as we did—
> It was a different tune—
> Herself to her a music
> As Bumble bee of June.
> Emily Dickinson, 14
> "One Sister have I in our house" (1858)

In December 1868, the 18-year-old Kate O'Flaherty attended a concert given by the famous Norwegian violinist Ole Bull in Saint Louis. The young artist wrote in her journal about the mesmerizing effects of his performance:

> To describe the effect his music had upon me would be impossible. It seemed the very perfection of the art, and while listening to him, I for the first time longed to be blind, that I might drink it all in undisturbed and undistracted by surrounding objects. (Toth et al. 63–64)

This deeply confessional impression shows Kate's descriptive creativity and how her exceptional aural perception was also linked to an unusual tasting experience: she could drink music. Her verbal depiction speaks of music in terms of taste, thus linking different sensory domains or, in other words, blending auditory with gustatory sensations in an overall synesthetic experience. Even more impressive is the young woman's lucid awareness of the ephemeral essence of the musical performance. The Saint Louis Sacred Heart Academy student wrote in her Commonplace Book about the influence of Christianity upon music, "that art so powerful as an agent in awakening the slumbering passions in the heart of man" (Toth et al. 34). In spite of her youth, Chopin's composition foreshadows what would become a distinct aesthetic aspect of her fiction: music as the pleasurable cognitive channel through which her characters awaken to strongly felt emotions that inspire a range of responses such as love, friendship, motherhood, artistic inspiration, or the quest for independence or personal fulfillment.

This chapter represents a shift from a focus on Kate Chopin's relationship and experience of music in the private sphere and in its representation in her fiction. Many critics have stressed the fact that the writer's passion for music is depicted in a pervasive way in nearly all of her most significant fiction: "thematically through the portrayal of individuals responding to the sensuous sounds and primal rhythms, and also formally through the narrative use of repetition, rhythm, lyrical language and melodic plots" (Thrailkill, *Affecting Fictions* 158). Nevertheless, the majority of them are unable to draw a clear description of the beginnings, the evolution, and the connections of Chopin's musical inspiration and, at the same time, analyze the sensorial implications of her unique synesthetic approach in her fiction. Moreover, it is important to take into account how the writer establishes a literary dialogue with the aesthetic and scientific currents of her time such as the impact in the arts of the Wagnerian "Gesamtkunstwerk" theory, the nineteenth-century romantic theories on artistic and sensorial synesthesia, and the turn-of-the-century groundbreaking cognitive research on how emotion mediated human experience of the exterior world. There are some critics who also suggest that Chopin's fiction can be read more fruitfully as "situated aesthetically, spiritually and even medically in a range of late nineteenth-century cultural discourses that plumbed the salutary effects of tuning the self to the cadences of the world both without and within the skin" (Thrailkill, "Chopin's Lyrical" 44).

Likewise, what interests me here is how Chopin experiments with altered states of consciousness and creates an enduring and multiple sensory synesthesia in *The Awakening* and in stories such as "Wiser than God," through the extensive use of music, in which one type of sensation is referred to in terms more appropriate to another. In this way, music, which provides the most powerful artistic leitmotif and sensation in these texts, evokes and blends not only images in the characters' minds, but all types of physical and emotional feelings that contribute, in a decisive way, to their transcendental metamorphosis.

As Nancy S. Ellis has concluded, "music becomes a thematic and symbolic expression in the lives of her characters. Whether male or female, conventional or defiant, the people of Kate Chopin's stories are influenced and changed by the power of music" (229).

Music was the significant genesis of Kate O'Flaherty's artistic education that in many ways developed her outstanding talent for the other arts. Her Franco-Irish family background prepared her for a gradual awakening to the outside world—to music, literature, and art in general. Her French great-grandmother, Madame Victoria Verdon Charleville, developed an unconventional homemade curriculum in which music played a preeminent role in the young lady's artistic education. The curious Kate O'Flaherty had a naturally gifted musical mind, and she demonstrated the capacities for hearing, understanding, and intuiting the interpretation of music. In this sense, her biographer Emily Toth highlights the fact that "when she was an adolescent she could repeat by ear any piece of music she heard" (113). Besides, St. Louis, her home town, "was one of the country's most musical cities. Some kind of performance went on every night of the week: philharmonic societies, German bands, touring Italian opera companies, and concerts of every description" (Toth 46). This exposure to music and her musical education also developed her artistic talents and she became not only an exceptional pianist and singer but also a composer; her first publication was "Lilia, Polka" (1888) for piano. Nothing is known about the emotions that inspired her to write the polka, other than her daughter's name being, Lélia, and the fact that polkas in those days, "were quite popular among the Germans and German Americans in St. Louis" (Toth et al. 195). It seems that H. H. Rollman, the publisher of the piano polka, probably foresaw its market value "and rushed to do business with Kate Chopin" (Toth et al. 195).

Chopin was also an opera lover (Boren 188), a convinced Wagnerite, and had the opportunity of attending the best performances at the Saint Louis French Opera House, the first in the United States to stage Richard Wagner's *Lohengrin* and *Tannhäuser*. As her notebooks illustrate, Chopin organized musical soirées at her home where she played the piano and she probably performed the popular keyboard transcriptions of Beethoven's and Wagner's orchestral works. All this outstanding musical training, performance, knowledge, and personal experiences doubtlessly account for Chopin's need to integrate music within some of her fiction protagonists' spiritual and artistic growth.

There are further examples of the relevance of music in Chopin's biography. For example, in 1896 she was writing a Christmas card for an unnamed acquaintance where she expressed poetically how she could know her better through her piano playing. This revealing short poem demonstrates a pattern that recurred through Chopin's personal and literary life: how music offered a sensorial channel for holistic cognitive perception. Therefore, when words failed to express relevant sensorial information, music spoke for her:

To a Lady at the Piano –Mrs. R-n.

I do not know you out upon the street
Where people meet.
We talk as women talk; shall I confess?
I know you less!
I hear you play, and touched by a wondrous spell
I know you well![1] (Toth et al. 193)

Chopin experienced life above all as a musician who lived in a world of sound images so realistic that they became part of her emotional experience. Likewise, her cognitive memory was connected with the auditory images that provoked an organic reaction in musical emotion. Nevertheless, the writer incorporates music in her fiction in various different and surprising manners: many of her central characters are brilliant music performers, such as the pianists Mademoiselle Reisz in *The Awakening* and Paula von Stolz in "Wiser Than a God." Both characters are professional pianists who believe in music as an enriching personal experience and as a creative path for women's social recognition. And as Nancy S. Ellis notes in her analysis of Chopin's major characters in three stories, each of them "experiences a significant self-discovery the author deliberately initiates through musical experience" (229). Music shapes the lives of many of her protagonists in the private and the public spheres. In fact, Chopin depicts in her fiction the transcendental presence of music in nineteenth-century American society among urban, middle-class people, as well as rural, alienated and underprivileged citizens in several short stories such as "At Chênière Caminada," "After the Winter," "A Very Fine Fiddle," "A Vocation and a Voice," "Wiser than a God" and "With the Violin." Notably, in these stories, some of her characters are physically and psychologically transformed by their sensorial involvement with music. Therefore, music provides not only a powerful sensation but a sort of cognitive path through which other sensory experiences are enhanced, just as the writer herself experienced music at the St. Louis concerts. Moreover, the young Chopin "tasted" music when she listened to it, which is characteristic of a prototypical synesthete's mind and perception. Thus, for Chopin as well as "for some individuals or synaesthetes, stimulation in one sensory modality may actually give rise to perceptual experience in more than one modality. This remarkable form of perception is labeled synaesthesia" (Sagiv et al. 294).

In one of Chopin's most musical short stories, "Wiser than a God" (1889), Paula von Stolz plays Chopin's "Berceuse" to soothe her mother who is an invalid widow. Paula's performance is so deeply moving that Mrs. von Stolz recalls the days when her deceased husband used to play the same musical piece for the family. More significant, "Berceuse" enables the mother's immediate recovery from her emotional and physical pain. The narrator describes the outcome of music in Mrs. Von Stolz's health using synesthetic imagery:

> Mrs. Von Stolz leaned her head back amongst the cushions, and with eyes closed, drank in the wonderful strains that came like an ethereal voice out the past, lulling her spirit into the quiet of sweet memories. (Chopin, *Complete Novels* 661–662)

This episode is reminiscent of young Chopin's description of Ole Bull's remarkable violin concert and her desire to become blind in order "to drink" that exceptional performance. In this case, it is Mrs. Von Stolz feels so entranced by her daughter's "wonderful strains" that her ultimate desire is also to "drink" that heavenly music like an elixir of life. But Chopin goes further in describing the healing effects of music by alluding to a well-known castrato singer, Carlo Broschi (1705–1782), known as Farinelli. In 1737 he was invited to sing for King Philip V of Spain, who suffered "melancholia." The favor of the king and queen soon secured him an important position at court because Farinelli's singing treatment had helped to stabilize the monarch's mental health.

Chopin's comparison between Paula Von Stolz's virtuoso piano playing with Farinelli's healing singing points to her belief in music not only as a supreme art but also as a cognitive channel for feelings and emotional states of consciousness. In this sense, the protagonist's passion for music motivates her to strive for artistic perfection and professional success. For Paula a triumphant concert tour is much more rewarding emotionally and physically than a marriage proposal.

In Chopin's most acclaimed novel, *The Awakening*, music becomes a powerful leitmotif that evokes transformation, awareness, and initiation. In various ways, the writer emphasizes the emotional power of music; in fact, Edna Pontellier's awakening is always accompanied by significant romantic or popular melodies throughout the novel. Thus, Edna's quest for a new transgressive and independent artistic self is linked to music because, in my view, it is the most relevant synesthetic channel through which other senses and arts such as painting, poetry, dance, theater, sculpture, architecture, operetta, and opera are explored in order to enable the protagonist's holistic transformation. Here too, Chopin uses "the musical sounds as an unworded vocal refrain heard at intervals throughout the story" (Ellis 224).

Although critics have pointed out the significant presence of music in the novel, they have surprisingly ignored its decisive role as a sensory structure and in Edna's rebirth as a new woman insofar as music is the natural auditory path through which the protagonist channels her emotions and her artistic creativity. Moreover, Edna feels music as a holistic cognitive experience that connects with the rest of the senses. The German physician and physicist Herman Helmholtz's seminal study *On the Sensations of Tone* (1954) documents the preeminence of music among the other arts from a psychological and a physical perspective, similarly to the ways Edna experiences music in the novel:

> Music stands in a much closer connection with pure sensation than any other arts. The latter rather deals with what the senses apprehend, that is the images of outward objects, collected by psychical processes from immediate sensation.... In this sense it is clear that music has a more immediate connection with pure sensation that any other of the fine arts, and, consequently, that the theory of the sensations of hearing is destined to play a much more important part in musical esthetics, than for example, the theory of *chiaroscuro* or of perspective in painting. (2–3)

Helmotz explains how music has significant sensory effects on the body, which Chopin's transgressive heroine in *The Awakening* experiences as a physical transformation. Thus Edna, like Chopin, appears to be a complete synesthete, as music evokes vivid visual imagery and other sensory combinations, including the tactile, the gustatory, and the olfactory. But there are still many other emotional implications for Edna's artistic and emotional quest as music is, in the narrator's terms, "an impress of the abiding truth" (71), which "penetrated her whole being like an effulgence, warming and brightening the dark places of her soul" (135–6). Such illuminating and meaningful descriptions demonstrate the ethic and aesthetic dimensions of music in Edna's life. Thus, Euterpe's art is much more than pure perception; it signifies creativity, authenticity, inspiration, revelation, sensual gratification, satisfaction, and many other emotional elements in the protagonist's sensorial experience. For her, music immediately triggers a spontaneous consistent response in another sensory modality, resulting in strong emotional effects. For that reason, Edna can see pictures in music; she experiences tactile sensations with melodies, like the taste of music, and, what is more significant, her emotional frame of mind is carried away when she hears her friend and pianist, the free and enigmatic Mademoiselle Reisz, play Frederic Chopin's piano pieces in the sensual atmosphere of the Grand Isle's hedonistic soirées:

> Edna was what she herself called very fond of music. Musical strains, well rendered, had a way of evoking pictures in her mind. . . . The very first chords which Mademoiselle Reisz struck upon the piano sent a keen tremor down Mrs. Pontellier's spinal column. . . . But the very passions themselves were aroused within her soul, swaying it, lashing it, as the waves daily beat upon her splendid body. She trembled, she was choking, and the tears blinded her. (72)

The turbulent romantic music of Frederick Chopin's impromptus not only creates pictures in Edna's mind; her very body becomes part of this synesthetic experience: she shivers, she weeps, she is transported to another spiritual and sensorial dimension of understanding and sensuality. In other words, the Polish composer's music with the free *rubato tempo* drives Edna into tears because he "mixed sounds as paints are mixed on a palette, and produced colors that had not been imagined before. He opened up new horizons of musical poetry," according to the Polish poet Kazimierz Wierzynski's striking synesthetic description (x).[2] Moreover, Edna's lack of control over her emotions reflects the illusion produced by Chopin's "Fantaisie-Impromptu," a very popular nineteenth-century piano composition intended to produce a fantasy of spontaneous improvisation and emotional agitation:

> Mademoiselle had glided from the Chopin into the quivering love notes of Isolde's song, and back again to the Impromptu with its soulful and poignant longing. The shadows deepened in the little room. The music grew strange and fantastic—turbulent, insistent, plaintive and soft with entreaty. The shadows grew deeper. The music filled the room. (116)

The significance of Frederick Chopin's passionate music is so pertinent in the narrative that Elaine Showalter has even argued that the structure of the novel mirrors that of the impromptu: "a musical form that seems spontaneous but it is in fact tightly organized" (76). The allusions to other romantic and popular composers such as Franz von Suppé, William Balfe, Eduard Grieg, Ludwig van Beethoven, and Richard Wagner, act as a powerful emotional leitmotif throughout the different scenes of the novel, providing a music accompaniment for each step of Edna's awakening and transformation.

However, there is an emphasis on Chopin's and Wagner's passionate compositions because the "writer imagistically mixes romantic desire with inevitable disappointment" to musically introduce Edna's emotional turmoil and final skepticism about boundless love (Dyer 129). Moreover, there is a powerful reason for the striking alternation of both composers' music: their connection to the romantic synesthetic tradition. They both believed in this sensorial fusion as an idealistic mechanism, allowing them to perceive more sublime levels of reality. Concretely, Richard Wagner's "Liebestod," the love-death song of *Tristan and Isolde*,[3] which is the type-myth of idealistic love and its frustration, announces Edna's romantic suffering, the deep emotional agony in her body for the loss of her beloved Robert Lebrun. The allusion to Tristan and Isolde, as the archetype of decadent lovers, connects Chopin's and Wagner's aesthetics with the symbolist movement.[4] Notably, Chopin was a convinced Wagnerite who followed the evolution of music theater in her city and discussed the musical impact of the opera composer in the cultural coteries, as Lynda S. Boren has noted (188–89). Moreover, she could have even read George Bernard Shaw's *The Perfect Wagnerite* (1898) while writing *The Awakening* (Black 110).

The nineteenth century was an aesthetic period that fostered the emergence of versatile composer-critics, such as Wagner, who engaged in the most significant artistic debates of the period. One of his relevant theories was the holistic and revolutionary vision of a music theater that represented the drama of classical antiquity, like the Greek classical tragedies, which would unite the arts of poetry, music, drama, dance, and scenery in a total performance. In other words, Wagnerian opera advocated for a concept of unified art work, "Das Gesamtkuntswerk," which meant the unified, total experience and the complete synthesis of music with the other arts, and their permanent interaction on stage.

But other derived aspects of his theory encompassed the infinite melody or the liberating and evocative power of the ever-present leitmotiv technique. These aspects of the composer's synesthetic aesthetics are fundamental in order to understand his transformation of nineteenth-century European opera and his crucial contribution to the total renewal of the music theater based on his attempt to synthesize romanticism with classicism. The significant echo of Wagner's music in *The Awakening* clearly illustrates Chopin's deep understanding and discussion of the current changes that were taking place in European music theater. The writer's transcultural literary dialogue with the aesthetics of the total artwork connects her work to the romantic mystical blending of the arts and its corresponding union with the senses. As a matter of fact, a great number of major musicians, painters, and writers of the period were either synesthetes or were overtly interested in exploring intersensory transfers in their own artistic fields: Alexander Scriabin, Richard Wagner, Charles Baudelaire, Arthur Rimbaud, Ludwig Tieck, John Keats, Mme. de Staël, Joris-Kar Huysman, E. T. A. Hoffman, Théophile Gautier, Ralph Waldo Emerson, Emily Dickinson, Walt Whitman, and E. A. Poe, among others.

Unfortunately, interest in artistic synesthesia declined for a short period of time in America and Europe as romantic dreams of sensory fusion faded with the emergence of literary realism and the socioeconomic transformation of postwar American society. But the emergence of new scientific research on the complex relationships between the human mind and body between 1880 and 1920 brought an innovative way of thinking "in which emotion was increasingly understood to mediate our experience of the exterior world" (Thrailkill, *Affecting Fictions* 8). These approaches attempted to solve the intricacies of the mind and its interactions with the body and its emotions, as well as "the connection between cognition (function) and anatomy (structure)" (Harrison et al. 59). From my perspective, Chopin's synesthetic approach was inspired by the scientists' crucial discoveries in this area in the closing decades of the nineteenth century and by the artists' contributions in their respective creative fields. But still, they were far from describing the fundamental mechanisms through which contemporary neuroscience explains empirically how the brain works in terms of its anatomical connections between the different sensory modules and the emotional results of that connectivity. However, the definitive confirmation of the writer's intuitive and literary synesthetic connections had to wait almost a century in order to be scientifically explained in the 1990s through the research of a cohort of neuroscientists (Baron-Cohen and Harrison; Campen; Cytowic; Cytowic and Engleman; Harrison; Sagiv, Dean and Bailes).

It is far more likely that Chopin's representation of sensory and artistic synesthesia were the visible result of her deep knowledge of the romantic ideals, seen through her use of the most frequent symbology of this period but, at the same time, her absolute creativity in the reinterpretation of synesthesia as an original sensorial metaphor. That is undoubtedly what the writer wanted to achieve with her most acclaimed novel *The Awakening*: the complete work of art, the novel that represented the transcendental significance of music as the supreme non-narrative and nondiscursive mode of expression described by the romantic and symbolist artists. Furthermore, Jane Thrailkill argues that Chopin also references an "influential nineteenth-century debate over the representational status of instrumental or 'absolute' music: music detached from any referential context and unaccompanied by the human voice" (*Affecting Fictions* 13). In this vein, she also examines how the novel "emulates music in its physiological effects on readers" through "the emphasis on repetition, rhythm, and the sound component of language" (*Affecting Fictions* 13). All these musical formal analogies are used to transform Edna Pontellier's body into a sort of "sounding board" (Thrailkill, *Affecting Fictions* 178), accounting for the importance of the links between mind, body, and emotion in the novel as well as among other realist writers. Thus, the narrative offers a significant display of different arts—painting, poetry, dance, theatre, sculpture, architecture, operetta, and opera—in a literary context in which music emerges as the most relevant and evocative art that, in many ways, is the interactive path through which the other arts are represented by the writer.

There are many instances in the novel, such as Edna's dinner party, where her friends are inspired by the subtle sound of mandolin music, a delightful accompaniment that arouses her friends' desire to dance, perform, and recite poems in a splendid architectural background. Here, music not only works as a liberating, inspiring, and creative force for Chopin's characters, but it becomes a sort of holistic connector that enhances interaction between different arts. One of the guests attending the gathering, Miss Mayblunt, loses her composure when she perceives the highly sensorial scene from a pictorial perspective instead of describing it in a verbal way, "Oh! To be able to paint in color rather than in words!" (146). It is reasonable to assume that Miss Mayblunt's professional activity as a writer could allow her to accurately describe with words such an appealing scene, but to many of the characters in the novel, being wordless becomes a habitual experience—a consequence of the altered states of consciousness experienced by them. That is, when words cannot express a mode of perception, arts such as music or painting can liberate individuals from the constraints of language. In the same way, Edna is not capable of uttering a word when her friend Mademoiselle Reisz finishes her memorable piano performance: "The young woman was unable to answer; she pressed the hand of the pianist convulsively, Mademoiselle Reisz perceived her agitation and even her tears" (72). The protagonist's extreme sensitivity enables her to express her emotional turmoil in a tactile way, which also underscores the failure of language.

In another example, music is the main stimulus in Edna's various sensory domains when she becomes the performer of her own music, that is, when she sings a melody that brings back her recollections of the recent and unforgettable past. This revealing moment of musical and painting releases a holistic sensorial response:

> Edna perceived that the young women's back and shoulders were molded on classic lines, and that her hair, loosened from its confining cap, became an inspiration. While Edna worked she sometimes sang low the little air, *"Ah! Si tu savais!"* It moved her with recollections. She could hear the ripple of the water. The flapping sail. She could see the glint of the moon upon the bay, and could feel the soft, gusty beating of the south wind. A subtle current of desire passed through her body, weakening her hold upon the brushes and making her eyes burn.... She was happy to be alive and breathing, when her whole being seemed to be one with the sunlight, the color, the odors, the luxuriant warmth of some perfect Southern day. (109)

Music moves Edna and induces her to new feelings, moods, states of mind, and spiritual vision. Besides, the evocative power of music is connected to her synesthetic capacities and to her aspirations of finding a new life out of her existential chaos. The regular rhythm of music is therapeutic and pleasurable for Edna, who finds in her own melody singing responses to her quest for emotional stability, even though there are certain moments in which she loses equanimity such as when she reads Robert Lebrun's letters:

> Edna did not at once read the letter. She sat holding it in her hand, while the music penetrated her whole being like effulgence, warming and brightening the dark places of her soul. It prepared her for joy and exultation. (135–6)

Further, under the artistic influence of Mademoiselle Reisz's virtuoso playing, Edna finds the proper inspiration not only to sing but also to initiate her quest for artistic achievement. As a result, she also decides to take up painting as a means to develop her creativity and independence. In fact, she begins her new life as a portrait painter of her friends and family. But above all she becomes a painter of her own desires and social expectations, insofar as she aspires to become an independent woman artist. In reality, at the beginning Edna finds in painting, as well as in music, a source of amusing gratification:

> Mrs. Pontellier had brought her sketching materials, which she sometimes dabbled with in an unprofessional way. She liked the dabbling. She felt in it satisfaction of a kind which no other employment afforded her. (55)

As it becomes more than pure improvisation, her painting undergoes a stylistic evolution; she is influenced by impressionism, which marks a new point in her artistic emancipation. Likewise, Chopin also found inspiration in the French impressionistic school of painting, particularly in its use of vivid color and bold brushstrokes. From a stylistic point of view, the influence of that fin de siècle school of painting can also be appreciated both in the descriptions of the refined party dresses worn by Edna and her friend Madame Ratignole and in the coastland of the Gulf of Mexico. Nevertheless, what also emerges is Edna's capacity to translate her impressions of nature, her memories, and her reactions to music into "pictures":

> First of all, the sight of the water stretching so far away, those motionless sails against the blue sky, made a delicious picture that I just wanted to sit and look at. The hot wind beating in my face made me think—without any connection that I can trace—of a summer day in Kentucky, of a meadow that seemed as big as the ocean to the very little girl walking through the grass, which was higher that her waist. She threw out her arms as if swimming when she walked, beating the tall grass as one strikes out in the water. Oh, I see the connection now! (60)

The above provides a relevant example of the complex web of synesthetic relations perceived by Edna: she describes the picture with the sense of tasting and the vision of the landscape results in "a delicious picture."[5] In other words, not only does she see or feel music or painting but also savors them all as well.[6] Moreover, her extremely complex sensory synesthesia permits her to transfer between two intimate and distant experiences: her adult's vision of the sea and her childhood's feeling of a Kentucky meadow. Thus, Edna ends up knowing and visualizing the connection as she is able to move from the sense of sight to the sense of touching, which is how a Kentucky meadow becomes a warm sea where she metaphorically swims. Similarly, Edna associates the race horse with her childhood, but again olfactory memory has considerable evocative power: "The atmosphere of the stables and the breath of the blue grass paddock revived in her memory and lingered in her nostrils" (128). In this way, *The Awakening* connects sounds, smells, colors, and visual images in a permanent transfer between two different contexts, producing synesthesia as a sensorial form of metaphor.

There are numerous instances in which Edna's feelings are described in terms of visual, sound, and tactile sensations, like when the narrator alludes to her passionless marriage, "no trace of passion or excessive and fictitious warmth colored her affection, thereby threatening its dissolution" (63). In opposition to the indifference she shows toward Leónce Pontellier, her beloved's voice reverberates in her mind and "it was musical and true. The voice, the notes, the whole refrain haunted her memory" (89). But Robert Lebrun's departure transforms the melodious echoes of his voice into unpleasant color and sound images, and the narrator compares Edna's unhappiness, using imagery that creates the illusion of a colorless picture, reinforced by a "faded garment" (95) that will be reinterpreted later as "pricking garments" (175), which she removes before her last embrace with the sensuous sea.

Likewise, the sensorial contrast occurs with the disagreeable sound of Madame Lebrun's sewing-machine that is repeated up to eight times in Chapter VIII, "Clatter, clatter, bang, clatter!" (67). The effect of the insistent onomatopoetic reverberation remains with the reader, and the powerful combination of this aural technique with the pictorial images clearly illustrates Chopin's method, which brings together the elements of sound, hearing, and touching to create sensorial atmospheres.

This manner of apprehending the sensorial world allows Edna to assimilate differing sensations into a holistic, visionary, and complex perceptive system that makes her an extraordinarily unique character in the history of American literature. Chopin's holistic approach affects Edna's unified sensory experience; the result of this singular cognitive process is that the author shows an authorial consistency in her most accomplished character, who is the outcome of a perfect correspondence between her desires and her ways of approaching the challenging circumstances that surround her. For this purpose, Edna swims in a sea of synesthetic imagery that reveals her joined perception and her holistic enjoyment of art and life.

In each example of sensorial synesthesia here, there are certain common perceptual elements that systematically elude conceptual language insofar as they speak of vision in terms of music, of music in terms of taste, and of vision in terms of touching, feeling, and smelling. Chopin elaborated on the use of aural, visual, and other sensory images in *The Awakening* as a means of successfully creating a poetical effect based on synesthetic metaphoric transfers in a text, where its apparent simplicity does not impede what I call "a sensorial universe of great beauty and refinement" (Piñero Gil 91–92). Nevertheless, in Edna's life not all her close friends and relatives truly appreciate her unique synesthetic experiences. Even though she finds in music and painting a liberating and inspiring artistic path, her husband, Léonce Pontellier, has no interest whatsoever in music. In fact, he has no musical training, no comprehension apart from his speculative business, but what is more surprising is the fact that he has no curiosity for her wife's sensorial and spiritual evolution—further evidence of the couple's detachment and unresolved marital conflict: "he said the music dispensed at her *soirées* was too 'heavy,' too far beyond his untrained comprehension" (121). The narrator uses the adjective "heavy" to describe Mr. Pontellier's lack of interest and his unpleasant and tedious physical perception of these particular musical experiences, which moves the description from the abstract experience of music to a concrete depiction of the physical effects these *soirées musicales* provoke in Edna's husband. But this passage exemplifies how music or the aural stimulus in one modality is experienced with sensations more associated with a second modality such as forms of feeling or touching, and it shows how Chopin draws from a number of adjectives to depict sensorial experience in which there is a synesthetic metaphoric transfer.

Toward the close of the novel, Edna's final celebration of her new life, her evening dinner party, is her own personal hedonistic climax, on her twenty-ninth birthday. The table is "extremely gorgeous" (142–43) and she wears a "cluster of diamonds that sparkled, that almost sputtered, in her hair" (143). The atmosphere of wine, fragrant roses, and color is a feast for the senses, a ceremony of artistic and sensorial synesthesia, as there is "the occasional sound of music of mandolin" (145), gorgeous clothes, exquisite food, theater, poetry, and dancing. This exceptional coup d'état, as her lover Arobin titles the event, is a social and sensual rite of passage that inaugurates her personal transformation and, at the same time, represents an unambiguous turning point.

The novel's ending reaffirms Edna's predominant belonging to the pleasurable realm of music and sounds: she goes back to nature, to the resonant waters of the Gulf because "the voice of the sea is seductive, never ceasing, whispering, clamoring, murmuring, inviting the soul to wander in abysses of solitude" (175). Her watery rebirth is a sort of sensual celebration and discovery of her naked body with the sea: "The touch of the sea is sensuous, enfolding the body in its soft, close embrace" (176). In this romantic way, Edna swims back into the sensory experiences of her youth where the sounds of her sister's and father's voices predominate but there were also "the hum of bees, and the musky odor of pinks filled the air" (176). In her final encounter with the natural rhythmic sounds of the sea, the scent and colors of pinks or Dianthus flowers (from the Greek "dios," god, and "anthos," flower) that were used in Greece to crown heroes clearly symbolize Edna's fearless and cathartic bath in the ocean with the allusive pagan divine image of "Venus rising from the foam" (173) of despair, solitude, and spiritual nakedness. Moreover, it is the ultimate heroic confirmation of her earlier courageous decision "to swim far out, where no woman had swum before" (73). As Lynda Boren concludes, "Edna drowns in a sea of sensations . . . and the predominant one, the sensation of sound overwhelms her" (181).

From the beginning of the novel to the end, Chopin develops a multiple sensory synesthesia, through the extensive use of music and sounds, in which one type of sensation is referred to in terms more appropriate to another. Music, the most powerful artistic leitmotif and sensation in Chopin's work, evokes and blends not only images in the characters' minds, but all types of physical and emotional sensations that contribute, in a decisive way, to their transcendental metamorphosis. To conclude, in Chopin's life and in her fictional world music occupied a pleasurable space of expression, emancipation, and a relevant cognitive synesthetic channel for her most transgressive characters who find in it an enduring holistic transformation.[7]

Notes

1. This anonymous pianist was probably a source of inspiration for the elderly concert pianist Mademoiselle Reisz. It should be noted that the nameless pianist's last name begins with R.
2. Curiously Frederick Chopin's piano music is often described by musicologists with striking synesthetic imagery, which combines colors with sounds.
3. Maureen Seaberg alludes to a significant anecdote referring to Wagner's synaesthetic perception of the music experience when he was rehearsing *Tristan and Isolde*: "Richard Wagner stormed off during a rehearsal of *Tristan and Isolde* because in the maestro's eyes the set's colors were all wrong; they didn't match his expectations,

given the music he'd written. His royal benefactor agreed and the opera opened with the new set" (24).

4. The English music critic Francis Hueffer (1845–1889), Ford Madox Ford's father, wrote a pioneering essay in which he states the importance of Wagner's innovative aesthetics in the sense that he was able to transcend the limits between the different artistic disciplines: "We must recognize the reformer who reunites the two arts of drama and music, which seemed to be separated by a profound chasm, and in reality are one" (qtd. in Beckson 276).
5. Edna's powerful physical relationship with the sensual world "finds its expression in the adjective delicious. Sometimes the adjective occurs more than three times on one page," as Douglas Radcliff-Umstead has observed (145). However, from my view, the adjective "delicious" is once again a clear example of Chopin's synaesthetic imagery or a concomitant manifestation of the abundant sensorial transfers in *The Awakening*. In this way, many of the auditory, visual, kinaesthetic and olfactory sensations described emphatically as "delicious" or as a gustatory experience highlight Edna's sensorial and emotional involvement with the surrounding world.
6. In Kate Chopin's "The Storm," the narrator describes Calixta's flesh with an overtly sexual synesthetic image: "Her firm elastic flesh that was knowing for the first time its birthright, was like a creamy lily" (Chopin, *Selected Stories* 284). This powerful image of sexual pleasure between Alcée and Calixta evokes the sense of taste and touch that predominate over the other senses in the story. The "creamy lily" metaphor heightens Calixta's white skin as well as her softness and her edible quality. Therefore, Chopin makes explicit allusions to female eroticism through the transfer of a visual image, the lily, to a tasting and tactile experience with the adjective "creamy," that is, to an exclusively luscious and fleshly encounter between the lovers.
7. This research is dedicated to the friendship and memory of Pepa Feu who inspired me with her amazing creativity. Her belief in music as the origin of language and as an essential part of human cognitive development encouraged me to explore literature from this enriching interdisciplinary approach.

Works Cited

Beckson, Karl. *London in the 1890s. A Cultural History.* New York: London, 1992. Print.

Black, Martha Fodaski. "The Quintessence of Chopinism." *Kate Chopin Reconsidered. Beyond the Bayou.* Eds. Lynda S. Boren and Sara deSaussure Davis. Baton Rouge: Louisiana State UP, 1999. 95–113. Print.

Boren, Lynda S. "Taming the Sirens: Self-Possession and the Strategies of Art in Kate Chopin's *The Awakening*." *Kate Chopin Reconsidered. Beyond the Bayou*. Eds. Lynda S. Boren and Sara deSaussure Davis. Baton Rouge: Louisiana State UP, 1999. 180–96. Print.

Chopin, Kate. *The Awakening and Selected Stories*. Harmondsworth: Penguin: 1985. Print.

———. "Wiser than a God." *Kate Chopin. Complete Novels and Stories*. New York: The Library of America, 2002. Print.

Cytowic, Richard E., and David Engleman. *Wednesday is Indigo Blue. Discovering the Brain of Synesthesia*. Cambridge, MA: MIT Press, 2009. Print.

Cytowic, Richard. E. *The Man Who Tasted Shapes*. Cambridge, MA: MIT Press, 2003. Print.

———. *Synesthesia: A Union of the Senses*. Cambridge, MA: MIT Press, 2002. Print.

Davis, Doris. "The Enigma at the Keyboard: Chopin's Mademoiselle Reisz." *The Mississippi Quarterly* 58: 1–2 (Winter 2004–2005): 89–104. Print.

Dickinson, Emily. *Poems by Emily Dickinson*. Eds. Mabel Loomis Todd and T. W. Higginson. Boston: Roberts Brothers, 1890. Print

Dyer, Joyce. "Symbolism in the Awakening." *Approaches to Teaching Chopin's The Awakening*. Ed. Bernard Koloski. New York: The Modern Language Association of America, 1988. 126–31. Print.

Ellis, Nancy S. "Insistent Refrains and Self-Discovery: Accompanied Awakenings in Three Stories by Kate Chopin." *Kate Chopin Reconsidered. Beyond the Bayou*. Eds. Lynda S. Boren and Sara deSaussure Davis. Baton Rouge: Louisiana State UP, 1999. 216–29. Print.

Harrison, John E. *Synaesthesia. The Strangest Thing*. Oxford: Oxford UP, 2001. Print.

Harrison, John E., and Simon Baron-Cohen, eds. *Synaesthesia: Classic and Contemporary Readings*. London: Wiley-Blackwell, 1997. Print.

Helmholtz, Hermann. *On the Sensations of Tone*. New York: Dover Publications, 1954. Print.

Piñero Gil, Eulalia. "Introducción." Kate Chopin. *El despertar*. Madrid: Cátedra, 2013. 9–12. Print.

Radcliff-Umstead, Douglas. "Literature of Deliverance: Images of Nature in *The Awakening*." *Southern Studies* 1.2 (1990): 127–47. Print.

Sagiv, Noam, R. T. Dean, and F. Bailes. "Algorithmic Synaesthesia." *The Oxford Handbook of Computer Music*. Ed. R. T. Dean. New York: Oxford UP, 2009. 294–311. Print.

Seaberg, Maureen. *Tasting the Universe: People Who See Colors in Words and Rainbows in Symphonies*. Pompton Plains, NJ: New Page Books, 2011. Print.

Shaw, George Bernard. *The Perfect Wagnerite: A Commentary on the Ring of the Niblungs*. London: Grant Richards, 1898. Print.

Showalter, Elaine. "The Awakening: Tradition and the American Female Talent." *Sister's Choice. Tradition and the Change in American Women's Writings*. Oxford: Oxford UP, 1994. 65–84. Print.

Thrailkill, Jane F. *Affecting Fictions. Mind, Body, and Emotion in American Literary Realism*. Cambridge, MA: Harvard UP, 2007. Print.
———. "Chopin's Lyrical Anodyne for the Modern Soul." *Kate Chopin in the Twenty-First Century: New Critical Approaches*. Ed. Heather Ostman. Newcastle upon Tyne: Cambridge Scholars, 2008. 33–52. Print.
Toth, Emily. *Unveiling Kate Chopin*. Jackson: UP Mississippi, 1999. Print.
Toth, Emily, Per Seyersted, and Cheyenne Bonnell, eds. *Kate Chopin's Private Papers*. Bloomington: Indiana UP, 1998. Print.
Wierzynski, Kazimierz. *The Life and Death of Chopin*. New York: Simon and Schuster, 1949. Print.

CHAPTER 6

Maternity vs. Autonomy in Chopin's "Regret"

Heather Ostman

In the 1894 short story "Regret," Kate Chopin presents the female character of Mamzelle Aurélie as a figure of conventional masculinity. In her "man's hat" and "old blue army coat," Chopin tells us, she is essentially alone, except for the companionship of her dog. However, when her neighbor Odile shows up one day and leaves her four children to stay with her for two weeks, Mamzelle Aurélie begins to learn there is more to mothering—to her surprise—than just feeding and sheltering children. Through the education of Mamzelle Aurélie, who is taught how to mother by her cook, Aunt Ruby, and especially by the children themselves, Chopin raises the question of women's essential nature. In contrast to other Chopin stories, such as *The Awakening* and "Athénaïse," which raise similar questions, "Regret" reconfigures conventional Victorian assumptions about woman's maternal "instinct" and suggests that it is the presence of children—not solely biology—that is the key to unlocking the maternal response. Through the character of Mamzelle Aurélie, Chopin constructs a far less conventional role for older women, one that draws upon the two predominant feminist schools of thought at the time: the essentialist and the antiessentialist approaches to woman's "nature." As a result, Chopin develops a mature female character whose newly found maternal instincts and inherent independence anticipate the New Woman of the next century and collapse the binary categories of feminist thought in the late nineteenth and early twentieth centuries.

"Regret" opens with a description of its main character, Mamzelle Aurélie, in masculine terms. With "ruddy cheeks" and a "determined eye," she wears men's clothes and runs her own farm. And although at 20 years old, "she had received a proposal, which she had promptly declined,... at the age of fifty she had not yet lived to regret it" ("Regret" 157). With the exception of her dog Ponto and the black workers on her farm, in addition to the various animals, "her gun (with which she shot chicken-hawks), and her religion," Mamzelle Aurélie, we are told, was "quite alone in the world" ("Regret" 157).

When her tear-stained neighbor Odile arrives at her door, Mamzelle Aurélie is less than pleased to receive the woman's four children. The mothering or nurturing of small children does not appear to come naturally or instinctively at first to Mamzelle Aurélie, who must deliberately think out her next step, "determining upon a line of action which should be identical with a line of duty"; she begins, then, by giving them food ("Regret" 158). However, the narrator explains:

> If Mamzelle Aurélie's responsibilities might have begun and ended there, they could easily have been dismissed; for her larder was amply provided against an emergency of this nature. But little children are not little pigs; they require and demand attentions which were wholly unexpected by Mamzelle Aurélie, and which she was ill prepared to give. ("Regret" 158)

The children's need for "attentions" is the key to eliciting the maternal response from Mamzelle Aurélie. What she begins to learn, from the children and from her cook, is that motherhood requires much more than simply feeding them. In the two weeks the children stay with her, she learns how to take care of them; for example, how to wash their feet, what stories they need to hear before going to bed, and even how to discipline them. The young Marceline tells Mamzelle Aurélie how to punish her brother for destroying her gardenias:

> " 'Tain't enough to tell 'im, ...," Marceline instructed her; "you got to tie 'im in a chair." ... [But] [t]he chair in which Mamzelle Aurelie tied Ti Nomme was roomy and comfortable, and he seized the opportunity to take a nap in it, the afternoon being warm. ("Regret"159)

Her cook, Aunty Ruby, as well, instructs her in childcare, telling Mamzelle Aurélie not to let children play with keys because it will make them "grow up hard-headed" ("Regret" 159).

Over the course of two weeks, though, the children's presence—or more precisely, their needs—transform Mamzelle Aurélie. She takes out "white aprons that she had not worn for years" and she grows used to Ti Nomme's "moist kisses—the expressions of an affectionate and exuberant nature" ("Regret" 160). She also removes her sewing basket from the upper shelf in her armoire, so that she could mend the children's clothes. Although it took a couple of days, she becomes, Chopin explains:

> accustomed to the laughing, the crying, the chattering that echoed through the house and around it all day long. And it was not the first or the second night that she could sleep comfortably with little Elodie's hot, plump body pressed close against her, and the little one's warm breath beating her cheek like the fanning of a bird's wing. ("Regret" 160)

Mamzelle Aurélie grows used to all of these things, only to realize the profound significance of them in her life once the children are retrieved by their mother at the end of two weeks. The children's departure leaves her with a deep sense of loss: once they are gone, her house is in "a sad disorder," but she does not at first begin to clean. Instead, she sits, puts her head down on her arm, and cries. The story ends: "Oh, but she cried! Not softly, as women often do. She cried like a man, with sobs that seemed to tear her very soul. She did not notice Ponto licking her hand" ("Regret" 161). Thus, "Regret" ends with Mamzelle Aurélie's return to her original state or, more precisely, the superficial appearance of it: she is an autonomous woman, described once again in masculine terms, as she cries "like a man," but her sense of herself has changed dramatically.

On one level, it appears that Mamzelle Aurélie learns to be maternal, as if motherhood was a role one can adopt. For she "certainly did not pretend or aspire to such subtle and far-reaching knowledge" of motherhood, and "she was glad enough to learn a few little mother-tricks to serve the moment's need" ("Regret" 160). The tricks she learns, though, are less practical and more emotional, as she comes to accept the children's kisses and sleeping bodies next to her. On another level, however, a stronger argument can be made for how the children's presence transforms Mamzelle Aurélie or, more precisely, returns her to some earlier, domestic, nurturing state, as we see when she takes out the aprons that she had ceased to wear many years before. And the tears she cries at the end of the story, while described in masculine terms, speak to the severity of the emotional loss she suffers, signaling a reluctant return to her former solitary state.

While Chopin seems to suggest that motherhood can in part be learned behavior, in "Regret" the deeper point she emphasizes through Mamzelle Aurélie is that the instinctive nature of motherhood can be evoked by context. In "Regret," the intimate care of children compels its emergence. So on the one hand, Chopin appears to depict motherhood as an instinct, yet on the other hand, she shows the "instinct" to be dependent on the specific presence of children and not merely the opportunity to care and nurture things, such as a dog, in Mamzelle Aurélie's case.

The two views of motherhood that emerge in "Regret" parallel feminist arguments that were present during Chopin's time and still exist to a certain extent today. In the late nineteenth and early twentieth centuries, two feminist perspectives predominated: reflecting an essentialist point of view, one school of thought believed that inherent social and psychological distinctions between the genders could benefit women's lives and power in society. But in another school, there existed a criticism of gender-based distinctions. These early arguments anticipated feminist developments in the late twentieth and early twenty-first centuries, when perceptions of women—as equal to men or as different from them—still find themselves at odds. More recent feminists of the "equality" camp believe "sexual difference ought to be an irrelevant consideration" in the public sphere, whereas feminists of the "difference" camp believe that "appeals on behalf of women ought to be made in terms of the needs, interests, and characteristics common to women as a group" (Scott 381).

The opposition of the two early feminist perspectives manifests in "Regret" and is illuminated by Chopin's novel *The Awakening*, where we are introduced to two kinds of mothers: the "mother women," such as Adèle Ratignolle, and the "not... mother-[women]," such as the protagonist, Edna Pontellier (*Awakening* 9), who unsuccessfully tries to define her identity independently of her role as a mother. Edna's mothering produces her independent sons, neither of whom was "apt to rush crying to his mother's arms for comfort" if he fell, but would instead, "more likely pick himself up, wipe the water out of his eyes and the sand out of his mouth, and go on playing" (*Awakening* 9). Her personality even before her "awakening" is considered distant by nineteenth-century Creole mothering standards, and yet she still cannot fully separate herself from the emotional bond and burden she feels for her sons. In contrast, mother-women, Chopin writes, "idolized their children, worshipped their husbands, and esteemed it a holy privilege to efface themselves as individuals and grow wings as ministering angels" (*Awakening* 9). Adèle's sensual nature and complete acceptance of her identity as a mother points to Creole essentialism of her time. Mary Bendel-Simso links motherhood in the context of the novel within a nineteenth-century Creole context as both biologically and institutionally based (40). She is, to use Virgina Ross's words, "the embodiment of maternity, defined by her current pregnancy and her ministration to her children" (55). Further, Adèle's maternal identity, like the other mother-women on Grand Isle, is linked directly to her wifehood. She worships her children; she worships her husband. Her entire existence is for her family.

Some critics argue that this construction of motherhood, that of the mother-women, is still simply that: a construction, one important in a class hierarchy—and particularly a racial hierarchy (Frye 46). Ivy Schweiter argues that such women "are defined by their reproductive capacity and social caretaking role. They are meant to discover their identity through intimate relationships of interconnection, rather than through independence, autonomy, and the self-definition of work" (169). However, Edna's presence at Adèle's delivery "serv[es] as the catalyst for Edna's recognition of her irrevocable biological identity as a mother, if not as a mother-woman [herself]" (Bendel-Simso 41). Adèle urges Edna to "think of the children" (*Awakening* 104) and in fact she does—she thinks of them and obtains her freedom through death, relinquishing the biological link between her and her own sons. Chopin writes:

> The children appeared before her like antagonists who had overcome her; who had overpowered and sought to drag her into the soul's slavery for the rest of her days. But she knew a way to elude them. (*Awakening* 108)

Edna eludes her biological sons through death—the only way to free the self; her experience of motherhood could not be more different than Adèle's, for whom motherhood defines all experience. Edna insists on trying to define herself outside of conventional gender roles, resorting to the extreme measure of suicide to achieve such self-definition.

Representations of motherhood in *The Awakening* emphasize the biological link between mother and children, even as that link, in Edna's case, prevents her from realizing her self-defined identity. The mother-women embody the essentialist assumptions of the time, which link women's domestic roles to their biological function, whereas Edna tries to construct an autonomous self, committed to the belief that such a thing existed for women. One could read the ending—Edna's swim out to the sea—as a successful realization of her autonomy, however grim, or one could read it as a failure to ultimately elude her essentialist maternal instincts. Either way, the essentialist view of motherhood that emerges within *The Awakening* supports the essentialism in "Regret," but also shows how the room for women's self-defined gender roles is rather broad. Before the children come, Mamzelle Aurélie's role is definitively not maternal: she dresses in men's clothing and works in a traditionally male occupation, running her own farm. Her identity is self-defined. She is the kind of woman Edna desires to become and very similar to the independent pianist Mademoiselle Reisz in the same novel. The presence of the four children incite a transformation in Mamzelle Aurélie, and what appears to be her instinctive nature, her capacity for maternal nurturing, emerges. Once it has surfaced—or resurfaced, perhaps—her former self-defined role no longer fits. Unlike Edna, her connection to the children is not biological, but their two-week presence is enough to change her so dramatically that their absence profoundly affects her. The children provide an opportunity for interconnectedness, which after some practice, recalls Mamzelle Aurélie to a former self. By the end of "Regret," she is quite the opposite of Edna in that the relationships she develops with the children leave her with a deep sense of loss, and she would never have intentionally severed the connection to them had their mother not returned to take them home.

While biological motherhood does not exist for Mamzelle Aurélie, her motherhood is experienced through the sensual experience of the children's presence—through their kisses and warm sleeping bodies. The sensuality of Mamzelle Aurélie's experience emphasizes the authenticity of her maternal essentialist self. In Chopin's story, "Athénaïse," the transformation of the protagonist offers another lens for viewing the sensual experiences of motherhood that Mamzelle Aurélie discovers in "Regret" and lends support to the notion that the presence of children evokes the maternal instinct, which may be dormant in their absence. Like the presence of Odile's four children in Mamzelle Aurélie's life, the presence of a child—or more accurately the mere anticipation of a child, changes Athénaïse into a sensual, maternal woman. This transformation is different, of course, from Edna, who awakens to the sensual life through the story of *The Awakening*—and after she has had children. In this story, Athénaïse rejects her husband, but returns to him once she discovers she is pregnant. Prior to her return, his physical presence offends her: "The marriage had been a blunder; he had only to look into her eyes to feel that, to discover her growing aversion" (427). But as Patricia Hopkins Lattin suggests:

> Athénaïse's "awakening" comes in a flash as soon as she realizes she is pregnant, and it sends her rushing back to her husband's arms, where she responds to his passion for the first time. Pregnancy has liberated her physically and caused her to accept her sexuality. (41)

When Athénaïse finally returns home to Cazeau, she, Chopin writes: "turned to him with an appealing gesture. As he clasped her in his arms, he felt the yielding of her whole body against him. He felt her lips for the first time respond to the passion of his own" ("Athénaïse" 454). Similar to "Regret, in "Athénaïse," motherhood plays a central role in the process of sensual transformation. For Athénaïse, the embrace of her sexual, sensual self and the acceptance of her husband are dependent on the knowledge of her pending biological motherhood. Athénaïse, in this regard, transforms into the mother-woman Adèle Ratignolle embodies, as she embraces her wifehood as an extension of the sensuality found in her motherhood. Her character demonstrates a transformation that parallels the changes in "Regret," where they occur in the character of Mamzelle Aurélie, both on the emotional and sensual levels. The great difference is that Mamzelle Aurélie's maternal experience is linked directly to the sensual experience of her living with the children; as a result, she sheds her original autonomy and becomes immediately comfortable with a far more interconnected life than she previously lived. Through the lens of "Athénaïse," Mamzelle Aurélie's transformation appears firmly grounded in the sensual experience of the children's presence. She, like Athénaïse, exchanges her autonomy for the interconnectedness offered by the presence of children—or, more precisely, the possibility of children in Athénaïse's case.

Importantly, the children do not remain with Mamzelle Aurélie, and thus she returns to her original autonomous state, which suggests that her autonomy is as authentic as her maternal response is. Another Chopin character, Charlie, from the short story so named, and Sarah Orne Jewett's character, Nan, of *The Country Doctor*, both offer further insight and an alternative perspective for considering the transformation of Mamzelle Aurélie. While sensual experience is virtually absent in both stories, the authors affirm a less conventional, more androgynous womanhood that models autonomy and self-assertiveness as acceptable elements of female behavior, which may shed light on the nature of woman in "Regret." In this story, the 17-year-old Charlotte, whose nickname Charlie indicates her transgressions of gender expectations, wears homemade trouserlets, "a costume of her own devising, something between bloomers and a divided skirt.... Canvas leggings, dusty boots and a single spur" (639). While accidentally shooting a young man lands Charlie at boarding school, where she learns ladylike accomplishments such as dancing and drawing, she is only temporarily changed into the appearance of conventional femininity in her new dresses and coifed hair. When news of her sister Julia's engagement throws Charlie into a fit of jealousy, she returns to her earlier, more familiar garb of trouserlets and boots and takes off on a wild ride on her horse Tim. She returns to her family's home, however, deeply changed:

> Shame and regret had followed and now she was steeped in humiliation such as she had never felt before.... The girlish infatuation which had blinded her was swept away in the torrents of a deeper emotion, and left her a woman. ("Charlie" 667)

Charlie returns "a woman," and importantly, she is a self-determined woman, who rejects the more recently acquired feminine accoutrements. Wearing her trouserlets, she asserts to her injured father that she can be his "right hand" on the farm ("Charlie" 667–8). As a result, the narrator explains:

> There is no telling what would have become of Les Palmiers that summer if it had not been for Charlie and Mr. Gus [a neighbor]. It was precisely a year since Charlie had been hustled away to the boarding school in a state of semi-disgrace. Now, with all the dignity and grace which the term implied, she was mistress of Les Palmiers. ("Charlie" 668–9)

Unlike Edna or Athénaïse, Charlie's transformation does not include a sensual change, but instead signifies a return to a more authentic self that is androgynous, independent, and nurturing, or in other words, to use Chopin's term, a "woman." Charlie comes back from her hard ride on her horse aware of the inappropriateness of her response to her sister's engagement announcement, but even more important, she returns with the ability to assert her will and take responsibility, not only for her own actions and behavior, but for the entire farm that sustains her family and their servants. For example, when her Aunt Clementine begins to dictate what will happen to her father's seven daughters, following his debilitating accident:

> "Please leave me out of your calculations, Aunt," said Charlie with a flash of her old rebellious nature. "Dad'll have something to say when he's able to bother about it, and in the meantime I propose to take care of myself and the youngsters and of Dad, and this meeting's got to end right here. ("Charlie" 665)

Despite her aunt's and her sister Julia's attempts to tell her what to do, they, as well as the other family members, obey Charlie's directions to leave the room.

Thus Charlie returns to her earlier androgynous clothing and demonstrates some of her "old rebellious nature," but now these aspects of her former self form an assertive, responsible female self. This self emerges from two events: the recognition of her misbehavior and the need of her father for her care, both as a nurse and as the manager of the farm. The construction of womanhood that emerges in "Charlie" appears to be one less dependent on conventional expectations for woman—in terms of dress and etiquette. Instead, when Charlie becomes a woman, she shows herself to be confident, assertive, and her womanhood develops upon being needed by her family. In the midst of a family crisis, she is able to step in, as both mother and father—nursing her father back to health and minding the younger children as well as managing the business of the farm. Charlie's androgynous clothing symbolically reflects this emergent self: her trouserlets draw from conventional male and female fashions, just as her behavior as a woman draws upon male and female gender roles. And while Charlie agrees to marry Mr. Gus at some unspecified point in the future and thus appears to agree to a formal, conventional gender role, her character shows that to be a woman, at least in this story, is to be independent and nurturing. In other words, she is a younger precedent to Mamzelle Aurélie, who finds herself at 50 to be capable of both. Charlie embodies the possibility of a definition of womanhood that is self-defined and draws from both conventional gender roles for men and women.

The portrayal of womanhood in "Charlie" in many ways parallels Sarah Orne Jewett's portrayal of Nan in *A Country Doctor* (1884), which helps illuminate the notion of an autonomous and nurturing womanhood in "Regret." Nan, like Charlie, does not conform to conventional expectations for her gender. She appears predestined to become a doctor, following in the footsteps of her guardian. Her attempts at fulfilling conventional, domestic roles are clumsy at best, but she flourishes when she is finally permitted to study medicine. In the course of the novel, Jewett suggests that instinct is as subjective as its beholder. She makes a distinction between the socially approved domestic "instincts" many women are said to demonstrate in the society of the novel and Nan's instinct to serve society as a doctor, because unlike her peers, Nan does not have "the natural instinct toward marriage" (Jewett 121). Jewett assures the reader that in spite of this lack, Nan still conforms to physical expectations for her gender, as her friends "assured themselves that their schoolmate showed no sign of being the sort of girl who tried to be mannish and to forsake her natural vocation for a profession" (122). Jewett's affirmation of Nan's avoidance of being "mannish" appears to dull the edge of Nan's daring, but it establishes a foundation for Nan's triumph at the end of the novel as a woman who has forgone marriage for studying medicine and presumably living a solitary life. Consequently, she appears ordinary in every other respect, not odd, and thus normalizes the choice she has made.

Nan's character, like Charlie's, demonstrates a different, less conventional woman, but one that appears to live within the bounds of social tolerance. Instinct exists in both characters; however, it is defined autonomously and outside of social convention. Nan explains to her aunt:

> I wish for your sake that I had been another sort of woman; but I shall never marry. I know you think I am wrong, but there is something which always tells me I am right, and I must follow another way. I should only wreck my life, and other people's. Most girls have an instinct towards marrying, but mine is all against it, and God knew best when He made me care more for another fashion of life. (239)

Significantly, Nan affirms the existence of her own instincts—she intuits her purpose in life, and it is contrary to the expectations of society. Her instinct for self-definition exists as equally as the maternal and domestic instincts exist for other women. Notably, Nan's instinct is for a vocation of caring, although becoming a doctor in 1889 was still very much within the realm of possibilities only available to men. Her desire at once draws upon her wish to serve and care for others, characteristics quite in line with conventional female gender roles, but also transgresses conventional gender roles by years of study and devotion to a profession, as opposed to devotion to one's family. Still, like Charlie, Nan emerges as a character drawn from elements of both conventional gender roles but identified solely as woman. To underscore the point, Jewett affirms Nan's vocational choice by locating it within the realm of the mother, as she closes the novel with the protagonist recalling her mother's journey to her hometown:

> There was a strange fascination about these river uplands; no place was so dear to Nan, and yet she often thought with a shudder of the story of those footprints which had sought the river's brink, and then turned back. Perhaps, made pure and strong in a better world, in which some lingering love and faith had given her the true direction at last, where even her love for her child had saved her, the mother had been still taking care of little Nan and guiding her. (260)

This final affirmation places approval of Nan's career choice through the invocation of the mother, who even in death "had been still taking care of little Nan and *guiding her*" (italics mine). Her decision to study medicine marks not a "disintegration of society"; on the contrary, asserts Jewett, "it must be acknowledged to belong to its progress" (247–8). Progress here, then, is the possibility of a woman entering a professional field, with such a possibility not only sanctioned by the mother but *bequeathed* to her daughter.

As indicators of progressive social developments, both the characters of Charlie and Nan call to mind the emergent Gibson Girl or the New Woman at the turn of the twentieth century, and as such, they are the legacy of such women characterized by the older Mamzelle Aurélie. The changing perceptions of women's physical abilities at the time emerged in this new construction of womanhood, which conveyed healthfulness and athleticism (Banner 22). In a 1910 issue of the *Atlantic Monthly*, Margaret Deland asserts that the New Woman was independent and more open about previously reserved topics:

> This young person—a wholesome, lovable creature with surprising bad manners—has gone to college, and when she graduates she is going to earn her own living. She declines to be dependent upon a father and mother amply able to support her. She will do settlement work; she won't go to church; she has views about the birth-rate, and she utters them without embarrassment; she occupies herself, passionately, with everything except the things that used to occupy the minds of girls. (291)

Inherent in Deland's description is a newly acceptable independence for young women, in thought as well as finances. The image of the Gibson Girl marked a new age of independence for women and a less squeamish environment for discussions about sex. And while it was expected that the Gibson Girl would get married, it was not shocking if she chose a career instead; however, career and marriage still presented mutually exclusive options for women (Banner 21), such as we see in the character of Nan.

The shifts in the cultural constructions of women's sexuality reveal that earlier assumptions of women's innate moral superiority were constructions themselves. As late as the 1910s, the younger generation of feminists and women activists appeared increasingly more sexually liberal, reflecting twentieth-century America's changing attitudes toward female sexuality, although the older generation, which preceded Freud's rise in popularity, frequently preferred celibacy or at least the freedom outside of marriage (Banner 52). The essentialists' conceptions of gender reiterated Victorian ideals of womanhood, which justified claims to women's moral superiority. However, with

Freudian theories helping to reshape cultural standards of sexuality and morality at the turn of the century, essentialists found themselves more often at odds with feminists who recognized gender-based divisions as cultural constructions. Then, as now, what seemed to define woman depended on social construction. Biology, at least as far as Chopin's "Regret" is concerned, was not enough to determine gender.

In the characters of Mamzelle Aurélie, Charlie, and Nan, biological determinism is secondary to another construction of womanhood, and Charlie and Nan, in particular, offer younger models of female autonomy at the turn of the twentieth century. Like Deland's description of the New Woman they do not depend on parents or anyone to support them. They are both, however, defined by their adoption of previously male-identified vocations, as such, and broaden the lens for viewing the 50-year-old Mamzelle Aurélie, who has lived independently, like a man would more likely be able, running her own farm for years. Charlie's androgyny, in particular, lends itself to an assumption of normalcy: to be a woman in a man's role makes it acceptable to act like one and to partly dress like one, much like Mamzelle Aurélie does.

There is, however, a limit to how much a woman can live and act like a man in any of these stories. The characters of Charlie and Nan are particularly helpful in illuminating the limitations placed on the character of Mamzelle Aurélie: despite their autonomy and self-assertiveness, both Charlie and Nan reassure the readers of their femininity by conforming to important conventional signifiers of gender. Charlie cares for family members and promises to marry, and Nan chooses a profession as a caretaker of the sick and, as mentioned earlier, the reader is told of her avoidance of being "mannish." These two characters affirm the little conventionality they have, assuring readers of the absence of total subversiveness. With the parallels to these two characters, Mamzelle Aurélie's appropriation of the motherhood role and her experience of loss and regret when it is over likewise affirm her partial conformity to social gender roles. In other words, she, like the other two women characters, demonstrates androgynous qualities; however, their authors rein them in from seeming radical by aligning them within socially sanctioned behavior codes.

Still, "Regret" is an anomaly among these stories. Its depiction of Mamzelle Aurélie, despite her disappointment and loss, does not subvert the premise of her androgynous identity, which is still intact by the end of the story. Like Adèle Ratignolle and Athénaïse, Mamzelle Aurélie is inducted into the sensual world of motherhood through the wonder of Odile's four children. On the other hand, once the children depart she returns to an earlier state of solitude and androgyny, in which she confronts her loss with tears like a man's, not a woman's, as Chopin makes the explicit distinction.

And while temporary—or rather, imposed—motherhood enables Mamzelle Aurélie to undergo a transformation of her identity, perhaps the change is best understood through the lens of surrogacy, such as the kind we see in Chopin's short story "The Godmother," where Tante Elodie risks everything to protect her godson Gabriel, after he has killed a man. In this story, the godmother's love for Gabriel compels her to cover up his crime. Yet the price is high. What she does out of maternal love turns him against her. Chopin writes: "He could not believe that any man was worth loving to such length, or worth saving at such a price. She seemed, to his imagination, less a woman than a monster, capable of committing, in cold-blood, deeds, which he himself could only accomplish in blind rage" ("Godmother" 185). On the contrary, the godmother's actions transform Gabriel's view of her; she is no longer the selfless, nurturing mother to him. Instead, she appears less than human—a heartless monster—to him, for which he rejects her. Gabriel's confession of his crime to his godmother changes her into a figure of determination and one for whom "all the soft womanliness had for the moment faded out" ("Godmother" 172). While transformation occurs in this story as in other Chopin stories, the more relevant point here is the issue of surrogacy. Tante Elodie is a kind of surrogate mother for Gabriel. Biology has nothing to do with her devotion to him, although her love for the young man stemmed from her earlier love for his father. For Tante Elodie, Gabriel's need—or apparent need for protection, for saving—compels her into action, but she had already assumed the maternal role prior to his crime.

"The Godmother" suggests a view of motherhood that illuminates a more nuanced view of essentialism in "Regret." In both stories, the surrogate mothers, Tante Elodie and Mamzelle Aurélie, assume the maternal role because of the presence of the child or children. It is the children's need that evokes the older women's nurturing, maternal behavior. Consequently, Mamzelle Aurélie's loss is deeper than the absence of the children. Her grief results also from her return to a solitary life. For example, now when her dog Ponto licks her hand, she does not even notice. Her pet cannot replace the children, and without them, her awakened maternal instinct has no outlet, no human relationship or child to nurture. She has been inducted to the world of her own maternal instinct. Importantly, she copes with tears like "a man's." Thus, in "Regret," Chopin poses the possibility that maternal essentialism trumps motherhood as a learned gender role.

But in the example of Mamzelle Aurélie, we see that it is the presence of children themselves that evokes the maternal instinct, suggesting that the instinct to mother is innate in women, but not necessarily linked to biological motherhood.

In "Regret," Chopin ignores the dominant binaries of feminist thinking of her day: Mamzelle Aurélie is neither a fully essentialist character, nor is she a socially constructed woman or mother. Certainly biology has nothing to do with her maternal response. The apparent negotiation in this particular story reflects the inauthenticity inherent within gender roles, such as is claimed in Joan Wallach Scott's argument that gender identification works to codify power relationships: "The core definition [of gender] rests on the integral connection between two propositions: gender is a constitutive element of social relationships based on perceived differences between the sexes, and gender is a primary way of signifying relationships of power" (167). Here, Scott implies that identifying woman as a category systematically disempowers women. But Chopin redefines woman in the examples of Mamzelle Aurélie and Charlie—two characters who draw strength from the binaries of conventional gender roles.

In fact, Mamzelle Aurélie, especially being older than the teenage Charlie, manifests an essentialist deconstructionist perspective implicit in the point Sandra Lipsitz Bem makes: "[I]f women are ever to have political and economic equality, what needs to change is not the psyche—or even the socialization—of the individual; what needs to change is the androcentric social structure that operates systematically and in the here and now to preserve male power" (135). To this end, Chopin identifies a new motherhood, which implicitly rejects patriarchal individualism. In Mamzelle Aurélie, the reader witnesses a character that shifts the essentialist notion of motherhood away from biological maternity and toward the experience of caring for children. In other words, the maternal instinct exists, according to Chopin, but it exists as freely as women's instinct for autonomy and self-determination, such as seen in "Charlie." In effect, she sets forth a new kind of womanhood that extends the premise of autonomy found in the construction of the younger New Woman to a character much further along in years, suggesting that a woman who exemplified the qualities of autonomy and interconnectedness existed long before the social fad.

Works Cited

Banner, Lois W. *Women in Modern America: A Brief History.* 2nd ed. San Diego: Harcourt Brace Jovanovich, 1984. Print.

Bem, Sandra Lipsitz. *The Lenses of Gender.* New Haven: Yale UP, 1993. Print.

Bendel-Simso, Mary M. "Mothers, Women, and Creole Mother-Women in Kate Chopin's South." *Southern Studies* 3.1 (1992): 35–44. Print.

Chopin, Kate. "Athénaïse." *The Complete Works of Kate Chopin.* Ed. Per Seyersted. Baton Rouge: Louisiana State UP, 1969. 426–54. Print.

———. *The Awakening.* Ed. Margo Culley. 2nd ed. 1899. New York: Norton, 1994. Print.

———. "Charlie." Seyersted 638–70.

———. "The Godmother." *A Vocation and a Voice.* Ed. Emily Toth. New York: Penguin, 1991. 164–88. Print.

———. "Regret." *A Matter of Prejudice and Other Stories.* New York: Bantam Classic, 1992. 157–61. Print.

Deland, Margaret. "The Change in the Feminine Ideal. *The Atlantic Monthly* 105 (1910): 8. Print.

Frye, Katie Berry. "Edna Pontellier, Adèle Ratignolle, and the Unnamed Nurse: A Triptych of Maternity in *The Awakening.*" *Southern Studies* 13.3/4 (2006): 45–66. Print.

Fuss, Diana. "Reading Like a Feminist." *The Essential Difference.* Ed. Naomi Schor and Elizabeth Weed. Bloomington: Indiana UP, 1994. Print.

Gordon, Linda. "Putting Children First: Women, Maternalism, and Welfare in the Early Twentieth Century." *U.S. History as Women's History.* Chapel Hill: U of North Carolina P, 1995. 63–86. Print.

Jewett, Sarah Orne. *A Country Doctor.* 1884. New York: Bantam Classic, 1999. Print.

Lattin, Patricia Hopkins. "Childbirth and Motherhood in *The Awakening* and in 'Athénaïse'." *Approaches to Teaching Chopin's* The Awakening. Ed. Bernard Koloski. New York: MLA, 1988. 40–6. Print.

Ross, Virginia. "Kate Chopin's Motherless Heroine." *Southern Mothers: Fact and Fiction in Southern Women's Writing.* Baton Rouge: Louisiana State UP, 1999. 51–63. Print.

Scott, Joan Wallach. "Deconstructing Equality-Versus-Difference: Or, the Uses of Poststructuralist Theory for Feminism." *Feminist Theory Reader.* Ed. Carole R. McCann and Seung-kyung Kim. New York: Routledge, 2003. 378–90. Print.

Schweiter, Ivy. "Maternal Discourse and the Romance of Self-Possession in Kate Chopin's *The Awakening.*" *Gendered Agents: Women and Institutional Knowledge.* Eds. Silvestro Mariniello and Paul Bové. Durham: Duke UP, 1998. 161–91. Print.

Yalom, Marilyn. *A History of the Wife.* New York: HarperCollins, 2001. Print.

PART II

New Pedagogical Approaches

CHAPTER 7

The "I Hate Edna Club"

Emily Toth

The Awakening had barely been published, in April 1899, when the first stirrings of Ednaphobia—the morbid fear and hatred of Edna Pontellier—began. The very first review, essentially a plot summary in Kate Chopin's hometown *St. Louis Republic*, called *The Awakening* "the story of a lady most foolish" and concluded that "the woman who did not want anything but her own way drowned herself" (Toth 220).

Another Ednaphobe was the young Willa Cather, who condemned Edna as one of the limited "women of the Bovary type" who "want the passion of love to fill and gratify every need of life" (Toth 223). Cather was 23 then and brash and in the closet, and she could not see heterosexual love as the center of a woman's life. If Edna thought it was, Cather says, Edna's a fool. Other Ednaphobes blamed Kate Chopin for showing nowhere "a single note of censure" for Edna's "totally unjustifiable conduct" (Toth 222).

What's interesting about the nineteenth-century condemnations is that they all appear to center on Edna's adultery, although some aren't clear as to whether she has one or two extramarital affairs. Neither are readers now, and it's not just a matter of an emotional affair (Robert) and a physical affair (Arobin). Because the language follows Victorian conventions, the sexual doings aren't clear to today's readers. High-school students in Louisiana, where I live, are told that Edna and Arobin don't "do it." Actually, they do. But one of my most recent students, not knowing that, wanted to know, "Why in hell didn't they do it?" This is a whole new version of Ednaphobia: the belief that Edna is a sexual coward, without the courage to follow her urges.

So to an earlier generation, mostly men, the sentiment was "I hate Edna because she's a slut." For at least some of the current hookup generation, mostly women, the sentiment is "I hate Edna because she doesn't do it when she wants to."

Damned if you do . . .

I sometimes think it could be a creative, challenging exam question: Is Edna a slut or a wimp? Explain your answer.

When *The Awakening* was rediscovered, a movement that's discussed in Bernard Koloski's *Awakenings: The Story of the Kate Chopin Revival*, the generation of new women in the 1970s embraced the book. But they didn't necessarily embrace Edna. They understood the competing desires and demands that can make a woman feel torn apart. But I can't remember anyone saying they really "liked" Edna.

I started teaching *The Awakening* in the 1970s, at Johns Hopkins University, where students saw Edna as a warning for their future choices: don't get stuck on the mommy track. My students were the very first women undergraduates at Hopkins, formerly an all-male undergraduate school. Those first women were ignored or harassed by male students, and they had to be tough cookies. Many of them are now judges, lawyers, and physicians who put their ambitions, and their new possibilities, first.

When I taught *The Awakening* at Morgan State, an historically black college, at the same time, my students felt that Edna had race and class privilege. She had a rich husband and servants. My African American students—mostly women juggling children and multiple jobs—criticized Edna for having first world problems. Their Ednaphobia took the form of "I should have the leisure to worry about my place in the universe."

Similarly, Bernard Koloski has told me that colleagues in other countries, especially developing ones, also hate Edna as someone whining about her privileges. When Koloski taught *The Awakening* in Poland, where there was an intense, immense housing shortage, students shrugged at Edna's adultery—but were fascinated and envious that she could move out and get an apartment of her own. That was the big fantasy. To Polish Ednaphobes, Edna was not a slut, but a space hog.

Different generations and different audiences have different varieties of Ednaphobia—depending on how they interpret Edna's struggle. What is she fighting for? In the 1970s we had no doubt. She's fighting sexual repression, we thought, since we ourselves were in the throes of the sexual revolution. Edna expands and grows like a sleek animal once she starts having her affair with the rake Alcée Arobin, a man who's obviously a better lover than her husband ever was. Some of my students in the 1970s took that to heart and, well, changed partners.

Women students identified with her struggle, then, but male students in the 1970s often did not. When I taught *The Awakening* at the University of North Dakota, some of my male students said, "Why didn't she just junk it all and go out West?" I suppose their ancestors had done so, but heading west doesn't seem to be an option for Edna. Robert leaves for Mexico, but women don't have geographical mobility unless they are like "Sylvano's wife," mentioned by the shrimp girl Mariequita in Chapter Twelve. That wife ran off with Francisco, and they took all of her husband's money, one child, and his boat—but that's not a possibility in Edna's social class. Edna cannot afford to do that. Ednaphobia could be defined as blaming Edna for not having the alternatives we have.

In the 1970s and the 1980s, I also had students who hated Edna because she doesn't succeed at romance. The year 1972 was a turning point in the United States, with a sudden leap in the divorce rate. There were many more career options for women, such as the opportunities seized by my Hopkins students. There was no-fault divorce, and the creation of battered women's shelters. All of these things meant that my students' mothers were leaving home—and many students were devastated.

And so, my students in the early 1980s at Penn State, for instance, wanted Edna and Robert to live happily ever after. They hated Edna because she failed to have a lasting romance with Robert. Of course, the truth is that Robert dumps her: He's the wimp who fails. And later interpretations have suggested that Robert is gay.

So I suppose you could also hate Edna for trying to "cure" a gay man.

That could be another creative exam question: Ednaphobia and homophobia.

But the largest "I hate Edna" group right now seems to be those who criticize her as a bad mother. That interpretation started coming up in my classes in the 1990s, with the daughters whose mothers had left their marriages to find themselves. Or the students were angry that their mothers weren't full-time stay-at-home moms anymore. We all want our mommies.

"The mommy wars" will probably always be with us, but nowadays my older students—the ones who've had children—frequently point out that Edna makes sure her children are well cared for, and they grow up self-reliant. She is not a stay-at-home mom, but that doesn't make her a monster mom.

Lately I've been talking with older women's groups about Edna—and with a wealth of life experience, they like to ponder whether

Edna is a good role model for women in search of love. This came up boldly a few years ago, when I spoke at an elderly women's book club. Member A said that Edna should be hated because she's unfaithful. Member B disagreed and said, "I'd like to have an affair, too." To which Member A retorted angrily: "Who'd have an affair with you? Your breasts are too small."

We don't know about Edna's breasts, but we do know about her arms. One of the sad features of university life today is that students often turn in papers plagiarized from the Internet—and according to one of these frequently-circulating papers, Edna is a masturbator. The evidence cited is in Chapter Thirteen, after Edna takes a nap on the jaunt to the Chênière. She wakes up and "She looked at her round arms as she held them straight up and rubbed them one after the other, observing closely, as if it were something she saw for the first time, the fine, firm quality and texture of her flesh. She clasped her hands easily above her head."

Personally, I like Edna and always have. I think she has a rare consciousness and a boldness that we should admire. But if I were to join the ranks of Ednaphobes, it would be because of the above passage. At the risk of seeming totally old-fashioned, or tacky, I have to note that masturbators do not put their hands above their heads. And so that could be one justifiable argument for Ednaphobia. She does not do right by herself.

Still, I would not condemn Edna Pontellier. As in so many things, she needs modern alternatives, modern education, and modern frankness. She needs to know herself. But if she did, we'd have no story.

Works Cited

Koloski, Bernard. *Awakenings: The Story of the Kate Chopin Revival.* Baton Rouge: Louisiana State University Press, 2012.

Toth, Emily. *Unveiling Kate Chopin.* Jackson: University Press of Mississippi, 1999.

CHAPTER 8

Pioneering Kate Chopin's Feminism: Elizabeth Stoddard's *The Morgesons* as Patchwork Precursor to *The Awakening*

Diana Epelbaum

In Elizabeth Stoddard's odd novel *The Morgesons* (1862), the sea stirs young Cassandra Morgeson, pulling to the surface a dormant sexuality, "murmuring softly, creeping along the shore, licking the rocks and sand as if recognizing a master. And I saw and felt its steady, resistless heaving, insidious and terrible" (63). Another, more famous, fin de siècle novel echoes this inner disturbance within its heroine in much the same terms, engaging the sea as a powerful symbol for sexuality and freedom. In Kate Chopin's *The Awakening* (1899), Edna Pontellier's love affair with the ocean is similarly characterized by an unleashing, first felt as a calm drifting and later as a violent storm. Edna is a boat unmoored, "borne away from some anchorage which had held her fast, whose chains had been loosening—had snapped the night before" (81). The sea, however, is only one representative element of the two closely related novels. While there is no evidence that Chopin read Stoddard's work, the two novels are thematic sisters, employing identical symbols, like those of water, food, music, and sleeping/waking, to probe common feminist themes. As patchwork of nineteenth-century fictional styles, and as early iteration of regional, realistic, and even naturalistic writing, *The Morgesons* stands firmly as a precursor to *The Awakening*. This chapter reads Stoddard and Chopin in tandem in order to model an enriching pedagogical approach to Chopin's canonical novel.

In 1899, *The Awakening* received much the same criticism *The Morgesons* would likely have received in 1862 had Stoddard not ended her book in marriage, sprinkled in antitemperance scenes, and left Cassandra's adulterous relationship with Charles unconsummated and, despite this fact, fatally punished.[1] Chopin's novel had the honor of being called "gilded dirt" by one critic, and "the sad story of a Southern lady who wanted to do what she wanted to do" by another (qtd. in Petry 52–53)[2]. While Stoddard's novel was unpopular, a few esteemed critics of Stoddard's day, namely Nathaniel Hawthorne, considered *The Morgesons* an achievement;[3] in its reissuances in 1890 and 1901, the highly realistic novel met with even better critical reception than it had in 1862,[4] but still suffered extremely poor sales.[5] Recently, however, Stoddard has enjoyed a revival of sorts (J. Harris 289). Critics comment on its unusual pacing, its lack of narrative cues, its terseness. Simultaneously conventional and radical for its day, *The Morgesons* leaves the reader with a vague feeling of discomfiture and incongruity. Called by Susan K. Harris "quite possibly the most radical women's novel to appear in the mid-nineteenth century" ("Projecting" 152), *The Morgesons*'s feminism, just like *The Awakening*'s, is channeled through the study of female psychology. Chopin and Stoddard sought to interrogate identity formation through individual characters using a singularly stylistic, yet publicly acceptable, expression of rebellious American womanhood.

Despite the decidedly subversive tenor of their work, Chopin and Stoddard still very much drew on an astonishing array of nineteenth-century female prototypes and participated in a women's fiction that continued, throughout the century, to mutate rapidly and by layers. Susan K. Harris defines three general periods in this fiction that she calls the "early didactic," which taught "readers how to accommodate themselves to the status quo," "exploratory," which began to "expand readers' horizons of acceptable female behavior [by positing] alternatives to conventional female roles," and "late didactic," which "reached out into the political realm... and plac[ed] women in the forefront of social reform" (200). Didactic novels often integrate concerns about marriage reform, wage slavery, and temperance; temperance novels usually centered around a double vow of marriage and temperance, a convention Stoddard draws on in *The Morgesons* (Claybaugh 93).[6] Conventional women's novels, as David S. Reynolds calls them, part of the early didactic genre, champion the idyllic, sentimentalized "cult of domesticity,"[7] a central interest of the reform novel that both Chopin and Stoddard spurn. Although domestic sphere literature gave women greater cultural "influence" than ever before, these novels saw the self as socially constructed: since self was part of society, and society relegated woman to the domestic realm, self was "itself a domestic site" (Baym xxvii, 36, xxi). The early, irksome realization that self cannot be imagined separately from society forms the greater part of the existential crisis Stoddard's and Chopin's female characters experience. At times, this understanding paralyzes Cassandra and Edna, ultimately inspiring their final decisions to give in and give up, respectively.

While in the final estimation rejecting reform and domestic conventions as inadequate for penetrating the complexities of her characters' lives, Stoddard still employs these conventions in *The Morgesons.* In the vein of reform literature, Stoddard fashions the two Somers brothers—Ben, who marries Veronica, and Desmond, who marries Cassandra—into alcoholics. While Desmond conquers his disease to make himself worthy of Cassandra's love, Ben dies of delirium tremens, leaving his illness-prone wife and their developmentally challenged baby without a husband and father. Amanda Claybaugh suggests that "drunkenness provided a way of describing the more general sufferings of marriage and sobriety" (Claybaugh 88); if read this way, the Somers' brothers' alcoholism becomes just one among many reform literature techniques Stoddard uses in her patchwork novel to comment upon women's lives. Cassandra does settle into domestic duty at the end of the novel, yet it is critical that the house she lives in is hers by legal right and that her marriage is an "equal" partnership.[8] The ending, although often read as conventional, betrays Stoddard's deep ambivalence about this resolution for her heroine.[9] Cassandra's acquisition of property stands as a symbol for self-proprietorship, and more broadly, by allowing Cassandra control over both the domestic and economic, Stoddard challenges the convention of separate spheres. Cassandra ironically admits that the "ownership of [the house] oppressed me, almost, there was so much liberty to realize" (Stoddard 248). Whereas most woman's fiction concludes with motherhood, Stoddard does not proceed into the work of mothering, keeping Cassandra childless and making Veronica's fate as mother one of ceaseless pain—thereby, as Lynn Mahoney points out, "reject[ing] the antebellum matriarch as the foundation for a modern feminine identity" (318).[10] Lawrence Buell takes it a step further by calling *The Morgesons* a "sophisticated parody" of women's fiction (362); ultimately, as Sybil Weir attests, the "domestic vision is fraudulent...family relationships are neurotic and destructive; women are neither moral paragons nor sexual imbeciles" (438).

Chopin too was indebted to the nineteenth-century feminist movement. In the 1870s, self-ownership, Edna's quest, would have translated into "voluntary motherhood" (Stange 22–23), or withheld sex at the woman's discretion. When Mr. Pontellier, Edna's husband, shares his concerns over his wife's behavior with the family physician, Dr. Mandelet, he complains: "'She's got some sort of notion in her head concerning the eternal rights of women; and—you understand—we meet in the morning at the breakfast table'" (Chopin 118). The conventional "cult of true womanhood," roughly analogous to Harris's definition of "early didactic" fiction, steadily transformed into "new womanhood," which redefined conceptions of sexuality and purity before and during marriage, and advocated moving beyond the domestic sphere (Radinovsky 10). These new conceptions, according to Elaine Showalter, made "room for interludes of fantasy and parable" (68–69). Markedly, Chopin was equally indebted to the conventional nineteenth-century woman, whose domestic fiction had to be written first in order for Chopin's protest to take form (67). Just one testament to this is Chopin's heroine's name, Edna, which resonates with the heroines in two popular nineteenth-century women's works, Edna Earl of Augusta Evans's *St. Elmo*, and Edna Kenderdine of Dinah Craik's *Woman's Kingdom* (71).

Just as *The Morgesons* straddles the space between the conventional nineteenth-century woman's novel and the feminist novel, so too does the book embody romantic, realistic, naturalistic, and regionalistic elements. Despite her adoption by William Dean Howells as one of his own—a realist—Stoddard objected that she was "*not* realistic—I am *romantic*, the very bareness and simplicity of my work is a trap for its romance" (qtd. in Opfermann and Roth xviii). The notion of the romantic individual is decidedly present in Cassandra's control over her own fate,[11] and in her final mastery over ambition and sexuality. Channeling an earlier genre of what David S. Reynolds calls "utopian feminism," largely written between 1800 and 1850 and portraying societies in which women and men had equal legal rights (389), Stoddard's men recognize and respect female autonomy, something none of the men in Chopin's later novel do. A further nod to Stoddard's romanticism is her use of the female Gothic, evident in the novel's thematic concerns with maternity/birthing, literary creativity, self-reliance, aberration, freakishness, the female body, and female hysteria.[12] Stoddard's secondary character Veronica is the novel's hysteric, plagued by mysterious illnesses and bruising on her arm from prophetic dreaming. Charles and Desmond, Cassandra's lovers, are the brooding romantic heroes, motivated by dark passions and inner demons. Physical decay is an obsession with Cassandra, who becomes fixated on her scars and crow's feet, and on Desmond's prematurely gray hair (Buell and Zagarell xxiii). Stoddard's work

> displays an interfusion of Victorian social realism with romance tradition, in particular that strain of it which present day feminist critics call "female gothic"...featuring male and female doubles [Ben/Desmond and maybe Veronica/Cassandra], intense physicality [Cassandra's bloody mouth after Charles's pronouncement of love, Cassandra's mother's death], violence [Charles's attack of an employee], and melodramatic heightening of sexual relationships [Charles's death scene] in order to suggest far-reaching connections between the heroine's physical and psychic development and her social reality. Stoddard, like the Brontës, depicts that social reality with a keen awareness of how kinship, marriage, property ownership, and inheritance intermesh. (Buell and Zagarell xvi)

Stoddard's romanticism overall, however, is problematic, since it takes on no one form and bases its romanticism on its opposition to realism (Radinovsky 23).

In spite of Stoddard's contrary claims, critics of her work generally feel that she presaged the realist and naturalist movements, and hence work like Chopin's. Cassandra's resignation to the "relentless...eternal monoton[y]" (Stoddard 252) that the ocean represents, the dark death of Ben Somers from alcoholism, and the bleakness of Veronica's future with her sick child in the closing scene of the novel all exemplify a final lack of control. There is no power to be had in this compromised life, so Chopin, some decades later, allows her heroine power in death. David S. Reynolds notes that Stoddard "anticipated the grimness and muted imagism" of naturalism (409), while Julia Stern feels that it is her characters' failure to negotiate their desires in satisfying ways that ultimately reveals the "antisentimental project in which their creator is engaged" (108).

Local color's defining nostalgia and resistance to change, as well as its emphasis on communal harmony and survival, was philosophically at odds with the naturalists, who dealt in their work with the corruption of these values, and stressed a predetermined universal Fate. Yet there are points of intersection between the two literary movements, so much so that local color steadily began, according to Donna M. Campbell, to "assimilate into naturalism" (47). Local color's nostalgia for a simpler past is depicted through regional community life, but naturalism betrays this same nostalgia in its more explicit critique of industrialization through the depiction of urban poverty. In both, "heredity and environment...have merged...until land and people seem but manifestations of each other" (10), the "land" itself the only variable—the country or village in local color work, and the urban landscape in naturalistic work. Most importantly, local color work imagined a romantic world in which female communities were self-sustaining, in this way radicalizing and complicating even its own realism.

The argument for Stoddard's realism, then, is as much in the local color, regional aspects of her work, as it is in her naturalism—and this, I believe, is what makes her resonate so deeply for Chopin scholars, readers, and teachers. Both subscribing to regionalistic conventions and deviating from New England regionalist work, *The Morgesons* continues to be a study in contrasts. The Morgesons are not a typical New England family obsessed with their ancestral lineage, deeply religious or otherwise very Puritan (S. Harris 156). Stoddard's concern, especially with Cassandra's character, is to chart Cassandra's passion against her traditional New England heritage. Lawrence Buell calls this special brand of New England regional writing "provincial gothic," defined by the consciousness of, but resistance to, change, the idea that New Englanders remain, in character, the same as they always were. This informs the prevalent themes of "entrapment," "ordeal," "suffering," "escape," which plague Cassandra so consistently and irrevocably. References to witchcraft (Cassandra is "possessed" in the opening line of the novel) and a preoccupation with decay speak to the "inherently grotesque" of that Puritan lineage (Buell 358–359). Stoddard felt acutely ambivalent about her hometown of Mattapoisset, Massachusetts, on which she based Surrey in *The Morgesons* (Boyd 78). Her only hope for reversing the particular brand of New England stagnation that revolted her is in Cassandra herself, who naturally does not succeed, but does try, to create change from within—suggesting that perhaps the agents of change in a stodgy, inert patriarchal culture must be women (Mahoney 318).

The Awakening, just like *The Morgesons*, cannot be neatly pigeonholed as a naturalist or regionalist novel. While it is abundantly clear that Chopin's novel is in the tradition of local color fiction, it defies regionalistic conventions by rejecting idealization and nostalgia, refusing the perspective of an elderly female narrator, and intermingling elements of impressionism, naturalism, feminism, and even, as I mentioned earlier, conventional nineteenth-century woman's fiction. Chopin's regionalism is readily on display in scenes like this one:

> Once in a while he withdrew his glance from the newspaper and looked about him. There was more noise than ever over at the house. The main building was called "the house, "to distinguish it from the

> cottages. The chattering and whistling birds were still at it. Two young girls, the Farival twins, were playing a duet from "Zampa" upon the piano. Madame Lebrun was bustling in and out, giving orders in a high key to a yard-boy whenever she got inside the house, and directions in an equally high voice to a dining-room servant whenever she got outside. She was a fresh, pretty woman, clad always in white with elbow sleeves. Her starched skirts crinkled as she came and went. Farther down, before one of the cottages, a lady in black was walking demurely up and down, telling her beads. A good many persons of the pension had gone over to the Chênière Caminada in Beaudelet's lugger to hear mass. Some young people were out under the wateroaks playing croquet. Mr. Pontellier's two children were there sturdy little fellows of four and five. A quadroon nurse followed them about with a faraway, meditative air. (Chopin 44)

However, strong naturalistic elements are at play, and even the scene above has a muted, suspenseful air. While Chopin entreats us to gaze at the scene she has so beautifully painted, we are simultaneously attuned to what might be outside the frame. We are essentially Edna, outsiders in this little Creole haven, and we know that we must end our stay sometime. When Edna does so by committing suicide, however, she eludes the "grinding, soul-denying denouement of the strictly naturalistic novel" (Leder 244). In other words, Edna's ability to choose her fate preserves her soul, a destiny hardly ever awarded to protagonists in naturalistic novels. Chopin's regionalism is equally unstable as a category: Chopin's use of local color is not a mode or genre at all, but a narrative strategy for depicting psychological tribulations without sentimentalism, moralism, didacticism, or melodrama (Gilbert qtd. in Showalter 71).

It is an exploration of sexuality's role in female identity formation and an erotics of language that *The Awakening* shares most explicitly with *The Morgesons.* Cassandra's charged sexuality is characterized by self-imposed restraint and Edna's by self-allowed liberation. Both women ineffectually navigate the realm of the forbidden. In direct contrast to reform novels, both texts excavate the impulse to commit adultery in nuanced ways, and hence, locate sexual license in a moral gray zone. It is Cassandra's self-repression that most strongly defines her, and of which she is paradoxically most proud, but it is not for herself, as in other early feminist literature, that Cassandra resists sex, but inversely in the interest of duty, loyalty, society, and a morality not hers. A full expression of the self would have meant an embrace of the sexuality that at moments threatens to consume her and perhaps even kill her through a literal and metaphoric consumptive disease.

Desmond finds "something animal in [her] eyes" (Stoddard 183) and she is "mad for the sight of him—mad to touch his hand once more" (200), but she resists. To Charles's admission of love, she responds with a "convulsive sob [that] choked [her]," and a "strange taste [that] fill[s] [her] mouth . . . [with] streaks of blood" (109). The accident in which Charles is killed and Cassandra's face is scarred is framed as orgasm: the horse moves "faster and faster" as a "splashing rain [falls]," his eyes are "glazed," "flakes of foam fl[y] from his mouth over his mane," "the flesh on his back contract[s] and quiver[s]," he is "leaping madly," and finally "fall[s] backward!" (121). In a revelatory conversation with her mother soon after the accident, Cassandra confesses the adultery she did not physically commit (Stoddard 133).[13] An instinct for Puritanical self-torture passionately stirs within her as she contemplates, in the context of her society's moral code, her lack of remorse for this imagined consummation (131–132), a remorselessness that condemns her to a life of self-repression without even the scanty comfort of guilt.

In Edna Pontellier's case, actions are unimportant in light of the thoughts and emotions that do or do not accompany them. Just like Cassandra, she believes that her thoughts have already committed the act; unlike Cassandra, she sees no moral barrier between fantasy and reality, for fulfilling the fantasy can be no more immoral than dreaming about fulfilling it. Her physical affair with Alcée Arobin is purely sexual—"a flaming torch that kindled desire," an "appeal to the animalism that stirred impatiently within her"—for "Alcée Arobin was absolutely nothing to her" (Chopin 131–9). Tellingly, it is not of Alcée or even of Robert she thinks as the shore recedes before her in the final scene, but of the cavalry officer, an adolescent infatuation who "melted imperceptibly out of her existence" (62), only to reappear at the unlikely moment of her death. It is to Robert, the man she is in love with, not her husband, to whom she at first feels she will have to answer for her affair with Arobin. But after consummation, Edna, like Cassandra, feels that "among the conflicting sensations which assailed her, there was neither shame nor remorse . . . only a dull pang of regret because it was not the kiss of love which had inflamed her" (139). It is the present, not the past or the future, that concerns Edna.

Edna's sexual awakening arrives quickly and consumes her quickly, whereas Cassandra's is gradual, and true to Stoddard's historical moment, repressed; both novels document this awakening through symbolic waking and sleeping. Edna is first rudely awakened by her inconsiderate husband, who reprimands her for taking poor care of the children. Soon, before even acknowledging her love for Robert to herself, she feels "a certain light... beginning to dawn dimly within her,—the light which, showing the way, forbids it" (Chopin 57). Following this light, Edna begins to grope for self-understanding: "Edna vaguely wondered what she meant by 'life's delirium.' It had crossed her thought like some unsought, extraneous impression" (107). While it was lovely to sleep, it is positively delicious for Edna to wake from that deepest of slumbers, to feel alive in a new world of her own imagining. She does not yet sense the pain wakefulness will mean: "Her eyes were bright and wide awake and her face glowed... 'How many years have I slept?'" (85), she asks Robert. In following scenes, wakefulness translates into self-knowledge. Edna cannot sleep after experiencing the "first-felt throbbings of desire" for Robert, to which she responds by standing up to her husband for the first time—"'I don't wish to go in, and I don't intend to. Don't speak to me like that again; I shall not answer you'" (77–8)—and later, she stays awake all night, in one position, after Robert leaves her. It is to Dr. Mandelet, perhaps the only person in her life aside from Mlle. Reisz who comes close to understanding her, that Edna confesses, using the metaphor of sleeping/waking, the terrible consequence of her journey: "'The years that are gone seem like dreams—if one might go on sleeping and dreaming—but to wake up and find—oh! well! Perhaps it is better to wake up after all, even to suffer, rather than to remain a dupe to illusions all one's life'" (171). In Cassandra's case, literal sleep is a stupor her body craves to combat the suffering of wakefulness. When Cassandra finds her mother dead, she cannot fend off a devouring sleep: "sleep overpowered me. I struggled against it in vain. It seemed the greatest good; let death and judgment come, I must sleep" (206). Cassandra's revelation upon waking parallels Edna's confession to Dr. Mandelet: "a mighty anguish filled my breast" (206).

Both novels likewise use the symbol of food to interrogate female sexual and emotional starvation and the expectation that women should "police and enforce their own psychological and emotional repression" (J. Harris 289). Veronica is Cassandra's virtually anorexic sister, eating little or nothing through her childhood, adolescence, and early adulthood; she is also persistently, mysteriously ill. Anorexia by the nineteenth century became a diagnosable illness tied to hysteria and "an expression of difficult interactions between young women and systems of social and sexual exchange" (Ryan 131). Food is a system of control for Veronica, who controls her illnesses equally well, and bears hunger and pain with epic courage.[14] In her embrace of illness, often explicitly invoked alongside her self-starvation,[15] Veronica denies her own existence, setting herself apart from her robust sister, so that "if Cassandra is 'possessed,'...then Veronica is the ultimate embodiment of *self*-possession" (Ryan 137). Considering that Veronica never plans to leave Surrey or her family home, her rejection of food is also a rejection of adult womanhood and sexual maturity, while at the same time a feminist embrace of "voluntary motherhood." Veronica continues to starve herself until Ben Somers, her future husband, begins to woo her. In direct contrast to Veronica, stands her passionate, appetitive sister, who makes many commentaries on her literal hunger. She taunts Veronica, who attests that she needs illness, with: "'As for me,' I said, biting my bread and butter, 'I feel well to my fingers' ends; they tingle with strength. I am elated with health'" (67). Again, she confesses, "I am afraid I am an animal" when she arrives for the first time to live with Charles and Alice in Rosville: "Did you notice how little the Morgesons ate?'" (71). After the accident, Cassandra begs Alice to supplement the "thin, impoverished liquid" she serves her with chicken, but when Alice does so, there is still too little chicken (124). Julia Stern notes that Alice's game with Cassandra's broth is a way of managing Cassandra's sexuality (118–121)—and Cassandra is often *very* hungry.[16]

In *The Awakening*, Chopin uses food to represent Edna's budding sexuality as well as her disdain for conventional womanly pursuits. The first day back in New Orleans that Edna scorns her "Tuesdays at home," or her duty to receive visitors, Léonce complains about the inedible dinner and storms off in a huff to have his dinner at the club. Edna sits and "finishe[s] her dinner alone, with forced deliberation. Her face was flushed and her eyes flamed with some inward fire that lighted them" (102). This dinner, which she eats out of protest, the food representing a life she can barely swallow, finds itself in direct contrast to her famishing hunger after falling asleep at Grand Terre and waking to a newfound sexuality: "She was very hungry...Edna bit a piece from the brown loaf, tearing it with her strong, white teeth" (85). Edna's going-away birthday dinner is a pivotal scene in the novel; she indulges on Léonce's tab before effectively abandoning the appearance of marriage and giving in completely to her own sexual volition. Immediately preceding her drowning, Edna's last conversation, with Victor and Mariequita, is about food: "'I'm very hungry...I hope you have fish for dinner" (174).

The sea is perhaps the most powerful symbol in both novels. Lisa Radinovsky feels that "Cassandra's boldest, most self-possessed erotic expression grows out of her relationship with the sea, rather than with a man" (104); the same is true for Edna. Tempestuous, passionate, never stagnant, possessed of inner turbulence, Cassandra is hopelessly drawn to the sea. Veronica, in her perpetual pre-pubescence, "could not bear to catch a glimpse of the sea, not to hear it" (26). While Cassandra's bedroom faces the sea, Veronica's faces in the other direction. After Rosville, Cassandra adopts the habit of

> consulting the sea as soon as I rose in the morning. Its aspect decided how my day would be spent. I watched it, studying its changes, seeking to understand its effect, ever attracted by an awful materiality and its easy power to drown me. By the shore at night the vague tumultuous sphere, swayed by an influence mightier than itself, gave voice, which drew my soul to utter speech for speech. I went there by day unobserved...(143)

The sea embraces Cassandra's depressive moods, as it does Edna's, and is ready to communicate fears and passions on equal footing. When Ben presses Cassandra to consider if the ocean reflects her own "powerful spirit," she wonders instead, "Is it power? It is pain" (160).

With Desmond, the connection between water and sexuality acquires greater transparency—he is explicitly associated with the sea, and his simultaneous presence (his love for her) and absence (his unworthiness due to alcoholism) is analogous to Cassandra's relationship to the sea, both soul-lifting and painful. She feels Desmond beside her, singing, and "I was where I saw the white sea-birds flashing between the blue deeps of our summer sea and sky, and the dark rocks that rose and dipped in the murmuring waves" (174). But Desmond does not always evoke images of a serene ocean; when seeing Desmond about to attack his mother, "anger raged through me like a fierce rain that strikes flat a violent sea" (186). Desmond, too, is a ball of contradictions and tumultuous passions. Cassandra wishes then, to marry herself, if marry she must. Cassandra's marriage—channeled through the symbolism of the ocean—should be read as only one step removed from Edna's final commitment to her own soul.

Finally, the sea represents great changes for the characters. For Veronica, her sexuality stirs as for the first time she consults the sea for prophecies—"if it was calm, she went away quietly; if the sea was rough, she was sorrowful" (233)—when she waits for Ben to come marry her. She is attuned to the motion of the water immediately after the horror of her mother's death—"'Where will they carry her?' she asked, shuddering, and putting her fingers in her ears. 'How the water splashes on the beach! Is the tide coming in?'" (206). And right before Cassandra discovers that her father has married Charles's widow, Alice, she walks home, with the sea "creeping quietly toward [the east] with a murmuring morning song" (243). The greatest change is Cassandra's moment of revelation, provoked by a conversation with the ocean:

> I climbed out to a flat, low rock, on the point;...stretched myself along its edge. Little pools meshed from the sea by the numberless rocks round me engrossed my attention.... the pool showed me the motionless shadow of my face again, on which I pondered, till I suddenly became aware of a slow, internal oscillation, which increased till I felt in a strange tumult. I put my hand in the pool and troubled its surface.
>
> "Hail, Cassandra! Hail!"
>
> I sprang up the highest rock on the point, and looked seaward, to catch a glimpse of the flying Spirit who had touched me...The wide, shimmering plain of sea...mingled its essence with mine. The wind was coming; under the far horizon the mass of waters began to undulate...The speedy wind tossed and teased the sea nearer and nearer, till I was surrounded by a gulf of milky green foam. As the tide rolled in I retreated, stepping back from rock to rock, round which the waves curled and hissed, baffled in their attempt to climb over me. I stopped on the verge of the tied-mark; the sea was seeking me and I must wait. It gave tongue as its lips touched my feet, roaring in the caves, falling on the level beaches with a mad, boundless joy!

"Have then at life!" my senses cried...Its roar, its beauty, its madness—we will have— *all.* (214)

The scene's erotic language culminates in sexual communion with the sea, which empowers Cassandra to search for "all." But only moments later, we discover that her "all" is a return to duty—a sacrifice of the self. She feels the fullness of possibility in the embrace of the sea, but shirks this limitless possibility in her embrace of duty—"I will reign, and serve also...I never shall have any more colds...never mean to have anything to myself—entirely, you know" (215). This revelation is baffling in the context of the previous passage, and it is when Cassandra sticks to this life—duty, marriage—that we learn the sea for her has lost its magical quality, and has become an "eternal monotone express[ing] no pity, no compassion" (252). It is no longer the sea that can readily drown her; it possesses no such power; it is a spurned, now indifferent lover.

Stoddard's metonymic treatment of the sea is radically expanded in Chopin's *The Awakening*, in which Edna can be positively described as having a love affair with the sea. This passage is repeated at the beginning and ending of the novel, with slight variation: "The voice of the sea is seductive; never ceasing, whispering, clamoring, murmuring, inviting the soul to wander for a spell in abysses of solitude; to lose itself in mazes of inward contemplation. The voice of the sea speaks to the soul. The touch of the sea is sensuous, enfolding the body in its soft, close embrace" (57, 175). The passage echoes the "seduction," "solitude," "contemplation," and "soul[fulness]" of Cassandra's final meeting with the sea. For Edna, the sea represents a budding sexuality grown out of a long-lost childhood: she remembers "a summer day in Kentucky, of a meadow that seemed as big as the ocean to the very little girl walking through the grass, which was higher than her waist. She threw out her arms as if swimming when she walked, beating the tall grass as one strikes out in the water" (60–61). It is this same Kentucky meadow, this "ocean of waving grass" that plays in Edna's mind as she swims out to her death. The liberation she feels as a young child traversing the boundless meadow is the limitlessness she feels when swimming for the first time at midnight with a group of carousers at Grand Isle. She feels "exulted," a feeling of "daring and reckless[ness]" overtaking her; she "want[s] to swim far out, where no woman had swum before" (73). The combination of Mlle. Reisz's earlier piano playing and the nighttime swim makes Edna feel as though she is "in a dream," as if those around her are "half-human beings," "spirits" (75). In a notable difference with *The Morgesons*, Edna, at the end of the novel, walks out to meet the "foamy wavelets curl[ing] up to her white feet,... coil[ing] like serpents about her ankles," while Cassandra feels the pull, and then retreats back into the prison of life. Edna's feels the "chill, but... walk[s] on. The water was deep, but she lifted her white body and reached out with a long, sweeping stroke" (176). Cassandra, as opposed to Edna, does not "confuse self and sex" (S. Harris, "Anomalies" 295),[17] and is therefore able to stow away her passionate nature and redirect her energies towards duty. Edna is finally unable to revert in any way whatsoever, desiring free sexual license and full self-proprietorship forever. She ultimately realizes that even the "thought of [Robert] would [someday] melt out of her existence, leaving her alone," and that she desires "no one thing in the world" and "no human being... near her" (175).

Through these symbols, Chopin and Stoddard interrogate woman's lot, women as individuals, and female relationships in revolutionary ways. Cassandra bitterly confesses to her father that men "require the souls and bodies of women, without having the trouble of knowing the difference between the one and other" (221). When Alice asks Cassandra what has become of her honesty, Cassandra attests that she is "more candid than ever... for I am silent" (153). Edna, her husband's "valuable piece of personal property" (Chopin 44) is in her husband's eyes "growing unbalanced" (108), hysterical, for what else could explain her irrational, unwomanly, behavior? In her sexual rejection of her husband, the stamping of her wedding ring, and the unshakeable sense that her small children are "antagonists" (175) seeking to drag her into the slavery of motherhood, Edna resists overly simplistic, male notions of womanhood like progressive Dr. Mandelet's: "woman . . . is a very peculiar and delicate organism . . . moody and whimsical" (119). Chopin's own voice on women's oppression is always prominent. It is her voice that pronounces sarcastically that mothers "esteemed it a holy privilege to efface themselves as individuals and grow wings as ministering angels" (51) and that men, like Edna's father, the Colonel, are blissfully unaware that they "coerce [their] own wi[ves] into [their] grave[s]" (125). The domestic role assigned to Edna is wholly unnatural to her—everywhere she turns a dreadful, world-weariness follows her. Early on, she feels an "indescribable oppression . . . like a shadow, like a mist passing across her soul's summer day" (49), an "idle[ness]," an "aimless[ness]" (61). She feels "no interest in anything about her" (104), that her life is simply passing her by, "leaving its promise broken and unfulfilled" (127), and that without Robert, life is totally "dulled" (95). Even at her birthday dinner, amid exciting conversation, warmth, and alcohol, the "old ennui" (145) overtakes her, and life becomes a simple going through of motions. In ecstatic moments, Edna feels grateful to be alive, but through it all knows that she is a "lost soul" (158).

Edna's ennui is matched by Cassandra's, and it too often manifests as depression: "I shifted the hours, as one shifts the kaleidoscope, with an eye only to their movement. Neither the remembrance of yesterday nor the hope of tomorrow stimulated me. The mere fact of breathing had ceased to be a happiness" (Stoddard 58). Suicidal thoughts accompany this ennui, as with Edna. All life for Cassandra is an "endur[ance] of aching, aimless melancholy" (213) and it is the prison of womanhood that Cassandra reacts to when she says, "if I turned my eyes inside the walls, I was aware of the yearning, yawning empty void within me" (250). Like Edna in her final epiphany, Cassandra feels that the future holds nothing of value: "My will was nerveless, when I contemplated Time, which stretched before me—a vague, limitless sea; and I only kept Endeavor in view, near enough to be tormented" (136).

Stunningly approached in *The Morgesons*, the relationship between sisters Cassandra and Veronica exemplifies the complexity and emotional depth of female relationships predicated on forced cohabitation and prescribed futures. In their new home, their adjacent rooms occupy a cul-de-sac-like structure set off from the house, and Veronica and Cassandra find themselves trapped together. This entrapment later becomes a metaphor for their relationship—their imposed closeness becomes a real closeness, a doubling almost, particularly in their final marriage of two brothers. During Veronica's few moments of immeasurable tenderness, Cassandra responds viscerally—"Veronica stooped over my hand and kissed it, unseen. It was more like a sigh upon it than a kiss, but it swept through me, tingling the scars on my face, as if the flesh had become alive again" (141). As for Cassandra's scars from her doomed love affair with Charles, Veronica shares them with her sister, [18] solidifying a bond that is deeply spiritual and sensory. In a final fusion of the sisters' lives, Veronica's intuition leads her to dream of Cassandra's lover Desmond, about whom Cassandra has never spoken, on the day of her own wedding.

Despite the oddity of Veronica and Cassandra's relationship, their first forced, then chosen closeness sustains them in a life of substantial isolation; Edna's female relationships function on the other hand to illuminate the self and soul, not as forgings of eternal dependencies. Adèle, Edna's "mother-woman" friend, is initially a source of pleasant escape from the dark thoughts that increasingly plague Edna, but quickly becomes Edna's foil. Adèle's perfectly harmonious relationship with her husband is nauseating to Edna, who leaves the spectacle of their marital concord with pity for Adèle, who is so simple as to be a "dupe to [life's] illusions." Adèle serves as a clear model for what is wholly unnatural to Edna, and therefore, in her own way, pushes Edna's awakening forward. Edna's only real friendship, with Mlle. Reisz, an aging, caustic spinster, challenges Edna to trust her internal sense of morality. Reisz is herself inspired by Edna's flight, but she also warns that the journey is dangerous: "She put her arms around me and felt my shoulder blades, to see if my wings were strong, she said. 'The bird that would soar above the level plain of tradition and prejudice must have strong wings. It is a sad spectacle to see the weaklings bruised, exhausted, fluttering back to earth'" (138). Mlle. Reisz, like Adèle, is for Edna a fearful outcome of a lost struggle, for Reisz is unsexed and alienated from the world. Both of these friendships move Edna closer to an understanding of herself, her desires, and her needs.

Finally, both novels invoke woman as artist as another form of self-ownership. *The Awakening* itself follows the narrative form of a Chopin piece.[19] Both Cassandra and Edna's passions are stirred by the piano playing of Veronica and Mlle. Reisz, respectively. Both pianists are musical geniuses, and the playing of both puts Cassandra and Edna into heightened sensory states that are simultaneously trance-like. Veronica's playing makes Cassandra feel as though she "woke from a dream, chaotic, but not tumultuous, beautiful, but inharmonious" (Stoddard 53). Later, she is moved to tears by Veronica's "wild lament that [made her] fathom [her] desires and despair" (141). Veronica's piano playing too then serves as a cryptic form of spiritual communication between the two sisters, reminding Cassandra of life's beauty and promise, even in her intense melancholy. Veronica is an artist whose fate is solitude, as is Mlle. Reisz's. Cassandra is in her own right an artist, for she is the narrator and implied author of *The Morgesons*. Lisa Radinovsky puts it this way: "as Cassandra settles into a dull domesticity toward the end of the novel, writing replaces both musical self-expression and vibrant erotic expression" (Radinovsky 115). Stoddard emphasizes that the "most realistic hope for women...lies in the power of self-definition through writing" (117), and that *The Morgesons* channels female power through stylistic experimentation that can compete with male writing (Reynolds 410). Veronica's musical genius is remarked upon as "a deplorable thing for a woman" by the elderly Mr. Somers. In frustration, Cassandra responds: "'a woman of genius is but a heavenly lunatic, or an anomaly sphered between the sexes; do you agree?'" (Stoddard 242).

In *The Awakening,* Edna dubs one of Mlle Reisz's pieces "Solitude," as she is rocked by the "very passions themselves [that] were aroused within her soul, swaying it, lashing it, as the waves daily beat upon her splendid body. She trembled, she was choking, and the tears blinded her" (71). Edna has the same reaction reading Robert's letter as Mlle. Reisz plays a "soft interlude," then the Chopin Impromptu. After Edna leaves, Mlle. Reisz finds Robert's letter "crumpled and damp with tears" (116) on the floor. Music and sounds stimulate and move Edna, as she persistently hears Robert's singing "haunt[ing] her memory" (89), and the sounds of a barking dog, the cavalry officer's spurs, and the buzzing of bees as she dies. Her own paintings progress from imitative work to highly original, presumably impressionistic portraits and drawings. Edna's portrait of Adèle, which "bore no resemblance" (55) to her subject, symbolizes both the expectation of a definable, limitable realism in contrast to an aimless, sensory impressionism (the drawing itself), and the blurred space inhabited by women, caught between the clearly delineated domestic sphere and an undefinable interiority. Adèle is disappointed in the painting's lack of realism, but Edna's disappointment is different. The painting has no soul; it does not represent or express the inner life of the artist, since it is yet a product of the artist's vague, unformulated consciousness, or "life's delirium." While she is highly critical of her own work, she is also at moments consumed by it, spending days on end drawing all the servants in her home, her father, her friends, and her lover, Arobin. It is especially important that her pigeon house contain an atelier and significant that she buys it partly from the proceeds from selling her paintings. Edna's painting is akin to Cassandra's authorship of her family's story—while both are artists, neither are geniuses in this work, and therefore their art is only one aspect of their greater lives, the pleasure they receive from the work hardly redeeming life's general misery.

The points of intersection between *The Awakening* and *The Morgesons* are many and provocative. Consider one final minor detail: that of pigeons. Cassandra witnesses her grandfather Warren shoot aunt Merce's pigeons, and later makes an explicit connection between herself and the murdered birds: "Well, don't shoot me, as you shot the pigeons." To this, her grandfather responds, "Pah, have pigeons a soul?" (47). This question is particularly apt if we apply it to Edna's inhabitation of the pigeon house. She is one of the pigeons shot by the Puritanical, sexist grandfather Warren; she is a woman whose existence as more than a body, as a soul, is consistently questioned by her patriarchal culture. Cassandra and Edna both fight to feel the impact of having a soul, even if, as in Cassandra's case, the result is a repression of the soul whose fullness she has known as many women of her day did not. Although a patchwork novel, *The Morgesons*'s early publication date of 1862 pioneers a brand of feminism *The Awakening* later takes up. Chopin moves many of the images, symbols, and themes more subtly explored in *The Morgesons* into wholly unchartered territory, leaving little room for the label of didacticism in a novel that explores head-on woman's "sinful" sexuality, self-discovery, and quest for self-ownership. Cassandra chooses the fate she was assigned, with the compromise of a marriage of love and equality and economic power through proprietorship. Edna refuses any compromise whatsoever, catapulting her author, Kate Chopin, into the next century, and forcing others to join her for a swim.

Notes

1. Susan K. Harris notes that "while Charles gets *his* just desserts by being killed, Cassandra escapes with physical and emotional scars . . . [that] ultimately aid rather than hinder her in finding a husband and signify her discovery of her own capabilities" ("Projecting" 163).

2. Reviews from *Providence Sunday Journal* (4 Jun 1899): 15 and *The Nation* 69 (3 Aug. 1899): 96. In the latter review, the male reviewer finds that had Edna "flirted less and looked after her children more . . . we need not have been put to the unpleasantness of reading about her and the temptations she trumped up for herself." Another case in point of male reaction to women's writing as "unwomanly" was the quite vocal opposition of the male literary establishment to women contributors to the intellectually rigorous *Atlantic Monthly*. The stories printed, meant to appeal to a female readership, "often influenced [male] perception of women writers as a whole" (Boyd 206). Cesare Lombroso's 1863 book *The Man of Genius* took this unsexing concept further: "there are no women of genius; the women of genius are men" (qtd. in Radinovsky 39). Radinovsky goes on to say that Stoddard herself "associated creative power with virility." On the other hand, a rapid dismissal of women's books as "feminine" did indeed preclude their inclusion in the canon. Early anthologies and critical treatments of American Renaissance writers either ignored women entirely or relegated them to the "feminine" sphere. See Charlene Avallone's discussion of "the language of renaissance," 1102–8.
3. Hawthorne offered this high praise: "There are very few books of which I take the trouble to have an opinion at all, or of which I could retain any memory so long after reading them, as I do of *The Morgesons*." See James H. Matlack for a full treatment of the relationship between the two writers.
4. See Lynn Mahoney and James H. Matlack for excerpts from critical reviews.
5. Stoddard wrote to her good friend Edmund Stedman in February of 1890 "that she had yet to make one hundred dollars from all three novels" that she wrote (Mahoney 331). Mahoney cites Matlack's book *The Literary Career of Elizabeth Stoddard* as proof that the second editions made Stoddard at least fifteen hundred dollars.
6. For an in-depth treatment of the reformist novel in all its shapes and forms, see David S. Reynolds's *Beneath the American Renaissance*, particularly Part One.
7. "The course of history dictated that the crusade for domesticity, unlike that for woman's parity with men, would be short-lived" (Baym 50).
8. "Egalitarian" marriage is a convention of women's writing, too, Baym claims (xxvi). Still, when Cassandra rescues Desmond from a life of alcoholism by marrying him, she takes on a stereotypically masculine role and is no longer a conventional female heroine (38).
9. Boyd notes that Stoddard herself was deeply ambivalent about marrying, not even immediately disclosing the event of her own marriage to her closest friends (57).

10. Baym puts it this way: "Children may be necessary for a woman's happiness, [but] they are not necessary for her identity" (38).
11. Just a few examples: she resists Charles's sexual advances while submitting to a private torturous desire, she chooses Desmond for a lover and waits until he takes the temperance pledge to marry him, she buys out her father from the family home and becomes its sole proprietress, she chooses sisterly love over petty differences.
12. For a full treatment of this genre, see Elaine Showalter's chapter "The American Female Gothic" in *Sister's Choice*, 127–44.
13. There is, however, reason to believe that, at least with Charles, Cassandra has in her own understanding already committed adultery. Alfred Habegger has argued that "the words 'I love you,'" words that Charles has uttered, "were linguistic representations of the act of copulation" (qtd. in S. Harris 165). Susan K. Harris notes that sexuality in nineteenth century women's writing is central, but usually manifests itself as "magnetism, a force emanating from the male that the female has the choice either to resist or accept" (165). It is clear that in Cassandra's mind, she has already accepted the indiscretion Charles has offered, but it is also important to note that she feels equally responsible for beginning the "affair." Incidentally, others around her consider her affair consummated as well. Ben Somers asks her to abide his alcoholism with this plea: "'why not leave me to God? Didn't you leave yourself that way once?'" (Stoddard 159).
14. "She acquired the fortitude of an Indian; pain could extort no groan from her;" "she was educated by sickness; her mind fed and grew on pain, and at last mastered it" (59); "I need all the illnesses that come" (67), Veronica admits.
15. For example, Veronica is overcome by her mysterious disorder after not having eaten the entire day (146).
16. Susanna Ryan notes that Stoddard "seeks to integrate self-possession and satiation through experiments with literary form and the forms of female appetites themselves" (145).
17. Susan K. Harris suggests that Edna is the only female character in nineteenth century women's literature that exhibits this confusion.
18. See Jennifer Putzi, 165–73, for an in-depth discussion of Cassandra's physical scars and how they are "a potentially empowering image that could enable women to claim their own bodies and the experiences they represent."
19. "Impromptu (opening theme), contrasting middle section, modified return to the melody and rhythm of the opening" (Showalter 76).

Works Cited

Avallone, Charlene. "What American Renaissance? The Gendered Genealogy of a Critical Discourse." *PMLA* 112.5 (Oct. 1997): 1102–20. Print.

Baym, Nina. *Woman's Fiction.* 2nd ed. Urbana: U of Illinois P, 1993. Print.

Boyd, Anne E. *Writing for Immortality: Women and the Emergence of High Literary Culture in America.* Baltimore and London: The Johns Hopkins UP, 2004. Print.

Buell, Lawrence. *New England Literary Culture: From Revolution Through Renaissance.* Cambridge: Cambridge UP, 1986. Print.

Buell, Lawrence, and Sandra A. Zagarell. "Introduction to *The Morgesons.*" *The Morgesons*, Ed. Elizabeth Stoddard. New York: Penguin Books, 1997. ix–xxi. Print.

Campbell, Donna M. *Resisting Regionalism: Gender and Naturalism in American Fiction, 1885–1915.* Athens: Ohio UP, 1997. Print.

Chopin, Kate. *The Awakening and Selected Stories.* Ed. Sandra M. Gilbert. New York: Penguin Books, 1986. Print.

Claybaugh, Amanda. *The Novel of Purpose: Literature and Social Reform in the Anglo-American World.* Ithaca: Cornell UP, 2007. Print.

Harris, Jennifer. "A Renaissance for Elizabeth Stoddard." *Canadian Review of American Studies.* 37.2 (2007): 283–92. Print.

Harris, Susan K. "Anomalies and Anxieties: *The Story of Avis, A Country Doctor, The Awakening, and O Pioneers!*" *Nineteenth Century American Women's Novels: Interpretative Strategies.* Cambridge: Cambridge UP, 1990. 199–210. Print.

———. "Projecting the 'I'/conoclast: First-person narration in *The Morgesons.*" *Nineteenth Century American Women's Novels: Interpretative Strategies.* Cambridge: Cambridge UP, 1990. 152–70. Print.

Lathrop, George Parsons. "Audacity in Women Novelists." *The North American Review* 150.402 (May 1890): 609–17. Print.

Leder, Priscilla. "Land's End: *The Awakening* and Nineteenth Century Literary Tradition." *Critical Essays on Kate Chopin.* Ed. Alice Hall Petry. New York: G.K. Hall, 1996. 237–50. Print.

Mahoney, Lynn. "Near the Edge: Elizabeth Stoddard and the Boundaries of Victorian Culture." Diss. Rutgers University, 1999.

Matlack, James H. "Hawthorne and Elizabeth Barstow Stoddard." *New England Quarterly* 50.2 (June 1977): 278–302. Print.

Opfermann, Susanne, and Yvonne Roth, ed. "Introduction to *Stories: Elizabeth Stoddard.*" *Stories: Elizabeth Stoddard.* Boston: Northeastern UP, 2003. ix–xxxi. Print.

Petry, Alice Hall, ed. *Critical Essays on Kate Chopin.* New York: G.K. Hall, 1996. Print.

Putzi, Jennifer. "'Tattooed Still': The Inscription of Female Agency in Elizabeth Stoddard's *The Morgesons.*" *Legacy* 17.2 (2000): 165–73. Print.

Radinovsky, Lisa M. "Gender Norms and Genre Forms: Elizabeth Stoddard's Challenges to Convention." Diss. Duke University, 1999.

Reynolds, David S. *Beneath the American Renaissance: The Subversive Imagination in the Age of Emerson and Melville.* Cambridge, MA and London: Harvard UP, 1988. Print.

Ryan, Susanna. "'Perversions of Volition': Self-Starvation and Self-Possession in Dickinson and Stoddard." *American Culture, Canons, and the Case of Elizabeth Stoddard*. Ed. Robert McClure Smith and Ellen Weinauer. Tuscaloosa: U of Alabama P, 2003. 128–48. Print.
Showalter, Elaine. *Sister's Choice: Tradition and Change in American Women's Writing*. Oxford: Clarendon Press, 1991. Print.
Stange, Margit. *Personal Property: Wives, White Slaves, and the Market in Women*. Baltimore: Johns Hopkins UP, 1998. 22–36. Print.
Stoddard, Elizabeth. *The Morgesons*. New York: Penguin Books, 1997. Print.
Stern, Julia. "'I Am Cruel Hungry': Dramas of Twisted Appetite and Rejected Identification in Elizabeth Stoddard's *The Morgesons*." *American Culture, Canons, and the Case of Elizabeth Stoddard*. Ed. Robert McClure Smith and Ellen Weinauer. Tuscaloosa: U of Alabama P, 2003. 107–27. Print.
Weir, Sybil. "A Neglected Feminist Bildungsroman." *The New England Quarterly* 49.3 (Sep. 1976): 427–39. Print.

CHAPTER 9

"I'm So Happy; It Frightens Me": Female Genealogy in the Fiction of Kate Chopin and Pauline Hopkins

Correna Catlett Merricks

On the plantation, the lives of black and white women were intricately intertwined in a complex hierarchical system; they often had sexual relations with the same men,[1] had children at the same time, and raised their children together. In this chapter, I explore the ways two women from different cultural and socioeconomic backgrounds express a shared identity. Kate Chopin's short stories, "Désirée's Baby" and "La Belle Zoraïde," work in conversation with Pauline Hopkins' sentimental novel, *Contending Forces,* to articulate a female-centered vision of the plantation south. Chopin and Hopkins experience a shared historical memory; each author reflects on the impact the plantation has had on the characters in her stories, and each author presents a new image of the changing plantation South. Pairing these texts can help students understand how Chopin's fiction destabilizes the patriarchal order of the plantation South by linking the past and present, exposing the frequent sexual exploitation of black women, and by blurring binary understandings of gender, race, and class. Pauline Hopkins's *Contending Forces* and Kate Chopin's *Bayou Folk* were published only a few years apart—*Bayou Folk* in 1894 and *Contending Forces* in 1900. These texts tell stories of women, their children, and the relationships between them, but they are also stories about the plantation in American culture and its far-reaching implications.

"Désirée's Baby," "La Belle Zoraïde," and *Contending Forces* are woman-centered; each text focuses on a mother–daughter relationship and privileges the voices of women over the voices of male characters. Because of these characteristics, I argue that these texts focus on female genealogy rather than a traditional patriarchal understanding of genealogical history. The image of haunting demonstrates the way these texts focus on genealogical history—the violence of the past seeps into the present and translates into pervasive anxiety; female genealogy is characterized by this anxiety, by synchronic connections between characters, and by an expanded definition of the mother–child relationship. In his book *Postslavery Literatures in the Americas*, George Handley discusses the differences between what he calls a diachronic and a synchronic reading of a postslavery text: "Genealogy, though traditionally understood to reach back through time, becomes a means of unveiling the latent heritage of the present" (14). In the plantation South, genealogical history is both diachronic and synchronic; there is more than simply past and present at work in these stories, and biological connections are only one way to trace family history. "Synchronic" is one way to describe the organic nature of the large plantation family; genealogy is not simply a straight line, instead a web of connections exists between members of the family. Exploring synchronic connections troubles the traditional understanding of the plantation as a patriarchal hierarchy and of race as a binary because it highlights moments of connection between the plantocracy and those they considered to be their "others." These texts include elements that allow readers to see when a linear understanding of the plantation is troubled: female characters who are orphans or foundlings, gothic imagery, and monstrous depictions of the female body shift the audience's gaze toward women, relationships between women, and the violence women experienced in the U.S. South.

"Désirée's Baby," "La Belle Zoraïde," and *Contending Forces* disrupt a binary understanding of the world by highlighting a culture in which individuals reflected on their identities as related to both the past and the present. Both *Bayou Folk* and *Contending Forces* were published in the late nineteenth century, close to 40 years after the Civil War ended, placing them around the time that Charles Aiken calls a "time of transition" between the Old South and the New South (6). Because the stories are written in the form of frame narratives, they explore connections between past and present for the authors.[2] Although both "Désirée's Baby" and "La Belle Zoraïde" depict life before the Civil War, their 1893 and 1894 publication dates connect them to anxiety about race in postbellum America. According to Katie Berry Frye, miscegenation was "a site of feverish anxiety in postbellum New Orleans" (47). *Contending Forces* has been rediscovered and canonized as a result of the efforts of critics like Hazel Carby and Claudia Tate.[3] Her fiction is not frequently anthologized, but teaching Hopkins's texts together with Chopin's can help students understand the deep impact of plantation culture and ideology. Chopin and Hopkins disrupt an understanding of time as linear; in the plantation South, the past reaches into the present to influence individuals. These two authors indicate the power of the past and its ability to affect present-day thinking, but they do not romanticize the plantation; instead, they demonstrate the insidious nature of the plantation's history, connecting the Old and New Souths.

In addition to recognizing the ever-reaching influence of the past, Chopin and Hopkins emphasize the importance of secrets and their relationship to genealogy in the plantation South. Secret histories indicate the importance of the past in present-day relationships. Chopin and Hopkins reveal the frequent sexual exploitation of black women that occurred in the plantation South by carefully describing women and children of various skin tones. Because it exposes what Handley calls "the ellipses of the planter's scheme, the moments of contact with those who have been excluded," the presence of women of color in these three texts disrupts a binary understanding of race and subverts the patriarchal order of the plantation South (15). The authors' insistence that women and motherhood are central in these stories brings the "concealed evidence of sexual contact" Handley mentions to light, pulling secrets that have been pushed to the side to the center of the story (3). Orphans, or foundlings, are central characters in each text: in "Désirée's Baby," Désirée, Zandrine, and Armand's mother are each either orphans or characters whose genealogical history is kept secret; in *Contending Forces,* Grace Montfort's racial history is concealed until she moves to North Carolina, and Sappho, another central character, has a covert history as well. The focus on orphans emphasizes the significance of secrets in the texts. Secrets tell the story of female genealogy—they tell the stories of women and the rape or violence they have experienced. Chopin and Hopkins lived in a society that found comfort in clearly drawn lines that created distance between races in spite of the fact that those lines were a construction.[4] Early twentieth-century American culture maintained the illusion that black and white were binaries, but Chopin and Hopkins pay detailed attention to both fair and dark-skinned African American characters.

"Désirée's Baby" emphasizes the significance of a secret history. Désirée's status as an orphan demonstrates the double standard that existed in the plantation South regarding genealogical purity, illustrates the way females and female bodies functioned as commodities in the plantation order, and connects her to other orphaned women and children in the text. The short story focuses on Désirée's relationship with her adoptive mother as well as her biological child, a son. Chopin upholds the mother–child relationship as primary throughout by focusing the story's surprising ending on the mother of Armand Aubigny, the plantation owner. Désirée's mother discovers her as a baby sleeping in the shadow of one of the plantation's pillars; she is associated with the white pillars of the plantation home from the beginning of the story. Because her history is unknown, she is passed from person to person and claimed as a possession. Désirée is transferred from her mother's ownership to her husband's, and the next step is to perpetuate the plantation system by becoming the mother of Armand's children. Armand takes a risk by marrying a woman with no history; he risks polluting his family's supposed genealogical purity, but as Chopin narrates, he "fell in love, as if struck by a pistol shot" (242). Armand's position as a male in power gives him a sense of overconfidence: "He was reminded that she was nameless. What did it matter about a name when he could give her one of the oldest and proudest in Louisiana?" (242). Armand's overconfidence also characterizes his demeanor as head of the plantation where his "rule was a strict one, too, and under it his negroes had forgotten how to be gay as they had been during the old master's easy-going and indulgent lifetime" (243).

Désirée is not the only individual in the story who does not know her genealogical history. We are also introduced to other plantation mother figures, including the "yellow nurse woman" named Zandrine, who cares for Désirée and Armand's new baby boy (243). Chopin weaves multiple connections between Désirée and Zandrine, demonstrating that both women are the victims of an insidious patriarchal system. Like Desireé, Zandrine's origins are unknown. Her yellow skin is never discussed; it is mostly taken for granted except for the fleeting moments when Désirée's mother carefully scrutinizes her grandson and then "looked as searchingly at Zandrine" (243). Zandrine serves as a double for Désirée since neither woman has a genealogy or a past, both illuminating the "ellipses of the planter's scheme" Handley mentions (3). By creating Zandrine as Désirée's foil, Chopin blurs the traditional dualistic understanding of race. Zandrine's hybridity illuminates the issues of genealogy Handley discusses and points out that Armand, whose racial purity is the source of his power in many ways, has had "moments of contact" with his "Other."

"La Belle Zoraïde" also explores the stories of orphans and secret histories, continuing the theme of "black" servants waiting on black mistresses, demonstrating that racial identity is muddled because ancestry is concealed. Manna Loulou tells the story of a beautiful, fair-skinned maid, Zoraïde, who has led the life of a house-slave and has been pampered and doted upon: "her fingers had never done rougher work than sewing a fine muslin seam; and she even had her own little black servant to wait upon her" (313). Chopin mentions that her owner, "was her godmother as well as her mistress" (313). Zoraïde's cafe-au-lait skin indicates that her genealogical history may include rape and violence, but her history is kept secret, making her an orphan. When she engages in a sexual relationship outside of her mistress' knowledge, she is not allowed to keep her baby, continuing the orphan narrative: "For the baby was living and well and strong. It had at once been removed from its mother's side, to be sent away to Madame's plantation, far up the coast" (315). Madame's love for Zoraïde and the mother–child relationship that she acts out are simply charades that place Madame in a paternalistic position over her slave.

Here, Chopin shows that the loving relationship between a mistress and her slave is a lie; the mistress's kindness ends when Zoraïde makes her own decision about her sexuality. Zoraïde is a commodity; her story can be representative of many women's stories, indicating that babies without mothers and mothers without babies are a result of the commodity exchange that occurred on the plantation. Light-skinned slaves like Zoraïde were considered more valuable than dark-skinned slaves, but the topic of how they came to be light-skinned was taboo. As Mary Chestnut writes, "Any lady is ready to tell you who is the father of all the mulatto children in everybody's household but her own. Those, she seems to think, drop from the clouds" (qtd. in Lundie 133). The loving relationship between Manna Loulou and her mistress could be seen as an image of the idyllic or rooted plantation, but the story Manna Loulou tells her mistress in order to help her go to sleep reveals the plantation as an insidious machine. Manna Loulou's story points back to herself; she is also connected to Zoraïde because she lives with and cares for a young woman who is not a member of her biological family. Manna Loulou and Madame DeLise have a complicated mother–child relationship that is similar to Zoraïde's relationship with her mistress.

With a similar emphasis on secrets, Hopkins questions the traditional binary understanding of race by centering her social drama around characters whose ethnicity is unknown. Sappho Clark's character is at the center of most of *Contending Forces*; the Montfort family's frame story hangs in the background, lending significance to the present-day tale and indicating Hopkins' intentions. Sappho's history is mysterious; she keeps her past a secret: "It was noticeable in these confidential chats that Sappho never spoke of her early life. Dora had confided to her friend every event of importance that had occurred in her young life…but all this had begot no like unburdening to eager ears of the early history of her friend" (127). We learn later that Sappho has a child as a result of a violent incestuous relationship, so she is keeping her sexual history a secret. Hopkins's careful construction of the frame narrative emphasizes the connections between characters, particularly between Grace Montfort and Sappho, indicating the synchronic nature of relationships in the novel, particularly relationships between women. Connecting the past and present works together with Hopkins's overall purpose because her frame narrative indicates that the insidious nature of the plantation continues to exist in late nineteenth-century Boston. She connects past and present, North and South, and in doing so she connects women who are victims of violence and racism.

While telling a story that fits within the form of a sentimental novel, Hopkins points out that often mixed-race persons have a story of violence as part of their genealogical past. Hopkins does not shy from indicating the pervasive sexual violence against African American women. Sappho marries Grace Montfort's great-grandson, but the women are also connected because they are both victims of sexual violence. When Sappho's past is revealed, another orphan becomes central to the story; Sappho has a son who was conceived as a result of an abusive sexual relationship. Sappho's son was conceived as a result of rape, and by telling her story, Hopkins reminds readers that many fair-skinned African Americans' genealogical history includes rape. Kate McCullough argues that

> Hopkins counters the post-Reconstruction racist white supremacist appropriation of the mulatto figure.… Using rape in place of "passing" as a figure for relations between the races, Hopkins self-consciously underscores the ways in which the white American imagination had linked sexuality to racial identity and had, moreover, figured a racial "threat" in sexual terms. (25)

Through the story of Sappho's secret history and her reunion with her son, Alphonse, who was housed in a convent and had been told his mother had died, Hopkins emphasizes the orphan narrative. She sheds light on the unjust stereotypes of African American women's sexuality that forced many women to keep their stories secret and to become separated from their children.

The image of the plantation as insidious also comes to life in the texts as the authors include elements of the Gothic genre, particularly in terms of genealogy, motherhood, and the female body. The Gothic is a vehicle for communicating the anxiety that centered around mixing and miscegenation in the New South. In her article, "Crossing Liminal Spaces: Teaching the Postcolonial Gothic" Gina Wisker explains that "postcolonial spaces, worldviews, writers, writings and reading are inevitably Gothic, since the... are haunted by the ghosts of those who were hidden and silenced in the colonial and imperial past" (402). Wisker's description of a haunted space could easily describe New Orleans. Ghosts and voices from the past rise to the surface in Chopin's and Hopkins's fiction, creating haunting and tension similar to Wisker's postcolonial Gothic. Understanding the U.S. South as a postcolonial space reshapes the conversation about the Gothic, as it links the U.S. South to its neighbors in the Caribbean, and also to its connections across the ocean.[5] These connections would have been fraught with anxiety for a late nineteenth-century reading audience because they unhinge the South from essentialism and blur the binary logic of the plantation. Reading "Désirée's Baby" and "La Belle Zoraïde" with their Gothic tendencies in mind illuminates the plantation's synchronicity—connections between characters are far more multifaceted than the white patriarchy would desire to acknowledge. Hopkins's *Contending Forces* also utilizes many traditional elements of Gothic nineteenth-century sentimental texts, including fainting spells, secret histories, and violent male predators. Chopin and Hopkins's texts are not ghost stories; elements of the supernatural are muted, producing texts that are not traditionally read as Gothic, although Charles Crow has argued that "Désirée's Baby" is in many ways emblematic of the American Gothic tradition.[6] Still, small details and descriptions evoke the Gothic and link the anxiety pervaded postbellum America.

In both "Désirée's Baby" and "La Belle Zoraïde," Chopin explores the effects of miscegenation that were a result of slavery. These stories consider slavery's impact on both white women and mixed-race women, and at times they implicitly criticize the upper-class women who were complicit in the abusive slavery system. This emphasis on miscegenation is indicative of Chopin's preoccupation with genealogy, similar to Hopkins's obsession with her characters' origins and family history. These two stories are unique in the canon of Chopin's work; she primarily focuses on the oppression white, upper-class women experienced.[7] In these texts, Gothic imagery indicates that hybridity is volatile; terrifying images surround the idea that the plantation hierarchy might be subverted.

Chopin characterizes the plantation by including Gothic imagery: Désirée appears to be a happy young mother at first, despite the dark descriptions of L'Abri, "a sad looking place... [where] [t]he roof came down steep and black like a cowl," but she later says "I'm so happy; it frightens me" (243–4). Désirée's happiness is a result of her husband's change in personality since the birth of her son: "Marriage, and later the birth of his son, had softened Armand Aubigny's imperious and exacting nature greatly" (244). Armand's personality becomes harsh again when he realizes that his son is mixed-race, and there is once again darkness surrounding the plantation. Désirée "awoke one day to the conviction that there was something in the air menacing her peace. It was at first too subtle to grasp"; her realization is followed by "a strange, an awful change in her husband's manner" (244). Detailed descriptions of skin color contribute to the ominous feel of the story; when Désirée glances over at one of the other children on the plantation, she realizes the reason for her husband's anger: "She looked from her child to the boy who stood beside him, and back again; over and over." (245). Désirée's recognition that her son is her "Other" indicates that she lives in the liminal space of the postcolonial Gothic; the dualistic world of the plantation South is blurred and becomes defined by hybridity. When Désirée realizes that her son is not white, she asks her husband, "What does it mean? Tell me" (245). According to Ellen Peel,

> The story takes place in an antebellum Creole community ruled by institutions based on apparently clear dualities: master over slave, white over black, and man over woman. Complacently deciphering the unruffled surface of this symbolic system, the characters feel confident that they know who belongs in which category and what signifies membership in each category. (224)

However, characters who appear to be white may not be a terrifying notion for the plantocracy that is heavily invested in the plantation economy.

Although she resists the connection, having a mixed-race son associates Désirée with the other women in her life, particularly La Blanche and Zandrine. When Armand points La Blanche out to Désirée, saying that her hand is "as white as La Blanche's," he disrupts signification because "La Blanche" literally means "the white one" (245). In fact, Chopin carefully crafts language describing the varied skin tones of each character in the story. Désirée is described as "fair" and "pale," Zandrine's skin is "yellow," and Armand has a "dark handsome face." The ending of the story reveals that it was Armand, after all who was not white. He realizes that his mother was mixed-race when he finds a letter she wrote that explains: "I thank the good God for having so arranged our lives that our dear Armand will never know that his mother, who adores him, belongs to the race that is cursed with the brand of slavery" (247). Female genealogy defines Armand and his family. Through the orphans and secret histories in the story, a hybrid world emerges.

In "La Belle Zoraïde," images of the grotesque and the monstrous connect to the ever-present fear of miscegenation. For Zoraïde, pregnancy and birth are marked with the understanding that she is not in control of her own fate; this lack of control connects to the idea of childbirth and reproduction as terrifying, a familiar theme in Gothic fiction.[8] When Zoraïde falls in love with a dark-skinned man, she commits a crime against the statutes of the plantation south because she chooses him rather than a mulatto man as her lover. She protests against the dualistic understanding of race when she tells her mistress about her love for Mézor: "'I am not white,' persisted Zoraïde, respectfully and gently. 'Doctor Langlé gives me his slave to marry, but he would not give me his son. Then, since I am not white, let me have from out of my own race the one whom my heart has chosen'" (314). Her mistress's response to Zoraïde's choice and to her pregnancy demonstrate Zoraïde's status as a commodity. The childbirth scene connects readers to a traumatic postpartum period rather than depicting birth as a fulfilling and hopeful event: "La belle Zoraïde's sorrows had now begun in earnest. Not only sorrows but sufferings, and with the anguish of maternity came the shadow of death" (315). As soon as Zoraïde gives birth to her baby, her mistress takes it away and tells Zoraïde that her baby is dead. Chopin includes the familiar Gothic trope of the mother who cannot let go of her dead baby's body when Zoraïde becomes obsessed with a bundle of rags she believes to be her child: "Night nor day did she lose sight of the doll that lay in her bed or in her arms" (316). Her insanity can be seen as the result of her decision to make a choice for herself: Chopin's contemporary audience would have easily recognized this link, since many of them may have been involved in the suffrage movement. As Adrienne Rich explains in *Of Woman Born,* "If education was supposed to atrophy the female reproductive organs, women's suffrage was seen as creating 'insane asylums in every county'" (170). Her insanity contrasts to the traditional nineteenth-century image of motherhood—what is normally seen as idyllic and peaceful has become horrifying and grotesque.

The image of motherhood in Zoraïde's story also contrasts with the complicated relationship between Manna Loulou and Madame DeLisle. Manna Loulou most likely breastfed Madame Delisle as an infant and cared for her throughout her life on the plantation, and after Madame's marriage, she has moved with her to her new home. This relationship gives us a new understanding of family in a post-slavery world—these two women are bonded very closely, but their connection is a slave–master relationship as well as a mother/child relationship. Patricia Yaeger writes about the slave–master breastfeeding relationship in these terms: "milk has the power to initiate new genealogies" (784). The relationship between Manna Loulou and Madame DeLise powerfully demonstrates this. She tells the story of Zoraïde to her mistress in order to put her to sleep, but "she told it to her mistress in the soft Creole patois, whose music and charm no English words can convey" (312). According to Handley, "The term *creole* or *criollo* in Spanish, originally was used in the New World slave market to refer to black slaves born in the Americas . . . but it later came to refer to white-identified Europeans born in the New World and suckled by black wet nurses" (47). The term demonstrates the complicated relationship between Manna Loulou and Madame DeLisle, and Zoraïde's story indicates the volatility of this relationship.

Hopkins was more politically driven than Chopin, and her novel is aimed toward a reading audience of white, middle-class women, with the purpose of encouraging them to become politically active on behalf of the African American community. She utilizes the popular Gothic genre to draw in her intended audience. She also includes detailed descriptions of lynching violence, feeding her readers' voyeuristic desires. These detailed descriptions are premissible in a sentimental novel because they are included as newspaper accounts or as part of activist meetings; including them in this form separates the author and the reader from the grotesque details. For example, one included newspaper account describes a man who "was bound to a tree, pieces of flesh were stripped from his body, his eyes were gouged out, his ears cut off, his nose split open, and his legs broken at the knees" (223). Grotesquely detailed but riveting descriptions invited her audience's voyeurism, too: Hopkins goes to an extreme here and in other places in *Contending Forces*, using language in order to create excess and to register the extremes of white panic.[9]

Hopkins's most subversive act is the creation of a "True Woman" in Sappho, who provides a twist on the female Gothic heroine because she experienced rape and sexual abuse before her narrative even began. Sappho's kind and gentle demeanor, as well as her domestic gifts and capabilities, draw the reader in, but Hopkins waits until the end of the novel to reveal that Sappho actually has a secret sexual history. And her story also involves a dark villain, but in this case his abuse is doubly horrifying because he both a white man and her uncle. The stereotypes of a black woman as "a hot-blooded, exotic whore" or a "cringing, terrified victim," as described by Frances Smith Foster in *Witnessing Slavery*, could have been applied to Sappho by members of the plantocracy, but Hopkins manipulates her readers by drawing them into relationship with her (131).

By making the villain a member of Sappho's family, Hopkins subverts the image of the plantation as nostalgic. The author describes the rapist as "an educated man, descended from a very wealthy family. His father had been his owner" (258). Monsieur Beauban's older brother is a powerful man who shares his father's affection for mixed-race women, and he was "extremely fond" of Mabelle, Beauban's oldest daughter. When Mabelle (known as Sappho when she is older) turns 14, her uncle kidnaps her, keeps her in a brothel, and rapes her repeatedly. Pregnancy is the terrifying result of rape for Mabelle. For Sappho, or Mabelle, pregnancy and birth carry the elements of the Gothic: guilt, dread, and flight. Her child is born in a convent, and raised by someone who loves him, but Sappho believes that she can never know the joy of motherhood, thus creating another foundling. By including Grace Montfort's story at the beginning of the novel, and by including characters throughout who do not know or do not claim their own family histories, Hopkins links Sappho's story to the stories of other African American women, indicating the synchronic connections that exist between individuals. Sappho's uncle experiences no grief over what he has done to his own relative; instead he offers to pay his brother one thousand dollars and "call it square" (259). This connects Sappho's uncle to the darkest Gothic predators, but in creating him, Hopkins also illuminates the darker secret histories of race relations in late-nineteenth-century America.

Exploring the connections between motherhood and genealogy in "Désirée's Baby," "La Belle Zoraïde," and *Contending Forces*, reveals connections between characters in these texts and undermines the patriarchal order of the plantation South. Comparing these three works helps the reader see the "persistence of slavery's legacies" (Handley 15) by demonstrating the ways women of different races and social statuses deal with the anxiety that surfaces when the plantation's hierarchy is questioned. Kate Chopin and Pauline Hopkins have crafted stories that center around women and privilege the female experience. Women are connected to other women, white and black, past and present, and these connections promote a vision of the plantation South as a hybrid space, rather than a space that submits to traditional binary logic. Chopin and Hopkins also portray the deep anxiety that surfaces as a result of the transition from Old South to New South by depicting miscegenation as dangerous and volatile. They show violent responses to threats to the plantation order—a baby is stolen from her mother, a woman is violently raped when she is suspected of having mixed ethnic heritage, and a husband abandons his wife because their son is not "white." These two authors weave connections between women across time, and they also connect women of varying classes and races. Chopin and Hopkins come from different racial and cultural backgrounds, but when their texts are paired, they work together to highlight synchronic connections between women, and these connections contrast with the traditional linear and hierarchical understanding of relationships that upheld the plantation.

Notes

1. The ideology of the plantation allowed a paternalistic relationship between whites and blacks, masters and slaves; it was possible to understand slaves as "family" members while abusing them. Sexual relationships between slave owners and their female slaves were not consensual, and contributed to an insidious system that was abusive toward black women.
2. "Désirée's Baby" is not a frame narrative, but as part of the short story collection, *Bayou Folk*, it reflects on the past. Some stories in the collection, including "Désirée's Baby," are set before the Civil War, and some are set after the war.
3. Hazel Carby discusses the rediscovery of *Contending Forces* in her book *Reconstructing Womanhood* (NewYork: Oxford UP, 1987) and Claudia Tate discusses the same in "Pauline Hopkins: Our Literary Foremother," in *Conjuring Black Women, Fiction, and Literary Tradition*, ed. Marjorie Pryse and Hortense J. J. Spillers (Bloomington: Indiana UP, 1985).
4. In "Edna Pontellier, Adèle Ratignolle, and the Unnamed Nurse: A Triptych of Maternity in *The Awakening*," Katie Berry Frye explains that late nineteenth-century New Orleans had a reputation for "quadroon beauties and interracial intimacy," but it also became "the setting of some of the harshest and earliest Jim Crow laws." Jim Crow laws applied to blacks regardless of whether or not they

had mixed ancestry because "miscegenation evinced a sincere and profound terror of the decline of the white population" (47).

5. I do not have the space to justify understanding the U.S. South as a postcolonial space as part of this chapter, but several recent texts have explored this possibility, including Melanie Benson's *Disturbing Calculations: The Economics of Identity in Postcolonial Southern Literature, 1912–2002* and Jon Smith and Deborah Cohn's *Look Away! The U.S. South in New World Studies.*
6. Further discussion of Chopin and the American Gothic tradition can be found in chapter 4.
7. I agree with Catherine Lundie, who acknowledges that Chopin's views on race were progressive for her time, but she argues that "it is important to recognize that [Chopin's] writing is that of a privileged white Southern woman" (129). Chopin could not have effectively described the injustices black women endured because she did not experience them herself.
8. In *Literary Women,* Ellen Moers uses Mary Shelley's *Frankenstein* as the seminal female Gothic text because, she argues, it is centered around the experience of giving birth. Moers says "Here, I think, is where Mary Shelley's book is most interesting, most powerful, and most feminine: in the motif of revulsion against newborn life, and the drama of guilt, dread, and flight surrounding birth and its consequences. Most of the novel…can be said to deal with the retribution visited upon monster and creator for deficient infant care" (93).
9. This use of excess resonates with Patricia Yaeger's article, "Circum-Atlantic Abundance: Milk as World-Making in Alice Randall and Kara Walker." See page 774 for more discussion of excess.

Works Cited

Aiken, Charles. *The Cotton Plantation South since the Civil War.* Baltimore: The Johns Hopkins UP, 2003. Print.

Allen, Carol. *Black Women Intellectuals: Strategies of Nation, Family, and Neighborhood in the Works of Pauline Hopkins, Jessie Fauset, and Marita Bonner.* New York: Routledge, 1998. Print.

Brown, Lois. *Pauline Elizabeth Hopkins: Black Daughter of the Revolution.* Chapel Hill: U of North Carolina P, 2008. Print.

Carby, Hazel. "'On the Threshold of Woman's Era': Lynching, Empire, and Sexuality in Black Feminist Theory." *"Race", Writing, and Difference.* Ed. Henry Louis Gates, Jr. Chicago: U of Chicago P, 1988: 301–16. Print.

Chopin, Kate. *Complete Novels and Stories.* New York: Library of America, 2002. Print.

Frye, Katie Berry. "Edna Pontellier, Adèle Ratignolle, and the Unnamed Nurse: A Triptych of Maternity in *The Awakening.*" *Southern Studies: An*

Interdisciplinary Journal of the South 13.3–4 (2006 Fall–Winter 2006): 45–66. Print.

Handley, George. "A New World Poetics of Oblivion." *Look Away!: The U.S. South in New World Studies*. Ed. John Smith and Deborah Cohn. Durham: Duke UP, 2004. Print.

———. *Postslavery Literatures in the Americas: Family Portraits in Black and White*. Charlottesville: UP of Virginia, 2000. Print.

Hopkins, Pauline. *Contending Forces*. New York: Oxford UP, 1988. Print.

Lundie, Catherine. "Doubly Dispossessed: Kate Chopin's Women of Color." *Louisiana Literature: A Review of Literature and Humanities* 11.1 (Spring 1994): 126–44. Print.

McCullough, Kate. "Slavery Sexuality and Genre: Pauline Hopkins and the Representation of Female Desire." *The Unruly Voice: Rediscovering Pauline Elizabeth Hopkins*. Ed. John Gruesser. Urbana: The U of Illinois P, 1996. Print.

Moers, Ellen. *Literary Women*. Garden City, NY: Doubleday, 1976. Print.

Peel, Ellen. "Semiotic Subversion in 'Désirée's Baby'." *American Literature: A Journal of Literary History, Criticism, and Bibliography* 62.2 (June 1990): 223–37. Print.

Rich, Adrienne. *Of Woman Born: Motherhood as Experience and Institution*. 2nd ed. New York: W.W. Norton, 1995. Print.

Russ, Elizabeth Christine. *The Plantation in the Postslavery Imagination*. New York: Oxford UP, 2009. Print.

Wisker, Gina. "Crossing Liminal Spaces: Teaching the Postcolonial Gothic." *Pedagogy: Critical Approaches to Teaching Literature, Language, Composition, and Culture* 7.3 (Fall 2007): 401–25. Print.

Yaeger, Patricia. "Circum-Atlantic Superabundance: Milk as World-Making in Alice Randall and Kara Walker." *American Literature: A Journal of Literary History, Criticism, and Bibliography* 78.4 (Dec. 2006): 769–98. Print.

———. *Dirt and Desire: Reconstructing Southern Women's Writing, 1930–1990*. Chicago: The U of Chicago P, 2000. Print.

CHAPTER 10

American Refusals: A Continuum of "I Prefer Not Tos" as Articulated in the Work of Chopin, Hawthorne, Harper, Atherton, and Dreiser

Patricia J. Sehulster

American history reverberates with refusals: I prefer not to . . . follow British rule . . . live within a prescribed social class . . . practice one, dictated religion . . . live any other way than freely, individually, and equally. American literature has reflected this rebellious reinvention through a myriad of voices. As teachers, we must lead our students to seeing the interconnectedness of those voices. As Kristeva has noted, "any text is the absorption and transformation of another" (qtd. Martin 148); as such, discovering intertextuality requires "attention to context—to what has gone before and to the ongoing conversation" (Bloome and Egan-Robertson 31). In asking our students to seek these interconnections, we expand the texts themselves and lead students to metacognitive processes (Elkad-Lehman 40). While Bloome and Egan-Robertson would have us believe that cultural rules exist for what texts can be related and therefore exclude certain sets of texts (312), I contend they err in this premise, and I use as my example here several not often related authors and their texts, spanning a 50-year period: Nathaniel Hawthorne's *Blithedale Romance* (1852); Frances Ellen Watkins Harper's "The Two Offers" (1859); Gertrude Atherton's "Pearls of Loreto" (1893); Kate Chopin's "Wiser Than a God" (1889), "A Respectable Woman" (1894), and "A Pair of Silk Stockings" (1896); and Theodore Dreiser's *Sister Carrie* (1900). Just as Toni Morrison has proposed the intertextuality of all American literature through her Africanist presence theory, I propose the lens of a female presence: an ongoing dialogue about how women in a nation founded on the values of individualism and freedom manage their lives when society consigns them predominantly to romance/sentiment, family, and community and so forces a quite American and constant tug between individual liberty and social cohesion that ultimately requires the annihilation of that binary construct.[1]

In demanding that students construct intertextual connections, I ask them to suspend what Gayatri Spivak has termed "the silent programming" encouraged by an American literary canon dominated by exclusions rather than inclusions (Mulford 108) and by relegating works to the status of minor and major. Instead, I guide them to embrace Louise Bernikow's assertion that a continuity and connection among male and female (as well as white and nonwhite) writers exists. Teaching such an inclusive canon—one that envelops but one rule to enhance our understanding of the American experience and the human experience—has become increasingly possible in this era of digitized texts, for even once obscure and out-of-print literature now survives electronically.

Whether we construct our American literature canon electronically or utilize a combination of standard anthology selections and the digitized pieces, we can frame our entire semester's study with the question of refusal. For example, in the syllabus description of my American Literature through the Nineteenth Century course, which I subtitle "A Continuum of Refusals?", I note that we will engage with several questions, including "What do our characters refuse to do, and what do those refusals say about the American culture in particular and the human condition in general?"[2] Though we can engage that inquiry from American literature's very beginnings, I focus here only on that narrow, almost 50-year span between 1852 and 1900. If we use Kate Chopin's work as a centering point within that period, we can easily see its intertextuality with works that have come before and after it, and we can focus that conversation on the female presence discourse.

While Chopin's works have gained "their proper place in the canon of American literature [. . .] squarely in the mainstream of nineteenth-century literary currents" (Lauter 413), and frequently critics view her short stories as thematic experiments that ultimately reach fruition only in *The Awakening* (1889), I contend her short stories offer their own value as presenting ways of refusing the male–female/individual–community binary, of offering what Bernard Koloski labels, people "yearning for something [Chopin] often calls 'rights of existence'—a chance for [. . .] physical and material freedom and fulfillment" (81). They posit both a refusal of the culture's patriarchy and a way of embracing a new discourse. In addition, in asking students to perceive Chopin's work in this manner—as a part of a whole, instead of as a separate, differently valued entity—we offer them an opportunity for improved understanding of Chopin's texts. While the most frequently anthologized works include "Désirée's Baby" (1892), "The Story of an Hour" (1894), "The Storm" (1898), and *The Awakening* (1898), "Wiser than a God", "A Respectable Woman," and "A Pair of Silk Stockings" provide readers with an easily accessible entry point to the dialogue with Hawthorne, Harper, Atherton, and Dreiser. They also offer us a glimpse of Chopin beyond those traditional categorizations of only southern regionalist writer, local color writer, realist writer, or feminist writer. And as I seek to move my students beyond such categories to encompass what Chopin, herself, valued as "human existence in its subtle, complex, true meaning, stripped of the veil with which ethical and conventional standards have draped it" (qtd. Koloski xiii), these stories serve well because they come less encumbered with preexisting assumptions than the often anthologized others might.

While "Wiser than a God" engages with nineteenth-century readers' assumptions about women's domestic roles and presents instead the possibility of what the *Mirror*'s William Marion Reedy termed woman's "evol[ution] from a doll into a human being [. . . who does not have to] sacrifice her individuality" (qtd. Toth 117), it presents perhaps the most optimistic view of female options Chopin would ever offer.[3] The character Paula Von Stoltz makes conscious and calculated choices to achieve her own vision of herself and her life; she wishes no less than that which her father has wished for her: to "be at the head" (Chopin, "Wiser than a God" 660). She refuses not just her suitor, George Brainard, but also society's definition of who she ought to become: a wife and mother content to use less than her abilities merely to entertain guests as a hostess—to act, in essence, as she does at the party that requires of her only a knowledge of dance pieces to serve as "the pleasing distraction of an idle moment" (668). She seeks instead to give into the temptation to "flights of originality" and the very entity the Steinway offers, "inviting possibilities" (661, 663). When George asks her to marry him, he makes the request more of a command as he shouts, "You will be my wife! From this moment we belong to each other!" (668). Though he also declares his love, he uses terms of ownership, and when she refuses his proposal, he warns her not to "speak like a mad woman" (668). George represents all of society in that single condemnation; for Paula to refuse to accept the standard domestic path for a woman to pursue instead a career and a life of fulfilled self-expression strikes others as an insane rejection of the norms. Yet, even Paula knows how much that standard courses through her own thinking, for she tells George to "Hush, don't tempt me further" (668) and ultimately runs from that temptation. In her running, she demonstrates a kind of self-knowledge that hastens her self- actualization (Weatherford 100). While Paula seems unable to envision anything beyond the binary—marriage–love or career–self-fulfillment, Chopin offers a vision beyond that constriction, for she ends the story with the line that Paula "is resting in Leipsic, after an extended and remunerative concert tour. Professor Max Kuntzler is also in Leipsic" (669). Paula has in fact managed to acquire fame, wealth, and love by following her own path and refusing what others would have demanded she follow.

On some level, Chopin's story follows a paradigm similar to that of Harper's "The Two Offers," written 30 years earlier than "Wiser than a God." While Harper provides a decidedly more didactic text than Chopin's, Harper articulates the same vision regarding choices for women. Harper does so by juxtaposing two female characters, Laura Lagrange and Janette Alston. Laura Lagrange represents the unliberated woman, the female tied to the old order because she does not so much choose domesticity as feel it provides the only viable way for a woman to survive. She receives two offers of marriage and cannot decide what she should do. Janette Alston, her cousin, tells her to accept neither offer because

> a woman who is undecided between two offers has not love enough for either to make a choice; and in that very hesitation, indecision, she has a reason to pause and seriously reflect, lest her marriage, instead of being an affinity of souls or a union of hearts should only be a mere matter of bargain and sale, or an affair of convenience and selfish interest (106).

In these few potent lines, Harper's rhetoric points to the fact that the wrongly motivated marriage becomes nothing more than a woman's sale of herself for reasons of her self-preservation. In spite of Janette's scathing indictment of marriage for economic surety, Laura replies, "But then if I refuse, there is the risk of being an old maid" (106). Janette immediately asks her "is that the most dreadful fate that can befall a woman?" (106). Janette cannot convince Laura that women need not become wives and mothers. Laura ultimately mocks Janette and accuses her of not understanding because, though she is kind and affectionate, she has never known love and so she cannot possibly understand Laura's predicament.

But Janette has, in fact, "known the mystic and solemn strength of all absorbing love [,... but as] an intellectual woman, whose genius gave life and vivacity to the social circle" (107), when she loses her love, she "finds calmness and strength [...and is] constantly developing" (108). She enjoys her life as a single, intellectual woman, and often, her freedom enables her to minister to the needs of others. That Jannette remains unmarried but has a superior intellect and education demonstrates her refusal to accept the standard her cousin does. Through her marriage, Laura ultimately discovers a worse fate than becoming an old maid, for her husband does nothing but break her heart, and she develops into a woman who can merely go through life weeping and whispering and finally, dying. Harper neither condemns marriage nor Laura or her husband, but uses the outside narrator to offer a different system for women:

> But woman—the true woman—if you would render her happy, it needs more than the mere development of her affectional nature. Her conscience should be enlightened, her faith in the true and right established, and scope given to her heaven-endowed and God-given faculties. The true aim of female education should be, not a development of one or two, but all the faculties of the human soul, because no perfect womanhood is developed by imperfect culture. (109)

Laura represents the antithesis of this ideal woman; she has cultivated only her love for her husband, and as a result, she has become a self-absorbed, weeping woman who experiences the "slowly wasting of vital forces, the sickness of the soul" (113). Conversely, Janette represents the woman who acts "too self-reliant to depend on the charity of relations [...and] endeavor[s] to support herself by her own exertions" (107). While Janette, unlike Chopin's Paula, never finds the fulfillment of having all possibilities—marriage, career, and her own earned wealth—she does consciously direct her own kind of fulfillment.[4]

Seeking such fulfillment becomes the text of Chopin's "A Pair of Silk Stockings," though the main character, Mrs. Sommers, enjoys that type of self-actualization only for the brief span of a day, very much in the present and without any contemplation of a future that offers the same kind of self-focus. As Koloski notes, Mrs. Sommers "concentrates on the present, following the instincts she does not consciously control" (74). Yet, in spite of this lack of conscious control, Mrs. Sommers does "find success specifically within her own, interior consciousness" (Kornhaber and Kornhaber 29). Though Chopin creates Mrs. Sommers five years after her invention of Paula, Chopin seems to have lost some of the optimism found in that story's outcome. In this text, we find a woman so immersed in her responsibilities as wife and mother that "For a day or two she walked about [. . .] really absorbed in speculation and calculation" regarding how to spend her fifteen dollar windfall (Chopin, "A Pair of Silk Stockings" 816). Initially, she contemplates all uses for her children, husband, and household, but as she begins her shopping, she instead finds herself "taking a rest from that laborious and fatiguing function and to have abandoned herself to some mechanical impulse that directed her actions and freed her of responsibility" (818). Mrs. Sommers finds a responsibility to herself alone; that Chopin marks this behavior as a "mechanical impulse," as if it were natural, as what ought to exist in the core of a human being. As Ewell has noted, Mrs. Sommers's "self-neglect is evident in her amazement, as she buys new shoes, that those pretty feet and ankles [are actually her own]" (142). In this single day of spending on herself—of using material accumulations to fulfill a need to tend to herself and escape the constant constraints of fulfilling the roles of mother and wife—Mrs. Sommers gives into the long-ago, premarriage self she can barely remember. When left to indulge herself—to refuse to accept her married role—Mrs. Sommers finds a confident person capable of making decisions for herself. But alas, like the play she sees, the "dream ended" (820), and Mrs. Sommers returns home with "a powerful longing that the cable car would never stop anywhere, but go on and on with her forever" (820). That Mrs. Sommers must leave that which moves exhilaratingly forward brings her great disappointment, for stopping that ride means arresting the life of her own fulfillment and self-actualization. Chopin offers here a life of such focus on selfhood as mere fantasy for women who marry.

A year prior to Chopin's fictional condemnation of the constraints of marriage, Gertrude Atherton offered the public a story that also convicts society's norms for women in "The Pearls of Loreto" (1893). In this piece, Ysabel, "haughty, passionate, restless, pleasure-loving" (305)—in other words, independent-minded, but not free to be independent—is so motivated to marry for economic reasons alone, that she declares that she will marry no man who does not bring her piles of pearls. Don Vincente de la Vega y Arillaga asks her if it is true: "That you have put a price upon yourself?" (304). Atherton's blatant use of the word "price" emphasizes her condemnation of marriage for economic reasons—the very system nineteenth-century society put into place by refusing women economic independence. Ysabel has, of course sold herself, and in doing so, she serves as an obvious exaggeration of what society has done by demanding that women not work and not have any semblance of independence. Don Vincente de la Vega y Arillaga, however, desires Ysabel so much that he decides to get the pearls, though first, he asks her to "swear to me that you will wed me when I return, no matter how or where I find those pearls" (306). Like Ysabel, he, too, embraces the expectations of society by demonstrating his will to go to great lengths to provide for this woman what she wants. Again, Atherton condemns through blatant hyperbole, for Don Vincente de la Vega y Arillaga does find the pearls, and he acquires them by desecrating a sacred statue of the Virgin Mary and by murdering the monk who catches him doing so. But Atherton also demonstrates the price these two and the community must pay for adhering to such expectations. Ultimately, the community members who own the statue track and find Don Vincente de la Vega y Arillaga, and to escape its members'—a suddenly wild, violent, inhuman mob—retribution, Ysabel and Don Vincente de la Vega y Arillaga jump off a cliff to their death. Atherton here steps beyond Chopin, for she paints the dependent woman as a source of moral depravity and so makes a moral argument for women's emancipation. In this case, not only Ysabel and De La Vega pay, but also the community from which the pearls come and the community to which Ysabel belongs. In this text, failure to refuse a corrupt standard taints everyone.[5]

The temptation faced by women who must live with a corrupt standard becomes the focus of Chopin's "A Respectable Woman." Even its title portends a sarcastic kind of condemnation. In this story, Mrs. Baroda moves beyond the small defiance of Chopin's Mrs. Sommers's spending a day and 15 dollars on herself by gaining the kind of consciousness of herself to contemplate thwarting societal norms by "modif[ying] Darwin's theory of sexual selection by choosing her own lover" (Bender 91). The very adherence to the convention of serving as hostess for her husband's guest actually brings her to an understanding of "options she had not much contemplated before" (Koloski 36). She initially flees, "being a respectable woman [. . . and] a very sensible one" (Chopin, "A Respectable Woman" 509), for she fears her own sensual reaction to the guest, Gouvernail, to whom she "wanted to reach out her hand in the darkness and touch [. . .] with the sensitive tips of her fingers" (509). Her running away from her own desire, however, ultimately leaves her time to do battle alone (509) by wrestling with her own feelings and longing. In her self-conscious discovery, she decides that she has "overcome everything! [...and she] shall be very nice to [Gouvernail]" (509). She has concluded that respectability does not really matter to her, for the label comes from a society that has conscribed her to the role and lover she does not necessarily want for herself. Chopin provides her with an alternative—a choice that touches upon the very sexual mores that have confined women to the role of passive, accepting vessel. Mrs. Baroda's mere contemplation of a future in which she does not adhere to this assigned role marks her refusal to accept a standard she has had no part in creating.[6]

Contemplation of such refusals of sexual standards for women came as early as the 1852 publication of Nathaniel Hawthorne's *Blithedale Romance*. While critics have more often focused on Hawthorne's *The Scarlet Letter*'s Hester and her relation to feminist theory, in the character of Zenobia, Hawthorne also offers a paradigm of refusal very parallel with Chopin's models. Though many critics sense in Hawthorne a canonized male author who shows us "female characters and relations between the sexes in a way that both reflects and contributed to sexist ideology" (Robinson 84), I contend in this case at least—in spite of Hawthorne's "damned mob of scribbling women" comment preceding the book's publication—Hawthorne actually presents a complex portrait of women. While Christophersen perceives all of the characters, including the females, as having a "lack of self-awareness" (82), I argue that Wolter, Dill, and Mills assess Zenobia more accurately; the free-loving Zenobia and virginal Priscilla stand as the antithesis of each other.

In many ways, Zenobia's self-awareness includes her conscious donning of some personas—her public name, her portrayal of beauty, and her acceptance of the domestic roles of Blithedale—to move her own agenda forward. While Chrisopherson notes that Zenobia's unconscious personas (veils) make it "impossible to live under the veil, yet potentially fatal to remove it" (89) and so help lead to her suicide, I note that from the very beginning, Zenobia unmasks her own personas, when, for example, she declares, "it may be that some of us, who wear the petticoat, will go afield, and leave the weaker brethren to take our places in the kitchen" (Hawthorne 16). Clearly, in this place set apart from society, she sees that possibility of leaving "the rusty iron frame-work of society behind" (19), and she includes as part of that rusty framework society's conspiracy to leave women unhappy "after discovering that fate has assigned her but one single event, which she must contrive to make the substance of her whole life [...while] a man has his choice of innumerable events" (60).

Repeatedly, Zenobia looks to Blithedale as a place that could at last expand that "sphere of ordinary womanhood [which she felt was] to be narrower than her development required" (190). Zenobia represents that woman who "trespasses against patriarchal privilege" and "masculine perogatives" (Mills 104), for she fully expects Blithedale—and its creators and inhabitants—to live up to its promises: "new roles, new relationships, and freedom as a woman" (Mills 99). Yet, when Zenobia discovers the treachery of Hollingsworth's false motives and his desire to marry Priscilla—the woman who "appears weak and has a need to please others, so fits authoritative tastes" (Dill 73)—and understands her own treachery in betraying her sister (an act akin to betraying herself and the general sisterhood of womanhood [Mills 115]), Zenobia can feel only a kind of hopelessness. Unlike Chopin's Mrs. Sommers, who does not even consider a future or Mrs. Baroda and Paula Von Stoltz, who look forward to a future, Zenobia has lost her will to look toward a future. She, who early in the text, embraces newness, realizes, "There are no new truths, much as we have prided ourselves on finding some" (Hawthorne 224), and she can see no softening to that reality. In facing that harshness, Zenobia refuses to move forward and "chooses" to end her own life, not because she has lost Hollingsworth, but because of the loss of the ideal of Blithedale and the ideal of herself. While Dill sees this suicide as an act of a sentimental woman "honoring the heart" (66), I suggest the suicide surfaces as the act of refusal to accept the world on its terms, for she feels "sick to death of playing at [. . .] progress" (Hawthorne 227). She makes a conscious decision to die on her own terms, for she bids farewell to Coverdale and leaves messages for others. She does not cast about irrationally, but makes a self-determined decision to leave a world unacceptable to her. She dies in the water, that place "symbolically tied to empowerment and rebirth" (Wolter 28). She takes the free choices of Chopin's and Harper's strong, female characters to the ultimate level: the free choice of refusing to live.

By 1900, Theodore Dreiser entered this discourse on women's choices in his *Sister Carrie*. In this novel, we find a woman who assumes control over her own objectification. She develops her own consciousness and discovers and applies her own agency, manages her own negotiations, and by the end of the novel, has even assumed full authority over the scripts she uses in her theatrical career. On some level, in her use of objects to create a kind of self-actualization, Chopin's Mrs. Sommers foreshadows Carrie Meeber, who "challenges woman's social objectification and commodification by using objects to make and remake the self" (Lemaster 41–42). Rather than refusing to participate in the system, she refuses to allow her objectification on its terms and instead uses the system's rules to her own benefit and to gain that fulfillment she desires. Carrie emerges in a "dual role of consumer commodity and commodity consumer" (Loranger 79). She has discovered that her sexuality can enable her to take charge of the very marketplace that would view her as a commodity because of her gender and turn it to her own advantage in acquiring the money that gives her the power she most desires. Carrie, like other women trapped in a role, "longed and longed and longed" (Dreiser 87), but she refused to leave that longing unanswered; she "was an apt student of fortune's ways" (75). Those studies enabled her to reverse the roles envisioned by society, for she could tell Drouet, "You thought only of what would be to your satisfaction. You thought you could make a toy of me—a plaything. Well, I'll show you that you won't. I'll have nothing more to do with you at all" (165). And Druet replies with a line most associated with a crying female: "Use everything and abuse me and then walk off. That's just like a woman" (165). In this instance, Carrie's behavior does encompass that of the modern woman, one who has "her own ability vividly brought to consciousness" (228). She had discovered that she, herself "was capital" (326). In that discovery dwells the crux of female progress, for while this text utilizes Carrie's physical body, physical beauty, and stage talents to make the point, Carrie's conscious, deliberate refusal to allow others to use these elements to profit from her and her choice to use them for her own gain mark her as a woman in control of her whole self and life. That in the end, she still "dream[s] such happiness as [she] may never feel" (369) may actually reflect more on her striving, capitalist nature than on her freedom as a woman.

Women's refusals to accept assigned roles have filled American literature for centuries. Different texts have broached the subject in different ways, through varying degrees of representation, yet all in discourse with one another. When we ask our students to see this kind of intersecting discourse, we ask them to think about American literature as a continuum instead of as a mere collection of literature by and about Americans. When my students engage in discussion forums, essay assignments, or the final original anthology project by leading with discussions of connections and relationships, with questions about continuity, and with challenges to their own initial perceptions, they have embarked upon a journey to understanding literature beyond mere words and plot. When the students who expressed deep disappointment in Hawthorne's Zenobia's final act suddenly understand "refusal as a conscious choice" after they read Chopin's "Wiser than A God", or a student dismissive of Chopin as "just another feminist writer" finally understands her as "somebody who conveys the American spirit of independence and individuality," I know that they have made connections that advance their thinking. When their final projects—electronic anthologies that must include works by authors we have not studied plus two original compositions of their own—come due, and I find that the students have paired such seemingly unconnected authors as Sarah Winnemucka and Henry James or Henry Adams and Charles Brockton Brown, under thematic questions such as "What does American exceptionalism really mean?" or "Capitalism or Idealism: An Eternal American Conflict?", they have begun to demonstrate the understanding of the interconnections among the texts; instead of simply understanding a collection of literary works, they have discovered an entire conversation. Like the characters in the works of Chopin, Harper, Atherton, Hawthorne, and Dreiser, they have developed a commitment to the Melvillian sentiment, "I prefer not to," for they will never perceive any single piece of literature in a vacuum again. In acquiring that skill, they will then understand every individual author from Chopin to Fitzgerald better than they might have.

Notes

1. I do not mean to imply here that this single, narrow focus offers the only way to read the texts discussed in this chapter, or even that in a semester I use only this single focus or only these texts. Rather, for the purpose of this chapter, I focus on but one example of the use of intertextuality. Each of the works discussed here offers a complex set of social and cultural issues, themes, and possibilities for consideration (including class, race, etc.), but a brief essay limits my scope to a single area.
2. Though I do not address these ideas in this brief chapter, I also include the following question: "What do our refusals—and acceptances—of some pieces of literature to the American literary canon say about our perceptions of America and its culture?"
3. See the following sources for information about nineteenth-century gender theories: Elaine Showalter, "Introduction: The Rise of Gender," in *Speaking of Gender*, ed. Elaine Showalter (New York: Routledge Press, 1989), 2; Linda Lindsay, *Gender Roles: A Sociological Perspective* (New Jersey: Prentice Hall, 1990); Robyn Wiegman, *American Anatomies Theorizing Race and Gender* (Durham, NC: Duke University Press, 1995), 1–8 and 21–78; Carole Pateman, *The Sexual Contract* (Stanford, CA: Stanford University Press, 1988), especially pages 5–17; Juliana Mach Nfah-Abbeny, *Gender in African Women's Writing* (Bloomington:

Indiana University Press, 1997), 17.For information regarding the Cult of True Womanhood and the debate about whether or not it existed for anyone other than white, middle class women and the ways black women reacted to and altered it, see: Barbara Welter, "The Cult of True Womanhood, 1820–1860," *American Quarterly* 18 (Summer 1966): 151–74 (the seminal essay); Hazel V. Carby, *Reconstructing Womanhood: The Emergence of the Afro-American Woman Novelist* (New York: Oxford University Press, 1987); Karen Halttunen, *Confidence Men and Painted Women: A Study of Middle-Class Culture in America, 1830–1870* (New Haven: Yale University Press, 1982); Ann Douglas, *The Feminization of American Culture* (New York: Alfred A. Knopf, 1977); Jane Tompkins, *Sensational Designs: The Cultural Work of American Fiction, 1780–1860* (New York: Oxford University Press, 1985); Nina Baym, *Women's Fiction: A Guide to Novels by and About Women in America, 1820–1870* (Ithaca, NY: Cornell University Press, 1978); Claudia Tate, *Domestic Allegories of Political Desire: The Black Heroine's Text at the Turn of the Century* (New York: Oxford University Press, 1992).Some scholarship has argued that the Cultof True Womanhood and the related theory of the separate spheres did not necessarily exist, or it existed for white, middle-class women only. See especially Cathy Davidson and Jessamyn Hatcher, eds. *No More Separate Spheres: A Next Wave American Studies Reader* (Durham, NC: Duke University Press, 2002). I note also that I have left unstated any information regarding the Cult of Manhood also prevalent at the time. Again, constraints of the narrow focus of this essay prevent me from doing so.

4. Harper continues to develop this theme in later works, especially *Minnie's Sacrifice* (1869) and *Iola Leroy* (1892), in each case offering characters who do ultimately maintain their individuality and self-actualization in addition to marrying.
5. Atherton develops this theme in several other texts as well: *Hermia Suydam* (1859), *The Doomswoman* (1892), *A Whirl Asunder* (1895), *His Fortunate Grace* (1897), and *Patience Sparhawk* (1897).
6. For a full discussion of sexual mores of the nineteenth century, see: Charles E. Rosenberg, 131–7, 140–1, and 145; Ruth H. Bloch, "Untangling the Roots of Modern Sex Roles: A Survey of Four Centuries of Change," *Signs* 4 (Winter 1978): 237–52; Carole Pateman, and John C. Spurlock, ed., 202–31.

Works Cited

Atherton, Gertrude. "Pearls of Loreto." *Before the Gringo Came Stories of Old California*. New York: J. Slewing Tait, 1893. 1–43. Print.

Bender, Bert. "*The Teeth of Desire*: The Awakening *and* The Descent of Man." *Kate Chopin—Updated Edition*. Ed. Harold Bloom. New York: Infobase Publishing, 2007. 89–101. Print.

Bloom, Harold. *Kate Chopin—Updated Edition.* New York: Infobasse Publishing, 2007. Print.

Bloome, David, and Ann Egan-Robertson. "The Social Construction of Intertextuality in Classroom Reading and Writing Lessons. *Reading Research Quarterly* 28.4 (October–November–December 1993): 304–33. *JSTOR*. Web. 30 November 2013.

Chopin, Kate. "A Pair of Silk Stockings." *Chopin Complete Novels and Stories.* New York: The Library of America, 2002. 816–20. Print.

———. "A Respectable Woman." *Chopin Complete Novels and Stories.* New York: The Library of America, 2002. 506–9. Print.

———. "Wiser than a God." *Chopin Complete Novels and Stories*, Ed. Sandra M. Gilbert. New York: The Library of America, 2002. 660–9. Print.

Christophersen, Bill. "Behind the White Veil: Self-Awareness in Hawthorne's 'Blithedale Romance.'" *Modern Language Studies* 12.2 (Spring 1982): 81–92. *MLA International Bibliography*. Web. 20 January 2014.

Dill, Elizabeth. "Angel of the House, Ghost of the Commune: Zenobia as Sentimental Woman in *Blithedale Romance*." *Nathaniel Hawthorne Review* 37.1 (Spring 2011): 62–87. *MLA International Bibliography.* Web. 2 January 2014.

Dreiser, Theodore. *Sister Carrie.* Ed. Donald Pizer. New York: W.W. Norton, 1991. Print.

Elkad-Lehman, Ilana. "Spinning a Tale: Intertextuality and Intertextual Aptitude." *Educational Studies in Language and Literature* 5(2005): 39–56. *Education Source Complete.* Web. 28 December 2013.

Ewell, Barbara C. "Barbara C. Ewell on 'A Pair of Silk Stockings' and 'Neg Creol.'" *Kate Chopin A Study of the Short Fiction.* Ed. Bernard Koloski. New York: Twayne Publishers An Imprint of Simon and Schuster Macmillan, 1996. 141–4. Print.

Harper, Frances Ellen Watkins. "The Two Offers." *A Brighter Coming Day: A Frances Ellen Watkins Harper READER.* Edited and with an Introduction by Frances Smith Foster. New York: The Feminist Press at The City University of New York, 1990. 105–14. Print.

Hawthorne, Nathaniel. *The Blithedale Romance.* New York: Penguin Books, 1986. Print.

Koloski, Bernard. *Kate Chopin A Study of the Short Fiction.* New York: Twayne Publishers An Imprint of Simon and Schuster Macmillan, 1996. Print.

Kornhaber, Donna, and David Kornhaber. "Stage and Status: Theatre and Class in the Short Fiction of Kate Chopin." *Kate Chopin in the Twenty-First Century: New Critical Essays.* Ed. Heather Ostman. New Castle upon Tyne: Cambridge Scholars Publishing, 2008. 15–31. Print.

Lauter, Paul. *The Heath Anthology of American Literature, Fifth Edition.* Stamford, CT: Cengage Learning. 2004. Print.

Lemaster, Tracy. "Feminist Thing Theory in *Sister Carrie*." *Studies in American Naturalism* 4.I (Summer 2009): 41–55. *MLA International Bibliography.* Web. 6 January 2014.

Loranger, Carol S. "'Character and Success': Teaching *Sister Carrie* in the Context of an Ongoing American Debate." *Dreiser Studies* 29.1/2 (1998): 74–84. *MLA International Bibliography*. Web. 6 January 2014.

Martin, Elaine. "Intertextuality: An Introduction." *The Comparatist* 35 (May 2011): 148–51. *Humanities Index*. Web. 30 November 2013.

Mills, Angela. "'The Sweet Word,' Sister: The Transformative Threat of Sisterhood and *The Blithedale Romance*." *ATQ* 17.2 (June 2003): 97–121. *MLA International Bibliography*. Web. 3 January 2014.

Mulford, Carla. "Writing Women in Early American Studies: On Canons, Feminist Critique, and the Work of Writing Women into History." *Tulsa Studies in Women's Literature* 26.1 (Spring 2007): 107–18. *JSTOR*. Web. 12 January 2014.

Papke, Mary E. "Mary E. Papke on 'The Story of an Hour.'" *Kate Chopin A Study of the Short Fiction*. Ed. Bernard Koloski. New York: Twayne Publishers, 1996. 132–4. Print.

Robinson, Lillian S. "Treason Our Text: Feminist Challenges to the Literary Canon." *Tulsa Studies in Women's Literature* 2.1 (Spring 1983): 83–98. JSTOR. Web. 12 January 2014.

Toth, Emily. "Kate Chopin on Divine Love and Suicide: Two Rediscovered Articles." *American Literature* 63.1 (March 1991): 115–21. JSTOR. Web. 26 November 2013.

Weatherford, K. J. "Courageous Souls: Kate Chopin's Women Artists." *American Studies in Scandinavia* 26 (1994): 96–112. American Studies in Scandinavia Online. Web. 26 November 2013.

Wolter, Jurgen. "Southern Hesters: Hawthorne's Influence on Kate Chopin, Toni Morrison, William Faulkner, and Tennessee Williams." *Southern Quarterly* 50.1 (Fall 2012): 24–41. *MLA International Bibliography*. Web. 13 December 2014.

CHAPTER 11

What Did She Die of? "The Story of an Hour" in the Middle East Classroom

Mohanalakshmi Rajakumar and Geetha Rajeswar

Kate Chopin's work is often read as a critique of nineteenth-century marriage and gender roles; it's also used in the curriculum because of its accessibility for beginning readers or nonnative speakers of English. In particular, "The Story of an Hour" has been taught in a variety of settings as an example of American short fiction. This classic example of form is concise, yet takes the reader on a great emotional journey; the surprise twist at the end is an excellent example of dramatic irony, which can also be used to assess reading comprehension. The reversal is indicative of the short story genre as established by early twentieth-century male writers including Guy Maupassant and O. Henry (Chongyue and Lihua 1). Despite its brevity, this narrative presents complex and subtle sentiments about marriage and the role of the wife in domesticity that often resonate with student readers. The idea that literature connects readers to their own life is not a new idea; readers respond to specific themes and focus their analysis around ideas that resonate with their own cultures (Diederich 116).

Through several scenes that take place in the span of a single afternoon, the short story depicts a marriage by revealing the inner emotions of the protagonist who is also a wife. Chopin presents a microcosm of "social, historical and cultural norms" through the main character, Mrs. Louise Mallard's, reaction to news of her husband's unexpected death (Ramos 117). As the story unfolds, the reader is given more and more information, challenging the notions she may have about the emotional state of Louise and Brently Mallard's outwardly happy marriage (Berenji 230). These nuances test reading comprehension as well as present points for active discussion.

My students, mostly of Arab or South Asian background, are studying in the branch campus of Virginia Commonwealth University in Doha, Qatar (VCUQatar). VCUQatar is the oldest university in the Education City project, the largest multiversity in the world, made up of a conglomerate of branch campuses from American universities: "The Qatar Foundation invited a series of American universities to open branch campuses in Qatar and to bring American-style higher education to the country. In less than ten years, six US universities set up campuses in Qatar and were admitting students in specific fields of study" (Kamrava 82).

Each university offers degrees in a few of their key areas; VCUQatar specializes in graphic, fashion, and interior design and has been matriculating students for over 15 years. Within the span of a century, Qatar, the home of the VCUQatar campus in particular, has moved from being a small pearl-diving nation, through a resource-based economy and is currently transitioning itself into a knowledge-based economy. Thus, the past three generations of Qataris have witnessed unprecedented economic, social, and cultural changes. At times there seems a disconnection between the knowledge and practices of the past and the present. While the "erosion of Qatari traditions" is often debated, concrete academic contributions to include issues and debates that are important to students will demonstrate the ability of academia to be relevant to these students' lives, not merely exist as imported ideas. In his introduction to *Qatar: A Modern History*, history professor Allen J.Fromherz explains that Qatar has managed to modernize its economy without major political or social change (5–10). While the commercialization of modern life is evident in cars, restaurants, and other global commodities, Qataris of all ages are fiercely nationalistic. As minority citizens in their own country, there exists a preoccupation regarding the preservation of traditional Qatari culture, mores, and values. All of these tensions and contradictions are present in the classroom as students grapple with American curriculum from their worldviews.

In the course material for Focused Inquiry 1 (UNIV 111), the first part of a two-course sequence in first year writing, I used Chopin to establish the conventions of the short story genre. UNIV 111 is part of the core curriculum and required for all majors; currently taught by the English department faculty, the course goals are the same university wide: "These skills include written communication, oral proficiency, critical thinking, information fluency, ethical and social responsibility and literacy" (Rajakumar Syllabus 1). As the introduction to the analysis of literature, the second unit in UNIV 111 is structured to give first year undergraduates the tools to discuss fiction, including the basics of literary devices such as plot, characters, and dialogue. The students also developed their understanding of how to construct a literary analysis using theme, figurative language, and symbolism. Students then went on to read other short stories by Arab writers from a variety of countries in the Middle East, using the principles, terms, and devices they learned from analyzing Chopin to explore the other stories in the unit.

The final assignment in unit two was to construct a literary comparison of any two stories in the unit. Students were asked to "demonstrate [their] ability to analyze and criticize literature, in this case, short fiction, in essay form in a paper of 3–5 pages" (Rajakumar Essay Guidelines). The charge was specifically to make their own arguments about disparate texts since Chopin was a different era and society than the three Arab writers whose work they read. I discovered Wadad Al Kuwari (Qatar), Nazar Jubran (Oman), and Sharifa Al Shamlan (Saudi) in *Arab Women Writers: An Anthology of Short Stories* (Cohen-Mor). I deliberately included these writers in this unit because often students in Qatar are asked to engage with material that is very eurocentric without any direct relevance to their own everyday lives or Middle Eastern contexts. This was the fourth time I have taught the course; in previous years I used texts from the *Beirut 39* anthology (Shimon), which celebrates 39 writers of Arab descent who are under the age of 39 (Shimon). Choosing such texts allows students to bridge between Western notions of the literary canon and adapt academic discourse, in this case literary analysis, to their own interest and environments. My aim in including these texts is to circumvent the importing of educational practices without contextualizing them. As Dr. Mehran Kamrava explains the challenge of the American classroom in the Middle East: "The pervasiveness of Western universities across the region, especially in Qatar, deepens the possibility that GCC societies become 'consumers, rather than producers, of knowledge, which continues to be generated externally'" (160). In years past, students have chosen two Arab writers to compare; often a theme is the idea of madness at a time of war as in the stories "Frankenstein in Baghdad" and "The Path to Madness" by Mansoura Ez Eldin (Shimon).

This time, however, nearly half of the students in the class chose to compare Chopin with one of the other Arab writers. Students constructed arguments that highlighted the main theme of "The Story of an Hour"—marriage and gender roles—examining how the author depicted freedom, autonomy, and individualism. In their comparisons, they used Chopin's character, Louise Mallard, as a contrasting figure for other protagonists, and created critiques of marriage practices in their own society. Their essays highlighted the similarities in treatment of women by Western and Arab societies with regards to gender expectations for wives and the restrictions placed on married women. They took up the challenge posed by the assignment, which was to "compose a thesis-driven essay which presents at least one of the following literary devices to create a thesis that compares or contrasts two of the stories we have read" (Rajakumar). With dire warnings against plot or narrative summary, they set off to tackle the important themes, symbols, or use of figurative language, creating a matrix of two stories and at least one literary device for analysis.

The essays from the Qatari students were illuminating in that the protagonist of Chopin's story became a foil through which they interpreted married women in their own society. Mrs. Mallard, as she is often referred to in the story, is emblematic of Qatari women who, as members of a collective society, are expected to keep their true emotions to themselves. The silent contemplation Louise undergoes upon receiving bad news is not unfamiliar to the female Qatari reader whose movements are monitored by family members and whose behavior is legally restrained. Qatari women are not allowed to travel abroad without permission from their families, nor are they permitted to enter nightclubs. One student explains Louise Mallard's life in the introduction of her paper: "In "The Story Of An Hour," Mrs. Mallard thinks that she is finally free from the misery of marriage when she hears that her husband has passed away, but when she discovers that he is still alive, the agony of not being free killed her" ("Set Me Free" 1). Another student explains a husband's death as the road to freedom:

> In this case when Mrs. Mallards's [sic] husband has died, she didn't break but grew stronger and was looking forward to live out the rest of her days all by herself and make the best out of it and seek all opportunities she will pass by in her leftover days. "She had previously dreaded the years ahead spent under the thumb of her husband" (paragraph 19) this conveys how much Mrs. Mallard was terrified of looking forward to the rest of her days with him. Also the use of thumb is the symbol of restrictions in her life. And referring to the word under, it shows power and pressure on her. Based on the story, Mr. Brently, Mallards's husband, wasn't really a wicked husband but because his belief agreed with the way he reacted and he thought he has all the right as a husband to guide and direct her life toughly ("Freedom! They Said").

Qatari female students hone in on the unhappiness of the wife and the social conventions that require women to marry, no matter their preferences otherwise.

Nicole Diederich's work supports these findings in her own experiences teaching this particular story. In her article, "Sharing Chopin: Teaching 'The Story of an Hour' to Specialized Populations," Diederich explains how this particular story allows readers to discuss beliefs about marriage and relationship practices in their own culture (117). Such connections are ultimately what are hoped for in the study of literature. Diederich's own use of the story with students in a paramedical professionals program found students' reactions to the protagonist's unexpected death had cultural underpinnings. Her conclusions, that the story allows for vibrant discussion about marriage and martial practices, were confirmed when I taught "The Story of an Hour" in a Middle Eastern classroom with female Arab students. My students felt the same way as contemporary Chinese readers did about the main theme of the story: "It is mainly an expression of women's desire for freedom in the man's world" (Chonguye and Lihua 3). Students from a variety of Arab societies related several of the protagonist's issues to their own culture. Teaching the "The Story of an Hour" in the Middle East classroom raised major discussions about marriage and gender inequality that are not discussed as directly in other fora.

Female Qatari students, in particular, connected the feelings of Mrs. Louise Mallard to their own sociocultural practices. Again and again, they highlighted similarities between Louise and the emotional state of married Qatari women. One student explained her surprise at the relevance of the story in the introduction to her essay: "'The Story of an Hour' was published in 1894, showing how odd this short story still relates to today's issues" ("Unresolved Women's Struggles" 1). Many Qatari women find themselves in companionate marriages similar to those of upper class women in the nineteenth century because of Qatar's emerging status as one of the world's wealthiest nations (Fromherz 5–10). The patriarchal nature of Qatari society means that all women are still under the expectations of traditional gender roles; girls live with their parents until marriage, at which point responsibility for them transfers to their husbands. In such a social context, readers are familiar with "the patriarchal pressures.... [that] posed severe obstacles for even the most privileged women" found in Chopin's writing (Ramos 145). This inequality and male domination is brought up in a student's essay. She explains that Mrs. Mallard hates her life because she must be entirely focused on her husband: "He would bend 'what she wants to what he wants,' force her 'to live the way he wants her to live' and 'do what he wants her to do'" ("Unexpected Deaths" 1). In a society where women are not allowed to travel abroad without a male relative as a companion, the student recognizes how stifling Louise's marriage could be. The ever-present pressures of patriarchy are familiar to the student. Qatari women have restrictions on their mobility to leave the country but also in terms of what is acceptable or unacceptable behavior within their own country; married or single, they often have curfews and are not legally permitted to enter any bar or nightclub. The student focuses on the independence Louise gains from the death of her husband:

> She admits that she loved him and he was kind and loving, she knows that she will cry in his funeral. But that does not mean she is not happy that he passed away. And she is finally free to live her life the way she ever [sic] wanted to. She views Brently's death as a release from cruelty. ("Unexpected Deaths" 2)

Like any wife would, Louise would be upset about her husband's death. She is not happy that he died, but happy to finally get what she deserves (i.e., her independence). For Louise, her freedom meant the world. After being in an oppresive relationship for a long time, her husband's death opened up a new chapter in her life; she can do what she wants to do, live the way she likes to live and make up for all the time she has wasted. The student reads the emotions of the character in relation to the space: "'There stood, facing the open window' representing the freedom and opportunities that await her after her husband died" ("Unexpected Deaths" 2). Therefore, Louise's new life begins with the demise of her husband.

Another student makes a direct comparison between the character, Mrs. Mallard, and women in her own society: "Women in society can relate to Chopin's short story through Mrs. Mallard because they are sometimes frustrated with their own husbands" (Unresolved Women's Struggles in Society). She says further that married Qatari women do not often receive enough "attention" or "love" from their husbands; marital dissatisfaction is also an emotion that Louise struggles with. According to Qatari traditions and culture, once a woman is married, she cannot meet nonrelative males and must completely submit to her husband. She must respect and love him irrespective of how she feels about him.

However, "The Story of an Hour" portrays a very different image of a married woman. The same student mentions in her essay that

Louise "did not love her husband as a typical wife would or else she would have been sobbing uncontrollably for losing him in a tragic way" ("Unresolved Women's Struggles in Society" 2). As a reader she finds similarities between Chopin and an Arab writer, Wedad Al Kawwari, who are both exploring women's place in society. The student explains the grounds for her comparison:

> Al-Kawwari and Chopin both display different women's issues that even after years from publishing their work, women still have similar issues till today. Both authors show how female protagonists deal with those issues and how these events can relate to almost all women across the world, making it universal and relatable. ("Unresolved Women's Struggles" 3)

For this student, the issues of mobility, happiness, and relationships are as current for the readers who were Chopin's contemporaries. She is able to connect Al Kawwari's work within the feminist framework of examining the everyday lives of women: "Both Al-Kawwari and Chopin use foreshadowing in their stories "Layla" and "The Story of an Hour" to portray the female protagonists' struggles with life and death. These struggles are still presented in society for women today" ("Unresolved Women's Struggles" 1). The student's pairing examines the ways in which Chopin and Al Kawwari depict social expectations for women in their respective societies. The student writer explores the similarities in gender roles for Western and Arab women; the protagonist in "Layla" is badgered by her family to become a mother much in the same way Louise feels restricted in her role as a wife. Two other students compared Chopin with Abderrazak Boukebba, who wrote the short story "Skin of Shadow." One student, in her paper, titled "Set Me Free," explores how the respective societies "oppress freedom" for the protagonists (1). In this instance, Louise Mallard's experiences are contrasted with that of Diab, a young boy who does not do the bidding of the Arab village elders. As another student explains the similarity: "'The Story of an Hour' and 'The Skin of Shadow' both represent self-determination and the restrictions they're facing" ("Freedom They Said!" 2). While the struggle is similar, she contrasts the way these struggles for freedom are resolved: "They both had the same concept but still differed with the complete opposite endings" ("Freedom They Said!" 3). These two students read the treatment of women and children, across these different societies, as similarly restrictive.

Chopin's fiction is driven by the desperation of women's marital problems. Most of the characters in her novels are wives who are frustrated with their husbands and take up extreme measures like suicide, adultery, or even desertion (Stein 52). "The Story of an Hour" focuses on the reaction of the character Mrs. Mallard to the news that she has become a widow. The distinction between public behavior and private emotion extends to inside the home; Louise is forced to pretend, even in front of her sister and friend, to mask her happiness at the years ahead of her. She is happy to gain freedom, even at the price of the death of her husband. As she grieves her husband's death outwardly, she is excited on the inside, which Chopin shows us through her thoughts. This contrast is not lost on a student reader who notes these emotions were her "private thoughts which reveals how forbidden this pleasure really is" ("Shattered Hearts" 1). After hearing about her husband's untimely death, Louise observed the "tops of trees that were all aquiver with new life" (Chopin 1). In "Shattered Hearts," the student notes this contrast as one that hints at possibilities for Louise, ones she dares not express, even in the privacy of her home, in front of her sister (1). In "Freedom They Said!" another Qatari student reads the silent scene at the window as symbolic of Louise's newfound freedom as she keeps repeating the word "free" while sitting before the opening. Chopin's story creates an interesting dialogue among the students about divorce and other types of relationship problems and their solutions (Deidriech 118).

The classrooms in Education City in Doha, Qatar, are very diverse in both ethnicity and religion. VCUQatar is no exception. In addition to Qatari students, there are students from around the Middle East as well as Asia. The way these students responded to the short story was an interesting contrast to the readings by the Qatari women. A female student of Indian descent described Louise Mallard as an example of a character who defies "the social expectations of women being weak" ("What Women are (Really) Made Of" 1). She constructs her analysis on the ambiguity of Louise's emotions when she first receives the news of husband's unexpected passing and interprets the symbols present in the scene of Louise's distress with more ambiguity than the Qatari students. Instead of focusing on the drudgery of marriage, the Indian student spends more time exploring how a husband's death could mean new life for Louise:

> Chopin uses the scenery outside Mrs. Mallard's window to symbolize her feeling of independence and freedom when she has found out her husband has passed away. [...] She sits in solitude to contemplate, watching the "trees that were all aquiver with the new spring life" outside her window. The season of spring is generally associated with new life, it is when the foliage begins to grow and there is birth of

> new life. She is grieved yet she sees "a peddler selling his wares" on the streets below her, a representation of everyday life going on, just as the peddler does. Instead of sorrow, she sees beauty outside, which is a reflection of her internal state. She has been struck by calamity yet she thinks optimistically of the years she has ahead of her. She is able to see the beauty of life, even though she is faced by woe. ("What Women are (Really) Made Of" 1–2)

The student interprets Mrs. Mallard as a vital character with a limited amount of resistance; she contrasts her to the institutionalized female protagonist in "Fragments of a Life" by Sharifa Al Shamlan (Cohen-Mor). She explains their similar treatment of struggling female protagonists: "Both Chopin and Al Shamlan use symbolism of settings to portray an emotional strength in their characters. Both authors are using the environment of the character as a cultivating factor for their characters' development into a emotionally strong state of mind" ("What Women are (Really) Made Of"). The student may not yet have the verbal dexterity this early in her academic career to outline the physical versus mental confinement of these two characters, but that is what she is uncovering in her analysis. While Louise Mallard is figuratively confined in a marriage, the staff at the mental facility physically restrains the unnamed protagonist in "Fragments of a Life." The two women use the private world of their minds, however, to escape encroachment on their individuality: "Both these short stories portray two very different characters and two very different types of emotional strengths being utilized. Mrs. Mallard's reactions have a positive connotation, while the unnamed narrator has reactions that may be classified as hostile, but are more suited to her situation" ("What Women are (Really) Made Of" 3–4).

My undergraduate research assistant, Geetha Rajeswar, with whom I worked on this analysis, was also once a student enrolled in the course. The essay on Chopin that she wrote for her literary analysis further demonstrates the contrast in emphasis and reading of the two types of students, Qatari and expatriate. Also of Indian descent, like the student who wrote "What Women are (Really) Made Of," Rajeswar took my class three years ago as a first-year student. Having studied abroad for a semester at the main campus of the university, her analysis is the closest to what we would consider a standard feminist critique from among the essays written by first-year students:

> Mrs. Mallard in Chopin's story is very unlike women today. She is portrayed as weak and oppressed by the patriarchal pressures. However, Mark Cunninghan argues that Chopin's decision to extricate the

> character Mrs. Mallard was correct. He says, "Louise's death occurs not because of Brentley's return but rather because of Louise's realization that her autonomy cannot last" (Cunningham 48). Louise's death extenuates the need for her freedom. We come to understand that for Louise, and any woman living in a similar kind of marital problem, will die of excitement literally. But what we're missing from this analysis is that she did not die of happiness but because she knows that her freedom is still not guaranteed. In the 19th century society setting, widows are treated worse when actually they need to be more looked after. They have no freedom and are often mistreated. All their happiness and freedom is taken away. Moreover, the thought of moving on is impossible because the society does not and will permit you further enforcing the decision to kill Louise in the end of the novel. Killing her saves her any humiliation and restriction that she might face even after her husband's death. Thus, her death is the opposite of what it stands for. Louise's death portrays the "futility" of her freedom. (Rajeswar)

According to Rajeswar, a junior interior design major, students interpret the character of Louise and her death differently. As a first-year student, she took my Focused Inquiry I course and remembers reading "The Story of an Hour." Her analysis is that readers from Arab societies understand Louise's death, occurring after the character and readers realize Brently Mallard is indeed alive, as attainment of freedom from a confined marriage. Rajeswar further explores the range of mixed feelings about the story's ending:

> Her death was not a solution to her problem. In today's society, where every individual is driven by the sole purpose of self-content and narcissism, death is not an option. In fact, death becomes a shortcut and divorce is the key and believed to be a best solution. Freeing oneself from a terrible marriage and living a life on one's own terms is preferred to death.

She wrestles with the morals of Chopin's era vis-à-vis contemporary society as a whole, peeling back another layer to look at gender and marriage in the Middle East.

> Women in the Arab society do take up such drastic steps irrespective of what the community things because freedom and choice is given utmost importance over slavery and bondage. I feel the way Chopin ended her story may not appeal to the married women in today's generation. However, the story is set and written during a time where divorce was not acceptable and a woman living alone after a certain age is frowned upon.

Her ruminations are echoed in an analysis by a male Arab student who defined Louise's ultimate death as a form of release. As the Palestinian male student explains in his paper:

> As the husband's death is considered a gift, his theoretical resurrection takes hope away from Mrs. Mallard's eyes because she is objectified again. Mrs. Mallard's death is blissful, as he does not own her anymore. Existentially, she can be whom she wants in her afterlife. Although devastation is the reason for her death, the damage is vanished when her death is the actually beginning of her new life: "When the doctors came, they said she had died of heart disease—of the joy that kills" (Chopin 3). Mrs. Mallard's secularity keeps her emotions well hidden from the doctors, as death gives life to her. ("Death is Blissful" 2)

While VCUQatar is a coeducational institution, there is a much smaller enrollment by male students due to stereotypes about design as a feminine major. Male students are generally one or two in classrooms full of ten or more female students. This particular first-year male was interested in women's issues throughout the course; his research paper centered on how Arab males cannot enjoy privileges that they do not give their sisters or female family members without being hypocrites. His equating Louise's death with freedom, and the doctor's definition of her "joy" as dramatic irony, demonstrates his reading of Arab society for women in unhappy marriages. And Rajeswar distinguishes such readings as different in comparison to those of non-Arab students', many of whom attribute Louise's death to health-related problems, such as her heart condition, as in the case of Deidriech's students.

"The Story of an Hour" evokes discussion of social and cultural gender roles that exist for women not only in the past century in America, but even today in the Middle East. In the nineteenth century, American women divorcees and spinsters were viewed negatively. Unlike modern Western society, where the stigma of divorce and spinsterhood may persist in some religious communities, they are no longer taboo for most western women. The last 50 years has seen massive social change in Qatari society; divorce and spinsterhood are tolerated without the crippling social isolation or stigma they once carried. Qatari society is more open in some ways and the changes for women continue incrementally. The pressure on becoming wives, and mothers, producing citizens for the state are still very much at the heart of Qatari women's experiences. The idea of an unhappy marriage or confined wife is not singular to Qatari society alone as demonstrated by the readings of students from other backgrounds in my first-year writing courses. The depth of their responses and ability to compare Chopin's brief story with other texts, and relate major themes to their societies is evidence of the relevance of her work for contemporary readers.

Works Cited

Berenji, Fahimeh Q. "Time and Gender in Charlotte Perkins Gilman's 'The Yellow Wall-Paper' and Kate Chopin's 'The Story of an Hour.'" *Journal of History and Culture and Art Research* 2.2. (2013): 221–34. Print.

Chongyue, Li, and Wang Lihua. "A Caricature of an Ungrateful and Unfaithful Wife." *English Language and Literature Studies* 3.2 (2013): 90–2. Print.

Chopin, Kate. "The Story of an Hour." *Virginia Commonwealth University. edu*. Web. 25 Jan 2014.

Cohen-Mor, Dayla. *Arab Women Writers: An Anthology of Short Stories.* Albany: State University of New York Press. 2005. Print.

Cunningham, Mark. "The Autonomous Female Self and the Death of Louise Mallard in Kate Chopin's 'Story of an Hour.'" *English Language Notes* 42.1 (Sept. 2004): 48–55. Print.

"Death is Blissful." 10 May 2013. TS. Virginia Commonwealth University Qatar. Class Assignment.

Diederich, Nicole. "Sharing Chopin: Teaching 'The Story of an Hour' to Specialized Populations." *Arkansas Review: A Journal of Delta Studies*, August 2012. Web. 23 Jan. 2014. 116–20.

"Freedom! They Said." 20 March 2013. TS. Virginia Commonwealth University Qatar. Class Assignment.

Fromherz, Allen J. *Qatar: A Modern History.* Washington, DC: Georgetown University Press, 2012. Print.

Kamrava, Mehran. *Qatar: Small State, Big Politics.* New York: Cornell University Press, 2013. Print.

Rajakumar, Mohanalakshmi. Focused Inquiry I Syllabus. 2013. Liberal Arts and Studies Department, Virginia Commonwealth University Qatar. Microsoft Word file.

———. Writing About Literature Essay 2 Guidelines. 2013. Liberal Arts and Studies Department, Virginia Commonwealth University Qatar. Microsoft Word file.

Ramos, Peter. "Unbearable Realism: Freedom, Ethics and Identity in The Awakening." *College Literature*, October 2010. Web. 25 Jan. 2014.

"Set Me Free." 2013. TS. Virginia Commonwealth University Qatar. Class Assignment.

"Shattered Hearts." 2013. TS. Virginia Commonwealth University Qatar. Class Assignment.

Shimon, Samuel. *Beirut 39: New Writing from the Arab World.* New York: Bloomsbury USA, 2010. Print.

Stein, Allen F. *Women and Autonomy in Kate Chopin's Short Fiction.* New York: Peter Lang, 2005. Print.
"Unexpected Deaths." 9 October. 2013. TS. Virginia Commonwealth University Qatar. Class Assignment.
"Unresolved Women's Struggles in Society." 2013. TS. Virginia Commonwealth University Qatar. Class Assignment.
"What Women Are (Really) Made Of." 2013. TS. Virginia Commonwealth University Qatar. Class Assignment.

CHAPTER 12

Teaching Kate Chopin Using Multimedia

Kate O'Donoghue

The Digital Humanities and Teaching Literature

Over a decade ago, when I decided to apply to graduate programs in English literature, I had to take the GRE English subject test. Studying for this test proved problematic. A cursory afternoon of research confirmed that the canon of Western literature had exploded sometime in the mid-twentieth century. I eventually stumbled upon a battered reprint of William J. Long's 1909 tome, *English Literature: Its History and its Significance for the Life of the English-Speaking World.* I purchased it, read it, took notes on index cards, and, given my own familiarity with works of American and English literature published after 1900, did reasonably well on the subject test. By the end of my first year in graduate school, however, shortly after I passed the first comprehensive exam, I forgot most of it. I no longer needed immediate recall of this information. The works of literature themselves had not diminished in importance, but the type of studying I performed to get into graduate school and pass its first exam ultimately had about as much relevance in twenty-first century graduate studies in the humanities as inkwells and vellum. There were so many other works to read and discover—forgotten authors, suppressed journals, recently discovered letters, exciting theories, radical philosophies, alternative histories, voices from oppressed or ignored groups. Indeed, if I had followed the subject test's lead, I never would have studied Kate Chopin. Nobody would have. Her name showed up just once on the test: as a possible multiple choice answer, and it wasn't even the right one (correct answer: Virginia Woolf).

I use this example to prove a point—two points, rather. The first is that for English as a discipline, there are no more absolutely authoritative texts, which complicates the traditional role of professor as master of knowledge. For example, in the introduction, Heather Ostman and I discuss Chopin's critical revival and her inclusion as requisite reading in both women's studies and American literature. Critical trends in twentieth-century literary studies broadened the field in provocative ways. Now, in the twenty-first century, digital humanities and technology have further expanded the field, especially in terms of methodology. Until recently however, much of the focus in digital humanities remained on scholarship, not pedagogy. In her chapter in this collection, Emily Toth emphasizes the cultural and political variability of student responses to Edna Pontellier over the decades. Toth relays that young women in 2014 think that Edna is not radical enough, while Edna's independence inspired women in earlier decades. As we emphasize in our introduction, readers and their relationships to texts matter. Moreover, as scholars and teachers of literature, our students as readers matter; most of us would probably agree that we want our undergraduates to develop enduring relationships with the texts we assign them.

In 2002, around the time I was filling in bubbles on the GRE subject test, Shari Stenberg and Amy Lee argued for new approaches in graduate teacher training. In "Developing Pedagogies: Learning the Teaching of English," the authors acknowledge that "we assume that professors develop in isolation, or in relationship to the scholarship we engage, but not as a result of collaboration with our students or with other teachers" (327). Stenberg and Lee find this stance troubling in the twenty-first century humanities classroom and join their voices with other scholars who advocate for more examined and interactive pedagogies. "We agree with James Slevin that…we need to question hegemonic conceptions of disciplinarity, where bodies of knowledge take precedence over activities of engaging knowledge with others" (327). Slevin implies that direct instruction of content in the humanities classroom, wherein the instructor tells the students what to read and how to read it, will never result in more institutional value being placed on teaching. This type of knowledge dissemination encourages the traditional role of professor as producer and master and knowledge, which emphasizes individual faculty research and publication instead of teaching and collaboration. Furthermore, Slevin also indicates that this practice implicitly privileges certain types of disciplinary information over others—in this mode, professors inevitably teach students to mimic their own thoughts (Stenberg and Lee 327).

The debate about how to impart knowledge to students most effectively harkens back to Socrates, perhaps even earlier. But technology complicates it. Even in the realm of digital humanities, this debate has been ongoing. Cathy Davidson, way back in 1999, asked readers of *The Chronicle of Higher Education* to "[i]magine if ideas in the humanities evolved in . . . the equivalent of a science laboratory . . . [where] discovery of one sort or another is the shared, overt goal ("What if Scholars in the Humanities Worked Together in a Lab?")." Yet, in his 2010 article "What Is Digital Humanities and What's It Doing in English Departments?", Matthew Kirschenbaum still felt the need to emphasize that "digital humanities is also a social undertaking" (3). The idea of collaboration in the humanities, and using computers to foster such, has been knocked around for decades. As scholar and educator Brett D. Hirsch points out in an introduction to the 2012 collection *Digital Humanities Pedagogy: Practices, Principles and Politics,* digital humanities "can trace its roots to research undertaken in the 1940s and boasts specialization in areas of humanities data archiving, preservation, and management" (13). The collaborative potential of the digital humanities, however, has not been fully tapped, despite the existence of organizations like Davidson's HASTAC, centers like MITH at the University of Maryland, or the New Media Lab at the CUNY Graduate Center.

In "Reclaiming Innovation," Jim Groom and Brian Lamb make the case that although early Web communities and Internet activity centered in universities, the advent and current widespread use of learning management systems implies that institutions of higher education limit the interactive and collaborative potential of the Web.

> Even after years of hype and widespread posturing about "openness" and "21st-century skills" as key values of contemporary higher education, most LMS implementations still lack elementary capacities to publish to and interact with the wider web and the public. By restricting online teaching and learning activity to these closed systems, colleges and universities make a mockery of oft-stated values such as social engagement, public knowledge, and the mission of promoting enlightenment and critical inquiry in society. ("Reclaiming Innovation").

The hierarchies of the learning management systems that Groom and Lamb refer to support the traditional knowledge dissemination modes in higher education assailed by Slevin, Stenberg, and Lee and reflect profoundly conservative political ideologies about teaching and learning.

Hirsch believes that by examining the ways they teach, and conflating the traditionally separated relationship between research and teaching, instructors in higher education can substantially enrich the field of the humanities, and place digital humanities in a continuum that assures its permanence. Hirsch quotes the renowned educational and cultural scholar Roger I. Simon, on the ideologies that undergird any teaching praxis:

> "[P]edagogy" is a more complex and extensive term than "teaching," referring to the integration in practice of particular curriculum content and design, classroom strategies and techniques, a time and space for the practice of those strategies and techniques, and evaluation purposes and methods. [...] [I]n other words, talk about pedagogy is simultaneously talk about the details of what students and others might do together and the cultural politics such practices support. To propose a pedagogy is to propose a political vision. In this perspective, we cannot talk about teaching practice without talking about politics (qtd in Hirsch 13–14).

Like Slevin, Stenberg, and Lee, Hirsch and Simon uncover the often unexamined politics and assumed ideologies beneath discussions of pedagogy and teaching practices. Research and pedagogy still remain separate entities in higher education: with one acting as manor lord and the other as serf. Recently, however, Hirsch has noted a revived interest in the pedagogy of digital humanities, after a decade in which research seemed to take precedence over pedagogy. Pedagogy, Hirsch argues, "stabilizes" the field, and therefore, "it is prudent for us, as a field, to start thinking critically not only about what we teach under the banner of 'digital humanities' and how we teach it, but also to consider the broader institutional implications and political consequences for doing so" (13–14).

Hirsch's words affirm what Slevin, Stenberg, Lee, and Simon point out: to change the way we teach the humanities means a reexamination of our ideologies about information. Throughout the twentieth century, the proliferation of what the discipline of literature encompasses radically enriched and altered the discipline of English. Matthew Kirschenbaum affirms another major change in the discipline for the twenty-first century in the increasingly expansive institutional nurturance of digital computing for the humanities, often featuring English departments. "Digital humanities," Kirschenbaum writes, "is now backed on a growing number of campuses by a level of funding, infrastructure, and administrative commitments that would have been unthinkable even a decade ago" (6).

While the actual body of knowledge university professors should apprehend in order to achieve so-called mastery abounds like mint in an untamed garden, technology and digital tools have become ubiquitous in the higher education environment. Even in classrooms not equipped with technology, computing presents itself as an important element of higher education and learning in the twenty-first century. For example, at City University's Baruch College, the majority of our students live in households with very limited financial resources ("2012 Student Experience Survey"). Yet in a survey conducted by Baruch's Center for Teaching and Learning in Spring 2014 to gauge student access to technology, most students indicated that they owned laptop or desktop computers (O'Donoghue and Waltzer). Students deem round-the-clock computer access as essential to success in their studies; even those from financially strapped households sacrifice, when they can, to purchase computers. This also confirms what any contemporary teacher already knows: students (and, let's be honest, instructors, administrators, and everyone in between) fervently and avidly "Google" anything and everything. This ready access to information further complicates the "most traditional model of professing at work, which holds that 'good teaching'...has more to do with the relationship one has to knowledge than to students" (Lee and Stenberg 330).

The second point I would like to make is that while this blossoming of what the discipline of literature and humanities encompasses has changed the practice of teaching, it also offers multiple paths for instructors to become producers of knowledge; however, simultaneously, students have increasingly become passive consumers of other people's knowledge. The ways many college students use digital tools mimics the way I studied for the English subject test. College instructors frequently complain about their students using the Web primarily as a shortcut to knowledge. Yet this is not always a bad thing—even in this age of innovation and experimentation college instructors tend to assign certain texts, such as *The Awakening*, and expect students to find certain elements, like Edna's discontentedness. After all, I needed the information in William Long's book for two very specific tasks: a standardized test and a comprehensive exam. Without memorizing portions of this information, I never would have succeeded in a graduate program that ultimately taught me think critically and question the very information I had learned to gain entry to it.

While we gripe about the loss of original research, we need to reflect on our own teaching practices. Students seek rote, Internet-ready answers if these answers are rewarded. If an instructor wants students to come up with a widely accepted interpretation of a work of literature, then the Internet is the best place for the student to find this information. If an instructor positions herself as a master of knowledge, and her students as passive recipients, then it makes perfect sense to use the internet in this superficial way. However, using this information as a jumping off point, as a beginning, changes the dynamic and makes the Web act not as a replacement of original thought, but a tool that leads to original research. As Groom and Lamb put it, "the choice of technology does not itself make teaching good or bad. Good teaching can happen in spite of bad tools, and good tools do not guarantee a good outcome. But it is facile to think that the technology makes no difference" ("Reclaiming Innovation"). Using a learning management system to post selected and instructor-vetted information online has its uses and conveniences, but it replicates a hegemony of knowledge and, as Groom and Lamb warn, it isolates students and learning from a larger, more exciting, context.

As Randy Bass articulates in "Engines of Inquiry," his influential 1997 article about the opportunities technology brings to teaching practices, "teaching and learning is not about perfect information, but often about imperfect information; indeed, learning is often about indirection, ambiguity, complexity, and multiplicity…[s]ometimes knowledge is too complex to be perfect" (10). Many educators in the humanities, when disparaging their students' uses of technology, mourn this loss of complexity and subtlety. Ultimately, most professors of literature do not want their students to parrot a "correct" answer about a text based on someone else's summary from a blog post or Internet guide. Literature and its study in higher education belies correct answers; indeed, the whole explosion of the traditional canon emphasizes this point.

Hirsch refers to Shari Stenberg's position advocating for "'a reevaluation of the function of the English professor as 'more than one who transmits particular knowledge'…expanding the role to include that of 'a facilitator of student projects, a co-inquirer, a learner'" (qtd in Hirsch 14). Using technology and digital tools to encourage students to become creators of knowledge creates an interactive and collaborative pedagogical practice, counteracts the passive consumption of knowledge, and conflates research and teaching in exciting ways.

Teaching students how to use digital tools to produce content radically alters pedagogy—instructional roles in the classroom become collaborative and less hierarchical. In my experience, as someone who considers herself technologically savvy but not expert, assigning multimedia projects means that I cannot position myself as a master of knowledge. However, the implications of incorporating technology in this way are complex and far-reaching. Instructors will have to challenge themselves to learn new technologies and materials. This brings up difficult labor issues. The learning and implementation of technology takes time; time that is at this point, largely unpaid. Contingent and full-time faculty already have overburdened schedules and workloads. Yet in many ways, the changes have already happened. Our students misuse technology because they think that's what we want.

After a decade spent teaching diverse groups of students at the City University of New York (CUNY), I have distilled a few objectives for all of my literature courses that transcend the specific goals of each individual class. Students should:

- learn some computer skills that they can bring with them into the professional world,
- experience the thrill of discovery through research,
- sustain their intellect through reading,
- realize the political and cultural implications of the production and dissemination of texts.

Part two of this chapter details an assignment series that seeks to provide a free and user-friendly way to make things with technology relevant to an undergraduate literature course, while attempting to target each of the goals listed above.

Mapping "Miss McEnders"

In the spring semester of 2013, I began work on a project with funding from the New Media Lab at the CUNY Graduate Center. I wanted to develop a simple but sophisticated way to introduce students to digital mapping techniques. Mapping fiction offers historical and contemporary foci to narratives and provides motive to students who may wonder why they read literature from decades and centuries before they were born, when the world around them seems more dynamic. The necessary geographical research that accompanies the actual mapping provides original and overlooked contexts that enrich the interpretations, analyses, and meanings of narratives. Mapping a story, when possible, also encourages students to use historical tools in a very specific way and thus breaks the common habit many students have of reductive generalization when analyzing a work of literature through a historical lens (i.e., "since the beginning of time, humans have . . . "). I also created a site through Wikispaces to use first as a drawing board during the project, but which will ultimately serve as an archive of the research process and a Web site to showcase students' work. When students place their work on the Web, the possibility of others seeing it emphasizes audience and sharpens their motivation. Moreover, wikis offer opportunities for students to execute group projects while developing a sense of process and to recognize the differences between collaboration and plagiarism.

Certain works of literature lend themselves more readily to mapping than others. Kate Chopin's 1892 short story "Miss McEnders" is ideal. In "Miss McEnders," Chopin highlights regional changes resulting from the social and economic inequality that developed in St. Louis after the Civil War. The stratification of American society remains as topical today as it was in the closing decades of the nineteenth century. When I initially conceived this idea, Occupy Wall Street occupied the nation's news. While editing this chapter for publication, a St. Louis suburb, Ferguson, made national headlines for the civil unrest there after a white police officer fatally shot an unarmed black teenager. In a *New York Times* op-ed piece from August 17, Jeff Smith indicts the exclusionary and polarizing urban planning of St. Louis that began in the late nineteenth century for creating the template for the current racial and economic dichotomies in the region:

> Back in 1876, the city of St. Louis made a fateful decision. Tired of providing services to the outlying areas, the city cordoned itself off, separating from St. Louis County. It's a decision the city came to regret. Most Rust Belt cities have bled population since the 1960s, but few have been as badly damaged as St. Louis City, which since 1970 has lost almost as much of its population as Detroit. This exodus has left a ring of mostly middle-class suburbs around an urban core plagued by entrenched poverty (Smith).

In "Miss McEnders," Chopin also indicts the urban structure of St. Louis for exacerbating class and economic tensions; mapping the story clarifies this critique and provides further evidence for the human toll that long-standing economic disparities enact, and how architecture, geography, and zoning all cement corrupt and unfair political structures.

While mapping fiction can highlight issues of enduring relevance for students, it helps when the narrative symbolically uses specific geographies to undergird its themes. Chopin built the narrative of "Miss McEnders" around a particular journey undertaken by its main character. Based on the true story of newspaper magnate James McKee, who went to jail for a Reconstruction-era corruption scandal known as the Whiskey Ring, Chopin uses the fictional tale of Miss McEnders to satirize McKee's daughter, Ellen, a contemporary of Chopin and a publisher, writer, and reformer in St. Louis. As Emily Toth confirms, Ellen McKee's activities would likely have rankled Chopin (198–199). The bourgeois Miss Georgie McEnders takes a journey to a poor part of town to visit Mademoiselle Salambre, who has recently acquired the business of making bespoke lingerie for her wedding trousseau. Georgie wants to visit the modiste out of a seemingly benevolent desire to "know the people who worked for her, as far as she could" (Chopin 204). This whimsy is quickly shown to be intrusive and judgmental, rather than altruistic and liberal: Georgie appears unannounced in Mlle. Salambre's room, interrupts her work, and discovers that the apparent "Mademoiselle" is the mother of a young girl. Miss McEnders is morally outraged and withdraws all her work from Mlle. Salambre. However, Mlle. Salambre returns the surprise visit, and defines Georgie's much older and corpulent fiancé as a rake and a libertine, a gilded age Lovelace, and Georgie's father as a cheat and a swindler. Both men achieved their ill-gotten wealth through exploitation and corrupt political maneuvering. Mlle. Salambre's declaration and corroborating evidence shatter Georgie's bourgeois complacency. At the end of the narrative, Georgie finds herself in a dilemma that mirrors Mlle. Salambre's: she must choose between economic security and self-respect.

My first hurdle to clear for my project involved deciding which software to use. I wanted free, user-friendly applications to reduce the amount of classroom time spent teaching software skills. I eventually decided to use two Google products: Earth and MapEngine. These applications use the familiar Google Maps interface but allow for more customized mapping. Next, I had to decide whether to use archival or contemporary maps. In the end, I used archival maps of St. Louis from the late nineteenth century as reference points to plot Miss McEnders's journey on a contemporary map. Jennifer Moore, the GIS/Outreach/Anthropology librarian at Washington University in St. Louis, generously shared their digital trove of Whipple fire insurance maps from nineteenth century St. Louis with me. Libraries and historical organizations increasingly digitize and store maps such as these, made in the nineteenth and early twentieth centuries by insurance companies for thousands of towns and cities in the United States. They offer rich opportunities for interested students to begin examining the social and political contexts of literature and to understand the importance and relevance of these contexts. Once I made a list of all the places that Georgie McEnders visits in the story, I plotted them on Google Earth and MapEngine. Then I researched each specific place, using a mix of Internet searches and library resources that students can easily access.

The McEnders' Home

The opening lines of the story establish the trajectory of Miss Georgie McEnders's journey, as well as her wealth.

> When Miss Georgie McEnders had finished an elaborately simple toilet of gray and black, she divested herself completely of rings, bangles, brooches—everything to suggest that she stood in friendly relation with fortune. For Georgie was going to read a paper upon "The Dignity of Labor" before the Woman's Reform Club; and if she was blessed with an abundance of wealth, she possessed a no less amount of good taste.
>
> Before entering the neat victoria that stood at her father's too-sumptuous door—and that was her special property—she turned to give certain directions to the coachman. First upon the list from which she read was inscribed: "Look up Mademoiselle Salambre."
>
> "James," said Georgie, flushing a pretty pink, as she always did with the slightest effort of speech, "we want to look up a person named Mademoiselle Salambre, in the southern part of town, on Arsenal street," indicating a certain number and locality (Chopin 204).

Georgie's exclusive control of a private carriage symbolizes the ease of access and movement afforded by her wealth—geographically, but also socially, politically and economically. Throughout most of the nineteenth century, St. Louis did not have mass transport, making it difficult for the working class residents to leave their neighborhoods. "For the wealthy, private carriages did a wonderful job of supplying transport from home. If you were a clerk or factory hand, however, your options were more limited. So most people chose homes within easy walking distance of work" (Sandweiss 3). This insularity of work and home also means that, to Georgie and the contemporary readers of this tale, Mlle. Salambre's residence offers important clues about her moral character and occupation.

The wealth of the McEnders family and their ostentatious residence in the northern end of the city, as well as Chopin's sardonic stance towards Georgie's wealth, establishes the Central West End as their likely location. A late-nineteenth-century enclave near Forest Park, Central West End developed as a respite from the increasingly industrializing city and its poor, working class residents. Although anachronistic to the setting of the story, this address punctuates both Chopin's contemporary jab at bourgeois reformers and her larger point about the postbellum stratification of St. Louis. Chopin critic Pamela Knights elaborates on the significance of textual clues that establish location in a critical edition of Chopin's fiction.

> *Arsenal Street*: a long street running west from the vast Anheuser-Busch brewery in downtown St. Louis: ethnically diverse, with a mixture of lodging houses, small business, and saloons, it represented in the 1890s an extreme contrast to the "too-sumptuous" McEnders home. Georgie, presumably, would have been pictured as living in one of the exclusive "private streets", the preserve of the St. Louis elite (Knights 382).

Historian Tim Fox confirms that this neighborhood and Forest Park, directly to its west, symbolized the economic and social changes in St. Louis, in which newly affluent industrialists and manufacturers sought to distance themselves from poorer sections of the city; residents of this exclusive neighborhood paid fees to maintain streets and amenities, and politically influenced zoning.

> By the late nineteenth century, the city's final western edge had become St. Louis' last setting for an upper-class enclave . . . those who had made their fortunes in distilling, flour milling, chemicals, iron and steel, textiles, utilities, tobacco, and shoe manufacturing built palatial mansions in the most extensive cluster of private places in St. Louis . . . [and] formed the original core of the Central West End (Fox 134).

Forest Park itself has an interesting relationship to social class. Created in 1876, its inception and subsequent changes throughout the remainder of the nineteenth century highlight public debates about accessibility of public lands, types of appropriate recreation, and class hierarchies, all of which are reflected in Miss McEnders. Georgie's assumptions about what poor women should do, her self-conscious yet complacent identification of her privilege (she realizes that she should remove her jewelry when speaking about working women, yet still assumes she possesses relevant information about these women's lives), and the leisure of having a carriage to bring her around the city underscores the debates about Forest Park, built in the late 1870s in a location which remained largely inaccessible to the working class neighborhoods in the southern part of the city until the construction of a new railroad route in 1885. The disjuncture between the setting of the story in the late 1870s and its publication date in 1891 underscores the park debate. The park had changed from a pastoral invention of leisurely pursuits and recreational events such as horse racing or winding carriage paths that were used primarily by wealthy citizens to its more plebeian and democratic accessibility in the early 1890s (Fox 122–127).

The Wednesday Club

When students edit the map, they use separate layers for different categories of data, such as the journey that Miss McEnders takes through St. Louis, Mlle. Salambre's residence, and places where Kate Chopin lived. Each layer has customizable markers in terms of both shape and color, and each marker can be annotated to display further information when clicked on. For example, students have added to a marker an explanation of the significance of a particular location and media such as photographs or videos. This type of visual information can help students identify a relationship between biography and content that goes beyond the superficial information that many struggle to integrate into their literary analysis by offering opportunities to see and hypothesize about interesting connections.

An example of such a connection in "Miss McEnders" is the Woman's Reform Club, the last stop of Miss McEnders's day. Quite likely, this club stood in for the actual Wednesday Club in St. Louis, an intellectual and reform-minded group of women with whom Chopin involved herself for a time. Apparently, the club earned Chopin's disdain. Emily Toth comments on the frustration Chopin felt with the unexamined zealotry and inefficacy of the bourgeois do-gooders in the group (127). Allen Stein further elaborates that Chopin deemed the club "irritatingly self-congratulatory and self-important as it stressed moral uplift for the general community" (78). The fact that Georgie gets her comeuppance from Mlle. Salambre before she delivers her hypocritical and uninformed lecture on the dignity of labor to this reform-minded group emphasizes Chopin's satirical take on such groups' often dubious agenda.

As Katharine Corbett explains in her book about women's history in St. Louis, the wide acceptance of distinct red light districts in St. Louis meant that working women living in or near those districts became suspected of prostitution by default and risked losing both employment and charity: "employers often required moral certification in letters of reference... [and] women suspected of immorality could not expect to receive private charity in times of need" (126). The lack of geographic mobility suffered by the working poor, and firms—like the fictitious Push and Prodem in "Miss McEnders," which Pamela Knights sees as an allusion to the aggressive tactics of St. Louis businessmen (378)— that kept wages ruthlessly low by outsourcing jobs such as Georgie's wedding trousseau to individual seamstresses, means that Mlle. Salambre resides in a geographic space that breeds economic instability. Even more unfair, labor historian Alice Kessler Harris reports that in the nineteenth century imagination, low wages were blamed for inducing working-class women to prostitution. "If women could not earn enough by dint of strenuous effort to support themselves, investigators thought, they would inevitably turn to prostitution" (Harris 104). Indeed, Georgie's journey downtown to Mlle. Salambre proves that the seamstress, at the very least, has had sex without being married. Yet Chopin presents Georgie's disapprobation of this woman as further evidence of her hypocrisy and silliness. When students realize, through mapping, that Chopin lived in adjacent neighborhoods to the Wednesday Club and to the likely locale of Miss McEnders, their comprehension of Chopin's satirical attitude towards the Woman's Reform Club deepens.

Mademoiselle Salambre's Residence

Since we know that Mlle. Salambre lives on Arsenal Street, and we meet her German landlady "redding bricks" in front of her boarding house, the Hill and Cheltenham neighborhoods are likely locations for Mlle. Salambre. Both featured German immigrants in the nineteenth century and nearby brick factories that employed residents (Fox 110–118). Redding bricks seems to be some type of brick postproduction task, which could entail adding a decorative glaze to the bricks (which may not have been naturally red) or cleaning soot from the bricks accrued in the kiln firing process ("General History of Brick Making," Sopko and Feister, "The History of Bricks and Brickmaking"). While her actions help to place the geographic location, the emphasis on the color red also suggests sexual digression and the sprucing up of the bricks implies that appearances can deceive. She also labors at the task, which emphasizes that these two elements—sex and attractiveness—mean work, not pleasure.

The southern edge of the Hill, at the corner of Arsenal and Sublette Park, further stands out as a plausible and interesting home residence for Mlle. Salambre. Between 1870 and 1874, St. Louis legalized prostitution with the Social Evil Ordinance; in 1873, the Hospital for Social Evil, on a tract of land that also contained the insane asylum and the women's House of Industry, opened at the corner of Arsenal and Sublette. This institution housed prostitutes who tested positive for sexually transmitted infections, and "reformers attempted to 'save' prostitutes in the House of Industry" although local news sources apparently reported that "[p]rostitutes resented being patronized and penalized by reformers (Corbett 126–127).

The Hill and Cheltenham neighborhoods have a further transgressive history. In the 1850s, a French utopian socialist group called the Icarians purchased a tract of land in this region shortly after the death of their leader, Etienne Cabot, and an exodus from Iowa. The group believed in "the principals of peace and justice" ("Etienne Cabot and the Icarians") and, to echo the title of Georgie McEnders pending lecture for the women's group, also in the "dignity of labor": the Icarians occupied themselves in skilled trades such as tailors, cobblers, and mechanics (Shaw 82–83). This context becomes interesting when one considers that Chopin distinctly emphasizes Mlle. Salambre's French origins, during a time period in which most recent immigrants to St. Louis were Irish, German, or Italian ("Peopling St. Louis: the Immigration Experience"). Moreover, the seamstress's final speech to Miss McEnders specifically indicts Georgie's bourgeois existence as immoral and dishonest:

> Very small, indeed, were her worldly possessions, she informed the young lady; but as Heaven was her witness—not a mouthful of bread that she had not earned. And her parents over yonder in France! As honest as the sunlight! Poor, ah! for that—poor as rats. God only knew how poor; and God only knew how honest. Her eyes remained fixed upon the picture of Horace McEnders. Some people might like fine houses, and servants, and horses, and all the luxury which dishonest wealth brings. Some people might enjoy such surroundings. As for her!—and she drew up her skirts ever so carefully and daintily, as though she feared contamination to her petticoats from the touch of the rich rug upon which she stood (Chopin 209).

Mlle. Salambre's disgust at Georgie stems not only from her wealth but also the young woman's unexamined ideology of morality and upward mobility and her lack of empathy for the working class—essentially, a Marxist rejection of capitalism's disregard for the destruction it wreaks and its privileging of consumer goods as measures of virtue and power.

Final Thoughts

When I began this project, I was not sure of how relevant this exercise would be in a classroom. However, I found that the mix of materials

I needed to use to find information—specific uses of the Internet, libraries, archival resources, how-to manuals on brick construction, and fire insurance maps—opened up the field of literary analysis in a way that engages students. Moreover, I find the possibilities of original discovery exciting; since students learn how to geocode, build a wiki, and customize maps, they gain valuable practical skills. In the classroom, students are divided into groups; each group is assigned a portion of the story. A sharable Google map of St. Louis serves as the base map on which multiple people work simultaneously. Individuals within groups have specific roles and must work together to make sure their information is cohesive. Each group makes annotated points on the shared map and has an accompanying Wiki page with more information, written analyses, and a Works Cited page.

Matthew Kirschenbaum argues that "the digital humanities today is about . . . a scholarship and pedagogy that are collaborative and depend on networks of people and that live an active 24/7 life online. Isn't that something you want in your English department? (6)." I would add that the separation of scholarship from pedagogy has for too long defined college-level teaching, and that asking ourselves and our students to begin experimenting together with the digital tools at hand has the potential to invigorate literary studies for the twenty-first century.

Works Cited

"2012 Student Experience Survey." *CUNY Office of Institutional Research and Assessment*, 2012. Web. 10 Aug. 2014.

Bass, Randy. "Engines of Inquiry: Teaching, Technology, and Learner-Centered Approaches to Culture and History." Introduction to *Engines of Inquiry: A Practical Guide for Using Technology in Teaching American Culture*. Ed. Randy Bass. Washington, DC: American Studies Crossroads Project, American Studies Association, 1997. Print.

Chopin, Kate. "Miss McEnders." *The Collected Works of Kate Chopin*. Ed. Per Seyersted. Vol. I. Baton Rouge: Louisiana State UP, 1969. 204–11. Print.

Corbett, Katharine T. *In Her Place: A Guide to St. Louis Women's History*. St. Louis: Missouri Historical Society, 1999. Print.

Davidson, Cathy. "What if Scholars in the Humanities Worked Together in a Lab?" *Chronicle of Higher Education*, 28 May 1999. Web. 10 Aug. 2014.

"Etienne Cabet and the Icarians." *Baxter-Snyder Center for Icarian Studies*. Western Illinois University, n.d. Web. 19 Mar. 2013.

Fox, Tim. *Where We Live: A Guide to St. Louis Communities*. St. Louis: Missouri Historical Society, 1995. Print.

"General History of Brick Making." *English Heritage Teacher's Kit*. English Heritage, n.d. Web. 3 Mar. 2014.

Groom, Jim, and Brian Lamb. "Reclaiming Innovation." *Educause Review.* 2014. Web. 23 Jun. 2014.

Harris, Alice Kessler. *Out to Work: A History of Wage-Earning Women in the United States.* New York: Oxford UP, 1982. Print.

Hirsch, Brett D. "Parentheses: Digital Humanities and the Place of Pedagogy." Introduction. *Digital Humanities Pedagogy: Practices, Principles and Politics.* Cambridge: OpenBook, 2012. Web. 10 Aug. 2014.

Kirschenbaum, Matthew D. "What Is the Digital Humanities and What Is It Doing in English Departments?." *ADE Bulletin* 150 (2010): 55–61. *Matthew G. Kirschenbaum.* Web. 10 Aug. 2014.

Knights, Pamela. "Miss McEnders: Explanatory Notes." *The Awakening, and Other Stories.* Ed. Kate Chopin. Oxford: Oxford UP, 2000. 381–3. Print.

O'Donoghue, Kate. Digital Images of Maps. *Mapping Miss McEnders (and Friends).* 20 May 2013. Web. 20 Aug. 2014.

O'Donoghue, Kate, and Lucas Waltzer. "Student Tech Survey: Strategies for Hybrid and Online Classes." *Baruch College Teaching and Technology Conference.* New York. 28 Mar. 2014. Presentation.

"Peopling St. Louis: the Immigration Experience." *A Preservation Plan for St. Louis Part I: Historic Contexts.* Missouri: The City of St. Louis, n.d. Web. 5 Apr. 2013.

Sandweiss, Eric. "Introduction." *Where We Live: A Guide to St. Louis Communities.* Ed. Tim Fox. St. Louis: Missouri Historical Society, 1995. 1–5. Print.

Shaw, Albert. *Icaria, a Chapter in the History of Communism.* New York: G. P. Putnam's Sons, 1884. *Internet Archive.* Library of the University of Illinois at Urbana-Champaign. Web. 16 Sep. 2012.

Smith, Jeff. "In Ferguson, Black Town, White Power." *The New York Times* 17 Aug. 2014. Web. 19 Aug. 2014.

Sopko, Joseph S., and Lois M. Feister. "18th- and Early 19th-Century Brickmaking at the John Jay Homestead: The Process, Products, and Craftsmen." *Northeast Historical Archaeology* 25 (1996): 51–68. *Digital Commons at Buffalo State.* Buffalo State: State University of New York, 16 Oct. 2013. Web. 18 Apr. 2014.

Stein, Allen F. *Women and Autonomy in Kate Chopin's Short Fiction.* New York: Peter Lang, 2005. Web.

Stenberg, Shari, and Amy Lee. "Developing Pedagogies: Learning the Teaching of English." *College English* 64.3 (2002): 326–47. *Jstor.* Web. 10 Aug. 2014.

"The History of Bricks and Brickmaking." *The Brick Directory.* N.p., n.d. Web. 10 Mar. 2014.

Toth, Emily. *Unveiling Kate Chopin.* Jackson: University Press of Mississippi, 1999. Print.

Contributors

Amy Branam Armiento is an associate professor of English at Frostburg State University. She serves as the coordinator for African American Studies and has published on women's studies and transatlantic nineteenth-century literature.

Diana Epelbaum is a doctoral candidate in English at The Graduate Center, City University of New York. Her dissertation explores eighteenth-century women's natural histories through the intersection of genre, gender, and early American studies. A 2009 recipient of *The New York Times*'s "Teachers Who Make a Difference" award, she holds a master's degree in literacy education and currently teaches composition.

Bernard Koloski has published books and articles about Chopin for many years. He edits the website *KateChopin.org*.

Correna Catlett Merricks is an assistant professor of English and Director of the Center for Academic Excellence at Asbury University in Wilmore, Kentucky. She specializes in late nineteenth- and early twentieth-century American women's fiction, focusing on representations of motherhood and the domestic life. She received her Ph.D. in English from the University of Mississippi in 2012.

Kate O'Donoghue earned her Ph.D. in English from the CUNY Graduate Center in February 2015. She specializes in nineteenth-century American women's fiction, digital pedagogy, and composition and rhetoric. She is currently a hybrid coordinator at Baruch College's Center for Teaching and Learning, where she advises faculty on hybrid and online courses and provides educational technology support. She also serves as a writing consultant and instructor for City University of New York-affiliated early college programs at Townsend Harris High School and the Queens School of Inquiry.

Heather Ostman is an associate professor of English and Director of the Humanities Institute at SUNY Westchester Community College in Valhalla, New York. She is the editor of *Kate Chopin* *in the Twenty-First Century* (Cambridge Scholars Press, 2008) and the author of *Writing Program Administration and the Community* College (Parlor Press, 2013). In addition to book chapters, she has written many articles, which have appeared in journals such as *College Composition and Communication*, *Prose Studies*, *Philological Studies*, *Women's Studies*, and others. She is the president of the Kate Chopin International Society.

Eulalia Piñero Gil is an associate professor in American Literature and Gender Studies at the Universidad Autónoma of Madrid. She has coedited *Voices and Images of Women in 20th Century Theater: Anglo-American Women Playwrights* (2002), *Women and Art: Visions of Change and Social Development* (2010) and *Breaking a Sea of Silence: Interdisciplinary Reflections on Gender Violence* (2013). In 2012, she translated and edited Kate Chopin's *The Awakening* (2012) in Spanish. She has published extensively on American modernism, comparative literature, women's literature, gender studies, music and literature, and nineteenth-century American literature. She is member of the Kate Chopin International Society Website Advisory Committee.

Mohanalakshmi Rajakumar is a writer and educator with a Ph.D. in literature. She has published numerous books and journals, including four novels. *An Unlikely Goddess* (2014) was recognized by She Writes with the New Novelist award. *Love Comes Later* (2012) was the winner of the Best Indie Book Award for Romance in 2013. Dr. Rajakumar is at work on her first crime novel, set in the Arabian Gulf

Geetha Rajeswar studied interior design at Virginia Commonwealth University in Qatar. As a member of Dr. Rajakumar's social science research group, she co-wrote articles such as the chapter that appears in this volume. She has also contributed to conference presentations related to race, gender, and writing pedagogy.

Aparecido Donizete Rossi is a professor of British Literature at UNESP (São Paulo State University), Araraquara, Brazil. His Ph.D. thesis, *Segredos do Sótão: Feminismo e Escritura na obra de Kate Chopin (Attic Secrets: Feminism and Writing in the Works of Kate Chopin)* addresses the intersection between Feminism and Deconstruction in the works of Kate Chopin. He is a member of the Kate Chopin International Society and editor of the Portuguese page of *KateChopin.org*.

Patricia J. Sehulster is an associate professor of English and the co-director of the Honors Program at SUNY Westchester Community

College. She earned her Ph.D. in American literature at Fordham University, and her work has appeared in *The Western Journal of Black Studies, The Journal of Black Studies*, and *A.T.Q.: 19th Century American Literature and Culture*, *Teaching English in the Two-Year College*, among other publications.

Emily Toth, a professor of English at Louisana State University, has published eleven books, including 5 on Kate Chopin. Her *Unveiling Kate Chopin* (UP of Mississippi) is the definitive biography, and her *Kate Chopin's Private Papers* (Indiana UP) comprises all diaries and letters. She edited Chopin's last story collection, *A Vocation and a Voice*, and writes the "Ms. Mentor" column online academic advice for the *Chronicle of Higher Education.*

Rafael Walker is a postdoctoral fellow at the University of Pennsylvania. He has published journal articles on American women writers and is completing a book on early-twentieth-century American literature, which is provisionally titled *Realism after Individualism: Women, Desire, and the Modern American Novel.*

Index